FOR ALL
Seasons

Copyright © 2012, Scepter Publishers, Inc.
P.O. Box 211, New York, N.Y. 10018
www.scepterpublishers.org

Quotations from *The Life of Pico* and *Dialogue of Conscience* are copyright of Scepter Publishers, New York, for modernized English translations.

Special thanks to Yale University Press, New Haven, CT for permission to reprint letters from Elizabeth Rogers' *Selected Letters of St. Thomas More* (letters 1, 4, 5, 6, 9, 11, 38, 43, and 44), as well as letters from the following volumes of the *Yale Edition of the Complete Works of St. Thomas More*: volume 3.1 (letter 4); volume 3.2 (letters 5a–b and 26); volume 4 (letters 9 and 15); and volume 15 (letter 19).

Permission is also recognized from Marie-Claire Phelippeau, editor of *Moreana*, the venerable and international journal of Thomas More studies, and the *Amici Thomae Mori* to reprint Clarence Miller's translations of letters to Francis Cranevelt (letters 35, 36, 37, 38, 41, 43, 44, 45, 46, 48, 49, and 50), originally published in *Moreana* Vol. 31 (1994).

Paintings reproduced in this book are courtesy of the National Portrait Gallery, London, which holds copyright thereto.

Cover / text: design and composition by Rose Design

Printed in the United States of America

ISBN: 978-1-59417-163-5

FOR ALL
Seasons

SELECTED LETTERS OF THOMAS MORE

edited by **STEPHEN SMITH**

 Scepter

ACKNOWLEDGMENTS

This collection of Thomas More's letters would not have been finished without the steadfast help of many friends and colleagues. First, I thank Gerard Wegemer, the director of the Center for Thomas More Studies, for his encouragement and support of this book from the beginning, and for his advice and friendship along the way. I would also like to thank Dr. Virginia Townley and Hillsdale College for their support of my work, and Mark Maier, the research librarian of Hillsdale College, for his tireless assistance in the preparation of the manuscript and his help with the many questions that arose during the course of this project. Thanks as well to my research assistant, Dennis Walton, whose labors and good cheer were much appreciated throughout the preparation of this book; to Marissa Wolfe and Mary Pawlowski at the University of Dallas for their help; to Russell Shaw for his modernization of the Frith letter; and to the students in my first Thomas More class here at Hillsdale, who likely do not know how much they have helped me better understand More, his drama, and its contemporary implications and significance. Finally and most especially, I thank Laura and my family for their encouragement, good cheer, and enduring love.

For permission to reprint various letters, I thank John Powers at Scepter Publishers, especially for the modernized texts from *The Life of Pico* and for the *Dialogue of Conscience*. I thank Marie-Claire Phélippeau, editor of *Moreana*, the venerable and international journal of Thomas More studies, for her permission to reprint Clarence Miller's excellent translations of Thomas More's letters to Francis Cranevelt, and I thank Yale University Press for their permission to reprint the translations for letters 1, 4, 5a–b, 7, 8, 9, 10, 12, 15, 19, 26, 27a–b, 47, 53, and 54. Thanks as well to Paulist Press for the permission to reprint a selection from their translation of Reginald Pole's *Defense of the Unity of the Church,* and to the British Library for permission to reprint an excerpt from their translation of the *Magna Carta.* Finally, I take this opportunity to thank Yale University Press for its support of Thomas More studies over the last forty years, and especially to congratulate it on the finished publication of *The Complete Works of St. Thomas More* (1963–1997), a labor of high scholarship and diligence that has provided readers with an invaluable standard edition of More's writings in English and Latin.

There is one last important note: In this book, Thomas More's letters are numbered in two ways. First, the letters are numbered simply, beginning with the number one, for the present purposes of this book and the general reader. In most cases, there is also a second number provided in square brackets. This second number directs the interested reader to the scholarly texts of these letters, including the original Latin, found in *The Correspondence of Sir Thomas More,* ed. Elizabeth Rogers (Princeton University Press, 1947). In the case of letters that are not in Rogers' volume, a new number has been assigned to each one to indicate where, approximately, the letter fits in Rogers' chronology. So, for example, letters 35–38, written by Thomas More to Francis Cranevelt, are now assigned the new numbers 106a, 106b, 106c, and 106d in square brackets, a numbering which places them now in order with the other letters written in 1521. As is perhaps evident, an updated and comprehensive edition of all More's extant letters, in both English and Latin, is a scholarly work greatly needed and "devoutly to be wished."

CONTENTS

FOREWORD

"No likeness of More can be truer than his own works, especially his letters"—so said the great Thomas More scholar Germain Marc'hadour who saw in these letters "every facet of More's many-sided personality." How More developed and integrated these many facets of his busy family, civic, professional, and spiritual life has always intrigued those coming to know this "man for all seasons," as More was called in his own lifetime.

More "seems to be born and made for friendship, of which he is the sincerest and most persistent devotee," writes Erasmus (letter 28). From Erasmus' perspective, this collection of letters might be subtitled: "Friendship in Action." That More worked consciously and diligently to exercise true friendship is evident from his earliest to his last letters, whether to his spiritual advisor Fr. John Colet or to his thirteen-year-old son John or to established professional colleagues such as the famous scholar Erasmus, the royal counselor Cromwell, or the powerful King Henry VIII. More's unique combination of kindness, intimacy, and artful truth-telling is indicated in letter 52 by More's long time friend and fellow ambassador Cuthbert Tunstall, bishop of London, who honors More "from among all my friends . . . on account of our intimacy and on account of your frankness; for I know that you will be pleased at whatever good it [Tunstall's book, which he is dedicating to More] may contain, warn me of whatever is imperfect, and forgive whatever is amiss."

In letter 2, for example, More confides to Fr. John Colet his ongoing struggle "to climb the narrow path of virtue," and he

thanks him for his "prudent advice, . . . pleasant company," and
"powerful sermons," all of which have edified and strengthened
him away "from almost the very gates of hell." He also encourages
Colet to return to his difficult work in London, especially since
he has won the city's trust and stirred their desire for virtue by his
own integrity, i.e., his consistency in word and deed.

In letter 39 to his children penned when away on business,
he teaches and encouraging them to write not just correctly but
with a joyful and loving refinement. In this letter addressed to
all of his children, he singles out the work of his youngest in
this way:

> The letter from my son John pleased me the best . . . because
> he seems to have given it a bit more labor and study. For he not
> only put out his matter . . . in fairly polished language, but he
> plays with me both pleasantly and cleverly, and turns my jokes
> on myself wittily enough. And this he does not only merrily, but
> with due moderation, showing that he does not forget that he
> is joking with his father. . . . By this diligence . . . there is
> nothing in itself so insipid that you cannot season it with grace
> and wit if you give a little thought to it.

Here More, famous for his affability and good humor, reveals
how he sought to teach these qualities to his own children, qualities requiring diligent labor done with joy: with hard work, "there
is nothing in itself so insipid," More instructs his thirteen-year-old
son, "that you cannot season it with grace and wit if you give a little
thought to it." Here we see that the "gladness of a virtuous mind"[1]
depends on hard work, good judgment, restraint, and the will to
give good cheer.

---

1. This phrase appears in rhyme royal poetry in More's first book published in English:
"You shall no pleasure comparable find / To th' inward gladness of a virtuous mind." See
Scepter's *The Life of Pico* (2010), p. 64, or Jeff Lehman's scholarly edition at *www.thomas-
morestudies.org*, p. 62.

Letters 5a and 5b to eighteen-year-old King Henry VIII are examples of More's most courageous but also most artful truth-telling. By that time, More had known Henry and Henry's tutors for ten years; More and his father had experienced firsthand what More considered the tyranny of Henry VII—and More saw the same tyrannical leanings in Henry VIII, as he indicates in the long poem he wrote in Latin for Henry's coronation. This poem is an intricate imitation of a classical form designed to instruct and encourage good rule, while calling attention to the dangers of power and pride. Just as bold is More's last letter to Henry (#61) when Henry's character had changed and hardened. Nonetheless, More appeals to Henry's past promises and reminds him that slander does the souls of the slanderers "more hurt" that it does More, that God will be the final judge of all, yet whatever happens he prays that he "should once meet with your Grace again in heaven, and there be merry with you."

In his letters to Henry's royal counselor Thomas Cromwell, to Erasmus, and to others, More goes farther in reminding Cromwell, the king, and all of Europe what had actually occurred before, during, and after his time as Henry's Lord Chancellor. More makes special note of Henry's promises to respect More's conscience, promises made before More first entered Henry's service in 1518 (letters 62, 79) and again when More accepted to be Lord Chancellor in 1529 (letters 62, 71). A year and a half before his imprisonment, More also published a clear statement of facts which included the public pronouncements of King Henry's repeated praise for More's service and of the public commendations in Parliament for More's long and unblemished public career (letter 56, with epitaph).

More also courageously sets forth in detail the interrogations leading up to his trial in letters 63, 77, and 79. In these and in letters 69–71 and 73 More shows clearly the issues of conscience he saw at stake in his trial; the great fear and suffering involved are indicated well in letter 74.

Courageous, however, are many of More's letters, revealing a friend who is no flatterer, a friend deeply concerned for the good of his wife, his children, his professional colleagues, and his country.

Letter 19 to the leaders of Oxford University is a masterpiece of diplomatic but forceful rebuke: polite and respectful, but devastating in the clear, lawyerly setting forth of facts—and of impending consequences. Letter 53 to theologian Martin Dorp is a similar strong and serious reprimand, so artfully done and so tailored to Dorp's character and situation that it led Dorp to correct publicly his position, as letter 54 reveals.

More's letters to Erasmus are particularly revealing of their many-sided friendship. They show More's practical efforts at helping Erasmus get money (letters 8, 12) and a horse (letters 10, 12), concern for Erasmus' health (letter 47), the joy of working together on *Utopia*'s publication (letters 8, 10, 12), encouragement of Erasmus's demanding intellectual work (letters 12, 54) as well as encouragement and support in the face of fear (letters 47, 56). More also reveals to Erasmus, guardedly in print but more fully in speech, the reasons for taking the dangerous position of Lord Chancellor: nothing less than "the interests of Christendom" (letter 53).

The most charming letters are those to his children, especially letter 26, playfully written in Latin verse supposedly while being "drenched by a soaking rain" on horseback and "bogged down in mud"; nonetheless despite "the mud, the miserably stormy weather, and having to urge a small horse through deep waters," he is "not able to distract his thoughts from" his children and his poem is proof "that, wherever he is, he thinks of" them. Yet even this letter has struck some as shockingly demanding. At the end of this poem, is he not requiring "accomplishments" if they are to earn his love? "Accomplishments" is actually *virtutibus* in the original Latin and, yes, More is using all of his wit and wisdom to encourage great virtue in his children—as he did with his friends.

One of the most moving letters is number 80, also one of the very last, written to the Italian banker Antonio Bonvisi, who seems to have been More's best friend throughout the whole of his professional life, a friend who took great risks to care for More during More's fifteen months of imprisonment.

The only letter to his wife that remains, letter 51, is perhaps the most revealing of all his letters, especially given the circumstances of composition: it was written spontaneously, in the face of a severe economic disaster for the family, with the prospect of losing their home and all their land. Nonetheless, More counsels "good cheer" and hearty thanks to God, "as well for adversity as for prosperity" for "His wisdom better sees what is good for us than we do for ourselves." This same response he will give to his daughter Meg in letter 69 when, for the third time, she tries to convince him to leave prison. In the concluding paragraph he says:

> And therefore, my own good daughter, never let your mind be troubled over anything that ever shall happen to me in this world. Nothing can come but what God wills. And I make myself very sure that whatever that may be, no matter how bad it seems, it will indeed be the best.

In stating that "I *make* myself very sure," More reveals the hard work of freely exercising his will to choose his response to adversity, in the light of a conscience formed by his deepest convictions. Characteristically, this choice was for More an act of loyal friendship with a God whom he had come to know as one who speaks clearly in the depth of conscience, but only in ways that invite free response.

Thomas More's dying words were "I die the King's good servant, *and* God's first," indicating the ideal that More learned from the example of John Colet (letter 2) early in life: true integrity of word and deed. Yet as these letters also reveal, to achieve and maintain such integrity requires diligent, courageous, and often heroic work—not only in the trials and difficulties of normal life but especially in prison during his final fifteen months. Until the very last moment, up through his final jokes with his guard and then with his executioner, he continued to *work* for integrity, an integrity that allowed him to calmly—and even merrily—say that he could "lose his head and have no harm" (letters 69, 73, 79).

When Pius XI declared More's sainthood in 1935, he summed up the impression of many when he said, "What a complete man!" Or as those petitioning for More to become Patron of Statesmen put it in 1999: "the idea that holiness is the fullness of humanity appears, in [Thomas More's] case, quite tangibly true." Or to use the words of John Paul II in his official Proclamation of 2000: "This harmony between the natural and the supernatural is perhaps the element which more than any other defines the personality of this great English statesman: he lived his intense public life with a simple humility marked by good humor, even at the moment of his execution." This humble good humor has been seen by many to be a model of refined statesmanship, cultured civility, human splendor, and even culture-changing charity. What does your reading of these letters reveal?

Gerard Wegemer, Director
Center for Thomas More Studies
July 6, 2011

PREFACE

The purpose of the present volume is to make widely available, for the first time in 40 years, a collection of Thomas More's correspondence for the great variety of readers. The last such edition was Elizabeth Rogers' *St. Thomas More: Selected Letters* (Yale University Press, 1961), based on her earlier and still indispensable *The Correspondence of Sir Thomas More* (Princeton University Press, 1947). Since the 1960s, there has been only one additional volume of More's letters published, *The Last Letters of Thomas More* (Eerdmans, 2000), edited with an excellent commentary by Alvaro Silva. Surprisingly, the Yale University Press edition of Thomas More's *Complete Works*, (hereafter *CW*) completed in 1997, lacks a volume (or volumes) devoted to More's letters, an omission that time and renewed scholarly interest on More will hopefully remedy in the years ahead.

Although the present volume of letters is not complete and exhaustive—some of the very long humanist letters, for example, are not included—the book nevertheless intends to provide for the general reader a "life in letters" of Sir Thomas More, from his youth to the great, historic drama of his last years and death. These letters remain an invaluable help in illuminating the character of this learned man—the husband, father, friend, statesman, and martyr—who was described in his own time as a "man for all seasons," and later praised by no less a judge than Jonathan Swift as "the person of the greatest virtue these islands ever produced." By reading and considering More's life through the testimony of his letters, one may begin to understand the justice of

Chesterton's striking judgment in *The Well and the Shallows*: "A mind like More's was full of light like a house made of windows; but the windows looked out on all sides and in all directions. We might say that, as the jewel has many facets, so the man had many faces; only none of them were masks."

Written from 1499–1535 in either Latin or English, the letters are presented here chronologically, with one exception (the two letters to Martin Dorp). The headnotes provide the historical context of each letter, as well as explanations of the many references and allusions in these rich letters; they also provide recommendations for further reading on the issues raised. In addition to the letters from More himself, the volume includes a selection of other relevant letters, such as letters from More's second wife, Dame Alice, and his daughter, Margaret, as well as texts from Erasmus, King Henry, and other players in the great drama of those times. Finally, the appendices furnish readers with materials helpful in studying and understanding better the King's "great matter," the breakdown of his marriage to Queen Catherine of Aragon and his remarriage to Anne Boleyn, as well as those particular legal documents—the acts, oaths, and laws—that played such a crucial role in More's imprisonment, interrogations, trial, and death. A contemporary account of his trial from *The Paris Newsletter* and two responses to his death are included, to round off the volume.

As indicated in the headnotes, a wealth of additional materials, texts, and study guides to Thomas More's life and writings are available online at the Center for Thomas More Studies website, *www.thomasmorestudies.org*, for interested readers, teachers, and writers.

Dr. Stephen Smith
Fellow, Center for Thomas More Studies
Townley Chair of English Literature,
Hillsdale College
February 7, 2012

Chronology of Thomas More's Life and Writings

Feb 7, 1477	Born in London to John and Agnes More
c. 1484–1487	Attends St. Anthony's School, London
c. 1489–1491	Page for Archbishop and Chancellor Morton
c. 1491–1493	Student at Oxford
c. 1493–1495	Pre-law student, New Inn, London
c. 1496–1504	Writes the English Poems, such as "Pageant of Life" and "Rueful Lamentation"
1496–c. 1501	Law student, Lincoln's Inn; called to the bar
1499	Meets Erasmus for the first time
c. 1501–1504	Frequents the London Charterhouse (Carthusians)
c. 1501	Lectures on St. Augustine's *City of God* ; begins the study of Greek
c. 1503–1506	Reader at Furnivall's Inn
c. 1504	*The Life of John Picus* (published 1510)
1504	Elected to Parliament
1505	Marries Jane Colt; Margaret ("Meg") born
1506	Publishes, with Erasmus, the translations of Lucian
1506	Studies intensely; visits Coventry; Elizabeth born

1518   Publishes the Latin Poems

1520   Field of Cloth of Gold; peace with France

1521   Knighted; undertreasurer; ambassador to Bruges and Calais; cautions Henry not to exaggerate the pope's secular authority; Margaret marries Roper; Buckingham executed

1522   Gives public oration welcoming Emperor Charles V; serves as Henry's secretary and cautions against war; war with France resumed

c. 1522   *The Four Last Things*

1523   Speaker of the House of Commons, proposes free speech; leases Crosby Hall, truce with France

1523   *Responsio ad Lutherum*

1524   High Steward, Oxford; moves to Chelsea; war with France resumes: "If my head could win [the King] a castle in France . . . it would not fail to go."

1525   High Steward, Cambridge; chancellor of Lancaster; Peasants' Revolt; peace treaty with France; Cecily marries Heron; Elizabeth marries Dauncey

1526   Appointed to royal council's subcommittee of four; urges Erasmus to complete writings against Luther; Turks invade Hungary; Tyndale's New Testament secretly distributed

1526   Writes "Letter to Bugenhagen" (not published until 1568)

1527   Accompanies Wolsey to France; sack of Rome; Henry consults More about divorce; More's daughters' dispute before Henry; Holbein paints the More family

1534   Henry asks for More's indictment (Feb. 21),
           but House of Lords refuses three times; More
           questioned by royal commission (March),
           interrogated at Lambeth Palace (Apr. 13), and
           finally imprisoned (illegally) for refusal to take
           Cromwell's oath regarding the Act of Suc-
           cession (Apr. 17); Chancellor Audley sends a
           warning to More (August)

1534   *A Treatise upon the Passion; A Treatise to
           Receive the Blessed Body; A Dialogue of Comfort
           against Tribulation*

1534–35   Spiritual Instructions: "Imploring Divine Help
           against Temptation"; "A Godly Instruction
           [on How to Treat Those Who Wrong Us]"; "A
           Godly Meditation [on detachment]"

1535   *Sadness of Christ;* "A Devout Prayer before
           Dying"

1535   Margaret visits while monks are led to execu-
           tion on May 4; More interrogated on May 7,
           June 3, and June 14; Richard Rich removes
           writing materials on June 12; More goes to trial
           on July 1

July 6, 1535   More executed

1557   *The Works of Sir Thomas More, Knight* pub-
           lished by William Rastell

Letter 1

To John Holt [2][1]

By 1501, Thomas More (1477–1535) was called to the bar after completing his law studies at Lincoln's Inn, London. At this time, the youthful and brilliant More began his study of ancient Greek, the classical philosophers, poets, and historians, and the Church fathers. Such academic pursuits, however, left his father Sir John More, a prominent and practical man of law, less than pleased and young Thomas nearly disinherited, according to Erasmus's later testimony. The young More also delivered lectures on St. Augustine's *City of God* at his parish church, St. Lawrence Jewry, "not from the theological point of view, but from the standpoint of history and philosophy," as the early biographer Thomas Stapleton attests. Around this time, he began to frequent the Charterhouse of the Carthusians, though he would eventually discern that the lay vocation of marriage and public service was his personal calling.

The addressee of this, More's earliest surviving letter, is John Holt, the schoolmaster and grammarian, an early humanist who held various posts in his career, such as fellow at Magdalen College, Oxford; teacher of Latin at Lambeth Palace; master of the Chichester Cathedral school; and tutor of Prince Henry, the promising youth later crowned King Henry VIII in 1509 (*ODNB*).[2]

---

1. Here and throughout, the number given in square brackets refers the interested reader to the critical edition of these texts in *The Correspondence of Sir Thomas More*, ed. Elizabeth Rogers (Princeton University Press, 1947).

2. Here and throughout "ODNB" refers to the magnificent and indispensable *Oxford Dictionary of National Biography*. The ODNB is the major source throughout this book for biographical and contextual information on the historical figures addressed or discussed in these letters. In each case, the abbreviation indicates the source and points the reader to the full entry on the given person. In the case of a direct quotation, the page number is provided.

"Grocin" is William Grocyn, the priest and humanist pioneer who brought the study of Greek to Oxford for the first time and taught the language to Thomas More; he was also a friend of Erasmus, John Colet, and the other prominent humanists such as Lily and Thomas Linacre, a physician who translated Galen from Greek to Latin (*ODNB*). Unfortunately "the comedy about Solomon" alluded to here is lost, though we know from Erasmus' letter to Ulrich von Hutten (see letter 28) that the young More took special delight in writing and performing in such plays. In the letter, "Celestial Hierarchies" refers to a mystical work written by Dionysius the Pseudo-Areopagite around the year 500; the work discusses the nine orders of angels (*ODCC*).[3]

This letter also celebrates an apparently "happy omen"—the arrival of Princess Catherine of Aragon (1485–1536) in London on 12 November 1501, a few days after which she married Arthur, Prince of Wales, with great and gorgeous ceremony. After Prince Arthur's untimely death on 2 April 1502, the widowed Catherine would languish in England for seven years before marrying Arthur's younger brother, the ruddy Prince Henry. This marriage, of such tremendous significance for English history, did not take place until King Henry VII first secured a dispensation from Rome. Queen Catherine's royal motto was "humble and loyal." During the later controversies over her marriage to Henry, Queen Catherine would solemnly swear on her conscience that the marriage between her and the 16-year-old Arthur was never consummated. During the trial over the royal marriage in 1527, she publicly stated: "I take God to be my judge, I have been to you a true and humble wife . . . " In 1531, when hope for the marriage was dying with the hastening minutes, she wrote: "What I suffer is enough to kill ten men, much more a shattered woman who has

---

3. Here and throughout "ODCC" refers to the *Oxford Dictionary of the Christian Church*. In each case, the abbreviation indicates the source and points the reader to the full entry on the given subject or person.

done no harm. I am the King's lawful wife, and while I live I will say no other" (quoted in Weir 229). See Appendix I for a discussion of the "Great Matter" of the King's marriage and divorce, and for the texts of two of Queen Catherine's late letters on the controversy. See Giles Tremlett's recent *Catherine of Aragon: Henry's Spanish Queen* (Faber and Faber, 2010), for a full contemporary biography of the Queen.

<LONDON

c. NOVEMBER 1501>

THOMAS MORE SENDS HIS GREETINGS TO JOHN HOLT:

I have sent you everything you wanted, except the additions I have made to the comedy about Solomon; those I could not send you at the moment, as I did not have them with me. I shall arrange for you to get them next week, along with any other of my materials you wish.

I am glad you have left Smarden, an unhealthy spot, and have moved to Chichester, which is a healthier location, with more sunshine. I suppose you will be glad you made the move; the local bishop, I hear, is very fond of you.

As for myself, thanks be to God, I am feeling quite well; and—something few people can say for themselves—I am living my life just as I desire; so please God, may my desires be good. You ask how I am doing in my studies. Wonderfully, of course; things could not be better. I have shelved my Latin books, to take up the study of Greek; however, while dropping the one, I have not as yet completely caught up with the other. But enough on that point.

Grocin, my instructor, recently made a very successful start on his lectures, at Saint Paul's, on the text of the "Celestial Hierarchies," the famous work of Saint Dionysius the Areopagite. It would be hard to tell which is greater—the acclaim for himself, or the profit for his listeners. His audience includes a group of students, whose numbers, unfortunately, are more impressive than their learning; but it also includes very many of the educated class. Several illiterates too are flocking to the lectures, some drawn by curiosity, some out of a desire to appear a little erudite. But the majority of self-styled intellectuals are not attending, so as not to give the impression of admitting their ignorance on matters of which they are ignorant.

Catherine, the illustrious daughter of the King of Spain and bride of our distinguished Prince, lately made her entry into London, amid a tremendous ovation; never, to my knowledge, has there been such a reception anywhere. The magnificent attire of our nobles aroused cries of admiration. But the Spanish escort— good heavens!—what a sight! If you had seen it, I am afraid you would have burst with laughter; they were so ludicrous. Except for three, or at the most four, of them, they were just too much to look at: hunchbacked, undersized, barefoot Pygmies from Ethiopia. If you had been there, you would have thought they were refugees from hell. Ah, but the lady! Take my word for it, she thrilled the hearts of everyone; she possesses all those qualities that make for beauty in a very charming young girl. Everywhere she receives the highest of praises; but even that is inadequate. I do hope this highly publicized union will prove a happy omen for England. Farewell.

Letter 2

To Rev. John Colet [3]

Humanist and priest, John Colet (1467–1519) was a close friend and spiritual counselor to the young Thomas More. Later the founder of St. Paul's Cathedral school in London and then Dean of St. Paul's, Colet praised More as *"Britannie unicum ingenium,"* the "the ablest man in Britain" (*ODNB*), or more accurately, "the only man of genius in Britain." In this early letter, the young More acknowledges his debt to Colet for his friendship, spiritual direction, and good company. More also shows his desire to resolve some of the more pressing questions facing the human being: What is the best way to live in this world? What are the best means to such a well-led life? Though More's critique of the difficulties of life in the city is strong, and his praise of bucolic bliss appealing, the letter nevertheless urges Colet to return to care for the abandoned city, which needs "the services of a physician" after the prudent and charitable pattern of Colet. The letter is also an early example of the importance More placed on human friendship. Erasmus praises More's gift for making and keeping friends in particular (see letter 28), and one of More's last letters is a tribute to the great grace of human friendship and the experience of a"certain loving kindness of God" through a lifetime of faithful friendship (see letter 80).

Some of the best classical texts on friendship are Aristotle's *Ethics* (book 8) and Cicero's *De Amicitia*. The biblical texts are rich in praise of friendship as well—see, for example, Exodus 33:11; 1 Samuel 23:15–18; Proverbs 17:17, 18:24, 27:9, and 27:17; Sirach 6:13–15; and John 15:13–14. Daniel Schwartz's illuminating book, *Aquinas on Friendship* (Oxford University Press, 2007), explores the importance of friendship across the writings of Thomas Aquinas, whom More called "the very flower of theology" and a "most learned and also most holy man" (*CW* 8 714 and *CW* 5 355). There are three prominent classical sources for More's intriguing allusion to the tale of Orpheus, the poet-son of Apollo, and Eurydice his lost love: the first is Plato's *Symposium* (179b); the second is Virgil's *Georgics* (book four); and the third is found in Ovid's *Metamorphoses* (book ten). In English Renaissance writing after More, the power of Orpheus's music "stands for a principle capable of transforming our limited, dull, chained human condition into something nearer the divine" while the figure of Orpheus himself is connected to the "theme of the poet as architect of civilized society" and even the "wise statesman" capable of leading men from savagery to what one later poet calls the "civil love of art" (Miles 58). This understanding of the poet's work seems reminiscent of Cicero's understanding of the ideal orator—that philosophical and political instrument of civilization building and ennobling—described in book one of *De Oratore*.

LONDON

23 OCTOBER < 1504 >

THOMAS MORE TO HIS DEAR JOHN COLET, GREETING.

As I was walking in the law-courts the other day, occupied with business of various kinds, I met your servant. I was delighted to see him, both because I have always been fond of him, and especially because I thought he would not be here without you. But when I heard from him not only that you had not returned, but that you would not return for a long time yet, my joyful expectation was changed to unutterable grief. No annoyance that I would suffer is to be compared with the loss of your companionship, which is so dear to me. It has been my custom to rely upon your prudent advice, to find my recreation in your pleasant company, to be stirred up by your powerful sermons, to be edified by your life and example, to be guided, in fine, by even the slightest indications of your opinions. When I had the advantage of all these helps I used to feel strengthened, now that I am deprived of them I seem to languish and grow feeble. By following your footsteps I had escaped from almost the very gates of hell, and now, driven by some secret but irresistible force, I am falling back again into the gruesome darkness. I am like Eurydice, except that she was lost because Orpheus looked back at her, but I am sinking because you do not cast a glance of pity towards me.

For city life helps no one to be good, but rather, when a man is straining every nerve to climb the narrow path of virtue, it tempts him with every kind of allurement and drags him down to its own level with its manifold deceits. Wherever you turn, what do you see around you? Pretended friends, and the honeyed poison of smooth flatterers, fierce hatreds, quarrels, rivalries and contentions. Look again and you will see butchers, confectioners, fishmongers, carriers, cooks, and poultrymen, all occupied in serving sensuality, the world and the world's lord, the devil. Houses block out from us a large measure of the light, and our view is bounded not by the round horizon, but by the lofty roofs. I really cannot blame you if you are not yet tired of the country where you live among simple people, unversed in the deceits of the towns. Wherever you cast your eyes, the smiling face of the earth greets you, the sweet fresh air invigorates you, the sight of the heavens charms you. You see nothing but the generous gifts of nature and the traces of our primeval innocence. But yet I do not wish you to be so enamored of these delights as to be unwilling to return to us as soon as possible. But if you are repelled by the unpleasantness of town life, then let me suggest that you should come to your country parish of Stepney. It needs your fatherly care, and you will enjoy there all the advantages of your present abode, and be able to come from time to time for a day or two into the city where so much meritorious work awaits you. For in the country, where men are for the most part innocent, or certainly not enchained in gross vice, the services of any physician, however moderate his attainments, can be usefully employed. But in the city, because of the great numbers that congregate there, and because of their long-standing habits of vice, no physician can do much good unless he be of the highest skill. Certainly there come from time to time into the pulpit at St Paul's preachers who hold out specious promises of help. But although they speak very eloquently, their life is in such sharp contrast to their words that they do harm rather than good. For they cannot bring men to believe that though they are themselves obviously in direst need of the physician's help, they are yet fit to be entrusted with the cure of other men's ailments. And thus when men see that their diseases are being prescribed for by physicians who are themselves covered with ulcers, they immediately become indignant and refuse to accept their remedies. But if, as observers of human nature assert, he is the best physician in whom the patient has the greatest confidence, it is beyond all doubt that you are the one who can do most for the salvation of all in the city. Their readiness to allow you to treat their wounds, their trust, their obedience, has been proved to you by past experience, and is, in any case, clear now by the incredibly strong desire and keen expectation with which all are looking forward to your coming. Come then, my dear friend, for Stepney's sake which mourns your long absence as deeply as a child his mother's, for your country's sake which should be no less dear to you than are your parents, and finally, though I cannot hope that this will be a powerful motive for your return, for my sake who am entirely devoted to you and anxiously awaiting your coming.

Meanwhile, I pass my time with Grocyn, Linacre and our dear friend Lily. The first as you know is the guide of my conduct, while you are absent, the second my master in letters, the third my confidant and most intimate friend. Farewell, and continue your love towards us.

LONDON.

Letter 3

TO JOYCE LEE [4]

Dedicated to the sister of More's family friend Edward Lee, this letter serves as the preface to the young More's *The Life of Pico*, his first major English work, a translation of the Latin biography of Pico della Mirandola, humanist and author, originally written by Pico's nephew Gianfrancesco. Still famous today for his "Oration on the Dignity of Man," Pico advocated a Renaissance vision of the self-fashioning wonder of the human being and his glorious liberty: "To man it is allowed to be whatever he chooses to be!" Pico writes with a kind of stirring fire. More's translation of *The Life of Pico*—often literal, yet also marked by provocative changes, alterations, omissions, and additions of More's own— explores both the wondrous promise and unfulfilled potential of this young humanist's life, work, and vocation, all cut short at the age of 31, when he died mysteriously, perhaps at the hand of one of his own servants. The biographical portion of More's *The Life of Pico* ends with the Florentine friar-statesman, Savanarola, claiming that Pico, after his death, languishes in the "dark fire" of purgatory, because he neglected to pursue his proper vocation, choosing to devote himself to pleasures such as his books and the sweet life of cultured ease while deferring the "especial commandment of God" to an ever later tomorrow. In addition to translating the *Life*, More includes three revealing letters from Pico on subjects such as public service and the contemplative-active life debate, and More concludes the work with a translation of Pico's "12 Rules for Spiritual Combat" and a collection of his own verses, "12 Properties of a Lover," wherein he reworks a list of the Petrarchan lover's virtues and applies them to the soul's love of God, addressed as "the very tender loving Father." The addressee, Joyce Lee, was a nun of the order of the Minoresses, or the Poor Clares. This letter and the following are from More's *The Life of Pico,* modernized by Russell Shaw. For the 500th Anniversary scholarly text of More's *The Life of Pico,* edited by Jeffrey Lehman, see *www.thomasmorestudies.org.*

<LONDON
c. 1 JANUARY 1505>

It is a custom of long standing, my beloved sister, for friends to exchange tokens of esteem or gifts at the opening of a New Year as expressions of their love and friendship. This gesture signifies as well each one's hope for the other that the year ahead, having begun so happily, should continue no less well and come to a prosperous ending.

Usually, though, the gifts friends exchange in this way pertain only to feeding or clothing or otherwise gratifying the body, so that one might suppose the friendship also to extend to material concerns and no further. The love and affection of Christian people ought, however, to be spiritual, not material. After all, as the apostle says, "We are not in the flesh but in the spirit if Christ abides in us" [Rom 8:9]. And so, as a token of my wish for your good fortune in this New Year, I have sent you, my dearly beloved sister, such a gift as may testify to my tender love and my eagerness for the happy continuation and gracious increase of virtue in your soul. Others' gifts tell of the worldly prosperity they desire for their friends. Mine tells of the godly prosperity I want for you.

These texts, more profitable than they are extensive, were composed in Latin by one Giovanni Pico, Earl of Mirandola, a member of the Italian nobility. I need not dwell here on his learning and virtue, since hereafter I shall expound on the entirety of his life, though briefly, as suits my limited ability, rather than in a manner suited to his merits. The works are such, dear sister, that, for their size, I believe none can be found more profitable for instilling temperance in the midst of prosperity or winning patience in adversity, for despising the vanity of the world or desiring the felicity of heaven. I would have no hesitation in urging you to accept them—except that their good matter (whatever might be said of the translation) is capable of delighting and gladdening anyone with any scant desire for and love of God, whereas for one of your virtue, the fervent zeal for God is so marked that you can be counted on joyfully to welcome anything that speaks, even clumsily, in reproach of vice, in praise of virtue, or to the honor and glory of God. I pray He keep you safe.

Letter 3b

FROM JOHN PICO TO ANDREW CORNEUS FROM THOMAS MORE'S *THE LIFE OF PICO*

The young Thomas More chose to translate this letter of Pico in his *The Life of Pico*. The letter is Pico's response to a friend who has challenged the philosopher to devote himself to "some real business." More will explore this very tension—between contemplation and action, or between pleasure and service—in his later masterwork of humanism, *Utopia*, first published in 1516. In that work, the wandering philosopher Raphael Hythloday will assert that the only "difference" between service and servitude is "one syllable," while More will urge him to participate in public affairs nonetheless: "Yet I think if you could bring yourself to devote your intelligence and energy to public affairs, you would be doing something worthy of your noble and truly philosophical nature, even if you did not much like it" (13). The bracketing in the letter indicates the portions Thomas More added to the original text as he translated it into English.

<PARIS
15 OCTOBER 1492>

⌐The Matter or Argument of Pico's Letter to Andrea Corneo

This Andrea, a distinguished man and particular friend of Pico's, had advised him in letters to give up studying philosophy, since he thought Pico had spent enough time on that and he judged it vain and unprofitable unless applied to the accomplishment of some real business. He therefore counseled Pico to leave off study and place himself among some of the great princes of Italy, with whom (so Andrea said) he would be occupied much more fruitfully than in forever studying and learning philosophy. Pico's answer, as appears in this present letter, thus means: It would follow from what is said that it was either servile or at least not princely to study philosophy for any reason except a mercenary one—meaning by mercenary all those things we do for pay or reward. Thus he makes philosophy mercenary and treats it as merchandise for those who study it with an eye to what may bring them some material gain or worldly advantage rather than the pleasure it gives ⌐or the instruction of their minds in moral virtue¬.

GIOVANNI PICO EARL OF MIRANDOLA TO ANDREA CORNEO, GREETINGS.

You exhort me by your letters to take up a public and active life, saying I have spent all this time studying philosophy uselessly and, as it were, to my reproach and shame unless I finally put that learning to use by engaging in some profitable activity and tangible business. Indeed, my dear friend Andrea, I would be rid of both the expense and trouble of these studies if I were convinced that in this matter I could find it in my heart to agree with you and take your advice.

This is a very deadly and monstrous notion that has entered into men's thinking, namely, that philosophical studies must either be entirely avoided by lords and princes or, at most, sipped sparingly and tasted lightly, more to polish up and show off their cleverness than to cultivate ⌐and profit¬ their minds. They take as absolute law Neoptolemus's saying that philosophy should be studied either not at all or not for long; but they regard as jokes, indeed as fables, the assertions of wise men that sure and lasting happiness resides only in the goodness of the mind, while outer things of the body or mere happenstance count for little or nothing with us.

But just here you will say to me: ⌐"It's fine with me that you study, but I would have you engaged with the world around you as well.¬ I don't want you to embrace Martha to such an extent that you give up Mary entirely. ⌐Love them and do them both: study and worldly business."¬

⌐Really, my dear friend,¬ on this point I don't deny what you say; nor do I find any fault with, or blame, those who do. But surely it's not the same thing to say that one does well in doing something and that one does evil *unless* one does it. There is a great difference between thinking it acceptable to move downward from contemplation to the active life— ⌐from the better to the worse, that is¬—and thinking it wrong to persist in what is better and not take that downward step. Should a man then be rebuked for desiring virtue and pursuing it only for its own sake—because he studies the mysteries of God, because he probes the wisdom of nature, because he makes constant use of pleasant leisure and rest, seeking no outward thing, despising all else, because the things that interest him are quite sufficient to content one who cares about them? By this reckoning it is something servile, or at least not princely, to study wisdom for any reasons but mercenary ones.

Who can hear this, who can abide it? Surely he never studied for wisdom's sake who studied for reasons that rendered him unfit or unwilling to do that in the future. A man acting thus was busy studying merchandise, not wisdom. You write me that the time now has come for me to place myself ⌐in the households of⌐ some great princes of Italy, but I perceive that you have not yet grasped how philosophers see themselves. In their eyes, as Horace remarks, they are kings of kings; ⌐they love liberty;⌐ they cannot bear the proud manners of people of high rank; they cannot serve. They dwell within themselves and are content with the tranquility of their own minds. Unto themselves they are sufficient, and more than sufficient. They seek nothing outside themselves. Things held in honor among common people are not honorable in their eyes. Whatever men's lustful desires thirst after or ambition seeks they set at naught and despise. And while all this applies to everyone, undoubtedly it pertains especially to those so generously favored by fortune that they can live not only well and prosperously but also nobly.

These great positions raise a man on high and put him on display, but it often happens that they throw down their master as a fierce and skittish horse throws his. Always, certainly, they grieve and vex him, tearing at him rather than bearing him up. What is desirable is the golden mean, ⌐the midpoint,⌐ which will more gently shelter us in its hands, obeying us and not playing the master to us.

Standing firmly by this opinion, I therefore attach more importance to my little house, my study, the enjoyment of my books, ⌐the rest⌐ and peace of my mind, than to all your kings' palaces, all your public business, ⌐all your glory,⌐ all the advantages you are so keen on, and all the favor of the court. Nor do I hope that my studies will result in my being thrust hereafter into the raging torrent of your worldly affairs; but only that I may finally bring forth the offspring I labor upon—bring forth for the common ⌐profit,⌐ that is, some books of my own that may contain something of the savor, if not of learning, then at least of intelligence and diligence.

And lest you suppose I've at all neglected or slacked off from my diligent efforts, let me tell you that after much hard work, with a lot of concentration and indefatigable labor, I have learned both the Hebrew and Chaldean tongues, and have now turned my attention to overcoming the great challenge of Arabic. Things like these, my dear friend, I have always thought, and think now, do pertain to a noble prince. ⌐Fare well.¬

Written at Paris, the fifteenth day of October, in the year of grace 1492.

Letter 4

To Thomas Ruthall [5]

In 1506, Thomas More published a collection of translations from the ancient satirist and comic author, Lucian of Samosata (c. 125–180), in collaboration with his friend, the Dutch humanist Erasmus. This letter is More's introduction to these translations, which he calls "the first fruits of his Greek studies." In More's judgment, Lucian is an author who fulfills the ancient Roman Horace's maxim in *Ars Poetica, or "The Art of Poetry,"* that the best poets both delight and teach their readers, especially through their "living words" (cf. ll. 305–322). Like other classical comic writers, Lucian delighted in representing and exposing to the reader's eyes the human tendency to prove ridiculous in one's words, desires, thoughts, and deeds. In Plato's *Philebus*, Socrates defines the "nature of the ridiculous" as ignorance of oneself; he calls it a "species of the genus 'badness' which is differentiated by the opposite of the inscription at Delphi. . . . 'by no means know thyself!'" (48a–b). Later in the English Renaissance, Sir Philip Sidney emphasizes the ridiculous as well in his astute comments on comedy in *A Defense of Poesy:* "Comedy is an imitation of the common errors of our life, which [the poet] represents in the most ridiculous and scornful sort that may be, so as it is impossible that any beholder can be content to be such a one" (229–30).

For his part in the literary project, More chose to translate three particular dialogues: *Cynicus, Necromantia,* and *Philopseudes, or Lover of Lies,* and he also contributed an original composition, a declamation in reply to Lucian's *Tyrannicide.* These early translations reveal some of More's key preoccupations as a thinker and writer, especially the difficulties of self-knowledge and self-rule; the metaphor of life as a drama and stage on which the human actor must learn to play his or her part well; the challenge of living truth and the comfort of living lies; the power of inordinate passion and the delusions of self-love; and most importantly the need for a citizen-leader capable of working to prevent tyrannies large and small, public and personal, in a free yet fragile country.

In More's lifetime, the Lucian translations were his most popular and successful publications. More, who was later called "Master Mock" by detractors, was particularly impressed by Lucian's gift for irony, which the Roman orator Quintillian defines as the rhetorical figure in which the author communicates "something which is the opposite of what is actually said" (*Institutes* 9.2.44). More uses just such "Socratic irony," named after its greatest practitioner, to fine effect in his later political and philosophical masterworks, *The History of Richard the Third* (1513) and *Utopia* (1516). Noticing first and then thinking through the significance of such ironic writing provides invaluable exercise to the willing reader; indeed, such exercise and intellectual endeavor, as More writes in his 1529 *Dialogue Concerning Heresies,* helps "make a man among other things well furnished in one special thing, without which all learning is half lame. . . . a good mother wit." Of note too is More's critique of alleged saints' lives that mislead readers about the real struggles of sanctification and inculcate in readers "foolish confidence and superstitious dread" instead. For the complete text of More's translations of Lucian and

his original declamation on tyrannicide, see volume four of the Yale
Complete Works of St. Thomas More.
The addressee of this letter, Thomas Ruthall (d. 1523), was educated at Oxford, and then served in a variety of important offices,
including secretary to both Henry VII and Henry VIII (1500–1519);
chancellor of Cambridge University (1503–1504); bishop of Durham
(1509–1523); and keeper of the privy seal (1516–1523) [*ODNB*]. In
the letter, "the rule of Critolaus" refers to a text from Cicero's *Tusculan Disputations:* "And here I ask what weight they think there is in
the balance of Critolaus, who having put the goods of the mind into
one scale, and the goods of the body and other external advantages
into the other, thought the goods of the mind outweighed the others so far that they would require the whole earth and sea to equalize
the scale" (5.17).

<LONDON

1506>

TO THE MOST ILLUSTRIOUS AND LEARNED THOMAS
RUTHALL, ENGLISH ROYAL SECRETARY, THOMAS MORE
SENDS GREETING:

If, most learned Sir, there was ever anyone who fulfilled the
Horatian maxim and combined delight with instruction, I think
Lucian certainly ranked among the foremost in this respect.
Refraining from the arrogant pronouncements of the philosophers as well as from the wanton wiles of the poets, he everywhere
reprimands and censures, with very honest and at the same time
very entertaining wit, our human frailties. And this he does so
cleverly and effectively that although no one pricks more deeply,
nobody resents his stinging words. He is always first-rate at this,
but in my opinion he has done it exceptionally well in these three
dialogues, which for this very reason I have chosen, from such

an abundance of exceedingly pleasant ones, to translate; though perhaps other persons might much prefer other dialogues. For just as, among girls, all men do not love the same one, but each has his own preference as fancy dictates and adores not the one he can prove is best but the one who seems best to him—so of the most agreeable dialogues of Lucian, one man likes a certain one best, another prefers another; and these have particularly struck my fancy, yet not without reason, I trust, nor mine alone.

For to begin with the shortest, which is called *Cynicus*, and which might appear unacceptable on account of its very brevity, did not Horace remind us that the greater strength is often to be found in a slight body, and did not we ourselves see that even the smallest jewels are prized: my choice of it is endorsed by the estimable approval of St. John Chrysostom, a man of the most acute judgment, of all learned men perhaps the most Christian and (at least in my opinion) of all Christians the most learned. So much did this dialogue delight him that he introduced a large part of it into a homily he composed on the Gospel of St. John. And not without reason: for what should have pleased that grave and truly Christian man more than this dialogue in which, while the severe life of Cynics, satisfied with little, is defended and the soft, enervating luxury of voluptuaries denounced, by the same token Christian simplicity, temperance, and frugality, and finally that strait and narrow path which leads to Life eternal, are praised?

Next *Necromantia*, for this is what the second dialogue is called—not very auspicious in its title but felicitous in content— how wittily it rebukes the jugglery of magicians or the silly fictions of poets or the fruitless contentions of philosophers among themselves on any question whatever!

There remains *Philopseudes*, which, with a measure of Socratic irony, is entirely concerned (as its title indicates) with ridiculing and reproving the inordinate passion for lying. Whether this dialogue is more amusing or more instructive is hard to say. I'm not much troubled by the fact that the author seems to have been disposed to doubt his own immortality, and to have been in the same error as Democritus, Lucretius, Pliny, and many others likewise were [i.e., by denying the immortality of the soul]. For what difference does it make to me what a pagan thinks about those articles contained in the principal mysteries of the Christian faith? Surely the dialogue will teach us this lesson: that we should put no trust in magic and that we should eschew superstition, which obtrudes everywhere under the guise of religion. It teaches us also that we should live a life less distracted by anxiety; less fearful, that is, of any gloomy and superstitious untruths. Very many of these are related with such a show of confidence and authority that some cunning rogue or other even induced the most blessed father Augustine, a man of complete sobriety and a zealous enemy of lies, to tell as a truth, as something that occurred in his own lifetime, that yarn about two *Spurinnae*—one coming back to life and the other departing from it—which Lucian made fun of in this dialogue, with only the names changed, so many years before Augustine was born.

You should not be surprised, therefore, if the common herd are taken in by the fictions of those who think they've done a great work, and put Christ in their debt forever, if they've feigned a story about a saint or a horrendous tale of hell to drive some old woman to tears or make her tremble with fear. And so there is scarcely a martyr's or a virgin's life which they have passed over without inserting some falsehoods of this kind—with pious intent, to be sure, for otherwise there was danger lest truth could not stand by its own strength but had to be bolstered with lies! They have not shrunk from defiling with their tales that religion which Truth itself established and which it intended to consist of truth unadorned; and they have not considered that fables of this kind, so far from helping at all, do more deadly harm than anything else. Surely, as the aforementioned father Augustine testifies, when the added falsehood is detected, the authority of truth is immediately diminished and weakened. Wherefore I have often suspected that a large portion of such fables has been concocted by certain crafty, wicked wretches and heretics whose object was partly to amuse themselves by the thoughtless credulity of the simple-minded (rather than the wise), partly to undermine trust in the true stories of Christians by traffic in mere fictions; since they often invent things so nearly resembling those in Sacred Scripture that they easily reveal that by playing upon those stories they have been ridiculing them. Therefore we ought to place unquestioning trust in the stories commended to us by divinely inspired Scripture, but testing the others carefully and deliberately by the teaching of Christ (as though applying the rule of Critolaus), we should either accept or reject them if we wish to free ourselves both from foolish confidence and superstitious dread.

But where am I headed? This epistle already rivals a book in length, yet I haven't said a word so far in praise of you; another man would have dwelt perhaps on that theme exclusively. I had abundant resources for doing so, without being open to the slightest suspicion of flattery. There is—quite apart from the rest of your virtues—your distinction in learning and your unsurpassed wisdom in practical affairs, attested by numerous diplomatic missions carried out in various lands with such difficult negotiations and with such success. Or there is your extraordinary trustworthiness and dignity. Unless he had regarded this as tried and tested, a sagacious prince would never have appointed you to be Secretary. But your singular modesty, which makes you unwilling to hear yourself praised for the praiseworthy things you so willingly do, balks at publication of your other virtues. Accordingly I spare your sense of propriety, begging only that you kindly accept these first fruits of my Greek studies and treat them as a token, in some sort, of my affection and my duty toward you. I have ventured to submit them to you with the greater confidence because, although your judgment is so keen that nobody would more quickly detect any error there may be, yet your nature is so kind that none would more readily condone it. Farewell.

Letter 5a

TO KING HENRY VIII [6]

This letter to the new King Henry VIII serves as a preface and introduction to More's *Coronation Ode*, originally composed in 1509, the year of young Henry's crowning. The first words of More's letter, "I fear," are indicative of the difficulty he understood in such communication with royal power, and they anticipate one reason for More's later request for "free speech," the first such appeal on record, made before King Henry during the 1523 Parliament (see letter 5d below for the text of Thomas More's "Petition"). Because the *Coronation Ode* itself is a letter of sorts in verse to King Henry, and certainly because of its intrinsic interest, the poem is included immediately following this letter. The *Ode* praises the young Henry, while making some daring critiques of his dead father, Henry VII, on behalf of the beleaguered nobility and "the people" of England, especially its leading citizens, who found the end of his reign rather taxing.

The *Coronation Ode* is a fascinating example of the art—and rhetorical challenge—of speaking to a young yet tremendously wealthy and powerful king. One perplexing thing about the *Ode* is that Henry was only 17 years old when he was crowned, and yet the poem seems to present him—a young man who has not yet ruled—as the best of all possible leaders. Such considerations have led scholars to wonder about possible ambiguities and ambivalences in this panegyric and to probe the several images of kingly rule it presents to the reader. How, for example, does the polished perturbation of a kingly crown bring with it "the character which deserves to rule"? What is the poem's teaching on "power"? And why does More liken the new king to Achilles when "he dragged Hector behind his Thessalian steeds"? This moment from Homer's *Iliad,* when the enraged Achilles refuses to allow Hector's body to be buried and insists on shaming him and desecrating his body, is not a particularly glorious one: in fact, the god Apollo observes that Achilles in the darkness of his passion has become "like some lion / going his own barbaric way, giving in to his power, his brute force, and wild pride" (24.48–50). What, then, is More's position on "unlimited power" in the poem? And how exactly does this poem counsel the youthful new king, who inherited power and wealth beyond the minds of most men? The *Coronation Ode* ends with the golden hope of peace and high praise for the new queen, Catherine of Aragon, who surpasses several classical women on account of her devotion, judgment, and eloquence, according to More. Later, after Catherine had fallen on the dark days of royal displeasure and divorce, Henry's minister Thomas Cromwell would remark: "Nature wronged her in not making her a man. But for her sex, she would have surpassed all the heroes of history"(quoted in Weir 252). For a complete analysis of More's *Ode,* see Wegemer's *Young Thomas More* (88–103), and for a study guide for the poem and its interpretive issues, see *www.thomasmorestudies.org.* For the text of the young Henry's Coronation Oath, see Appendix II.

<LONDON
c. JUNE 1509>

I fear, most glorious prince, that while I was trying to win favor for my awkward verses by the addition of color (like maidens who have insufficient confidence in their beauty), I may have robbed them of that characteristic by which they could have given you the greatest pleasure—I mean timeliness. For when I had finished writing them at the time of your coronation and had handed them over to an illuminator for decoration, an attack of the gout, no less, by which the illuminator was most inopportunely afflicted immediately upon undertaking the task, has caused me to present my verses to you only now, considerably later than the circumstances seemed to require. And so (if, in accord with your inherent kindness, you give me leave to deal informally with the matter) I do not know whether greater charm was given to my verses by the illuminator's hands or taken from them by his feet. In any case it is because of his feet that I am constrained to fear that my expression of joy may seem to you no less late, no less untimely, than, in antiquity, the famous expression of sorrow by the citizens of Troy seemed to the Emperor Tiberius. The Trojans commiserated with the Emperor on the loss of a son who had been dead for a long time. The Emperor with ready wit made fun of their condolences by saying that he too sympathized with them in their loss of that noble warrior Hector. But their effort, directed at a grief that was not merely fading but had wholly passed away, could not be anything but ridiculous. Mine, however, is preserved from this defect by the immeasurable rejoicing occasioned by your thronged coronation; for since that joy has filled the hearts of all with an emotion so strong and lasting that it cannot fade even in a whole lifetime, the result is that this offering of mine seems to have arrived, not late and when the event was past and forgotten, but in time and while the event is still with us. Farewell, most glorious and (although this title is strange and rare for kings) most beloved prince.

Letter 5b

THOMAS MORE'S CORONATION ODE TO KING HENRY VIII

On the Coronation Day of King Henry the Eighth,
Most Glorious and Blessed King
Of the British Isles, And of Catherine
His Most Happy Queen,
A Poetical Expression of Good Wishes
By Thomas More of London

<LONDON
c. JUNE 1509>

If ever there was a day, England, if ever there was a time for you to give thanks to those above, this is that happy day, one to be marked with a pure white stone and put in your calendar. This day is the [end] of our slavery, the beginning of our freedom, the end of sadness, the source of joy, for this day consecrates a young man who is the everlasting glory of our time and makes him your king—a king who is worthy not merely to govern a single people but singly to rule the whole world—such a king as will wipe the tears from every eye and put joy in the place of our long distress. Every heart smiles to see its cares dispelled, as the day shines bright when clouds are scattered. Now the people, freed, run before their king with bright faces. Their joy is almost beyond their own comprehension. They rejoice, they exult, they leap for joy and celebrate their having such a king. "The King" is all that any mouth can say.

The nobility, long since at the mercy of the dregs of the population, the nobility, whose title has too long been without meaning, now lifts its head, now rejoices in such a king, and has proper reason for rejoicing. The merchant, heretofore deterred by numerous taxes, now once again plows seas grown unfamiliar. Laws, heretofore powerless—yes, even laws put to unjust ends— now happily have regained their proper authority. All are equally happy. All weigh their earlier losses against the advantages to come. Now each man happily does not hesitate to show the possessions which in the past his fear kept hidden in dark seclusion. Now there is enjoyment in any profit which managed to escape the many sly clutching hands of the many thieves. No longer is it a criminal offense to own property which was honestly acquired (formerly it was a serious offense). No longer does fear hiss whispered secrets in one's ear, for no one has secrets either to keep or to whisper. Now it is a delight to ignore informers. Only ex-informers fear informers now.

The people gather together, every age, both sexes, and all ranks. There is no reason why they should lurk in their homes and not take part while the king, after completion of the proper ceremonies, undertakes, amid happy auspices, the rule of Britain. Wherever he goes, the dense crowd in their desire to look upon him leaves hardly a narrow lane for his passage. The houses are filled to overflowing, the rooftops strain to support the weight of spectators. On all sides there arises a shout of new good will. Nor are the people satisfied to see the king just once; they change their vantage points time and time again in the hope that, from one place or another, they may see him again. Three times they delight to see him—and why not? This king, than whom Nature has [shaped] nothing more deserving of love.

Among a thousand noble companions he stands out taller than any. And he has strength worthy of his regal person. His hand, too, is as skilled as his heart is brave, whether there is an issue to be settled by the naked sword, or an eager charge with leveled lances, or an arrow aimed to strike a target. There is fiery

power in his eyes, [Venus] in his face, and such color in his cheeks
as is typical of twin roses. In fact, that face, admirable for its ani-
mated strength, could belong to either a young girl or a man.
Thus Achilles looked when he pretended to be a maiden, thus he
looked when he dragged Hector behind his Thessalian steeds.

Ah, if only nature would permit that, like his body, the
outstanding excellence of his [soul] be visible to the eye. Nay
but in fact his virtue does shine forth from his very face; his
countenance bears the open message of a good heart, revealing
how ripe the wisdom that dwells in his judicious mind, how
profound the calm of his untroubled breast, how he bears his
lot and manages it whether it be good or bad, how great his care
for modest chastity. How serene the clemency that warms his
gentle heart, how far removed from arrogance his mind, of these
the noble countenance of our prince itself displays the indubi-
table signs, signs that admit no counterfeit. But his justice, the
skill he has in the art of ruling, his sense of responsibility in the
treatment of his people—these can easily be discerned from our
faces, these must be perceived from the prosperity we enjoy. In
that we are treated thus and are gaining our liberty, in that fear,
harm, danger, grief have vanished, while peace, ease, joy, and
laughter have returned—therein is revealed the excellence of
our distinguished prince.

Unlimited power has a tendency to weaken good minds, and
that even in the case of very gifted men. But howsoever dutiful he
was before, his crown has brought our prince a character which
deserves to rule, for he has provided promptly on his first day
such advantages as few rulers have granted in extreme old age.
He has instantly arrested and imprisoned anyone who by plots
had harmed the realm. Whoever was an informer is closely fet-
tered and confined, so that he himself suffers the woes which he
imposed on many. Our prince opened the sea for trade. If any
over-harsh duties were required of the merchants, he lightened

their load. And the long-scorned nobility recovered on our prince's first day the ancient rights of nobles. He now gives to good men the honors and public offices which used to be sold to evil men. By a happy reversal of circumstances, learned men now have the prerogatives which ignoramuses carried off in the past.

Our prince without delay has restored to the laws their ancient force and dignity (for they had been perverted so as to subvert the realm). And although formerly each rank in the state was changing character completely, now at once every rank is restored. What if, in the hope of being kind to his people, he decided to retract certain provisions of the law which he knew his father had approved? In this he placed, as he should, his country before his father. This preference does not surprise me; what could lie beyond the powers of a prince whose natural gifts have been enhanced by a liberal education, a prince bathed by the nine sisters [i.e., the Muses] in the Castalian fount and steeped in philosophy's own precepts? The whole people used to be, on many counts, in debt to the king, and this in particular was the evil they feared. But our king, though he could have inspired fear in this way and could have gathered from this source immense riches, if he had wished to do so, has forgiven the debts of all, and rendered all secure, removing all the evil of distressing fear. Hence it is that, while other kings have been feared by their [people], this king is loved, since now through his action they have no cause for fear.

O prince, terror to your proud enemies but not to your own people, it is your enemies who fear you; we revere and love you. Our love for you will prove the reason for their fear. And thus it is that, in the absence of sycophants, your [people's] love and your enemies' fear will hedge you round in peace and safety. As for wars beyond the borders—if the French, for instance, join with the Scots—no one is afraid, provided that England is not divided. And internal strife there will not be, for what cause, what reason, is there to provoke it? Most important, concerning your right and title to the crown, there is no opposition, nor can there be. You, all by yourself, represent both sides of the quarrel which usually arises; the fact that both your parents were high-born disposes of this problem. And anyway the anger of the people, a wicked thing, common source of civil disturbance, is even more remote from you. To all your subjects you are so dear that no man could be dearer to himself. But if perchance wrath were to bring powerful chieftains to war, your nod will promptly put an end to that wrath, such reverence for your sacred majesty have your virtues justly created. And whatever virtues your ancestors had, these are yours too, not excelled in ages past. For you, sire, have your father's wisdom, you have your mother's kindly strength, the devout intelligence of your paternal grandmother, the noble heart of your mother's father. What wonder, then, if England rejoices in a fashion heretofore unknown, since she has such a king as she never had before?

And then there is the fact that this joy, apparently as great as it could be, was increased by your marriage—a marriage which the kindly powers above arranged and in which they planned well for you and yours. In her you have as wife one whom your people have been happy to see sharing your power, one for whom the powers above care so much that they distinguish her and honor her by marriage with you. She it is who could vanquish the ancient Sabine women in devotion, and in dignity the holy, half-divine heroines of Greece. She could equal the unselfish love of Alcestis or, in her unfailing judgment, outdo Tanaquil. In her expression, in her countenance, there is a remarkable beauty uniquely appropriate for one so great and good. The well-spoken Cornelia would yield to her in eloquence; she is like Penelope in loyalty to a husband. This lady, prince, vowed to you for many years, through a long time of waiting remained alone for love of you. Neither her own sister nor her native land could win her from her way; neither her mother nor her father could dissuade her. It was you, none other, whom she preferred to her mother, sister, native land, and beloved father. This blessed lady has joined in lasting alliance two nations, each of them powerful. She is descended from great kings, to be sure; and she will be the mother of kings as great as her ancestors. Until now one anchor has protected your ship of state—a strong one, yet only one. But your queen, fruitful in male offspring, will render it on all sides stable and everlasting. Great advantage is yours because of her, and similarly is hers because of you. There has been no other woman, surely, worthy to have you as husband, nor any other man worthy to have her as wife.

England! bring incense, and an offering more potent than all incense—loyal hearts and innocent hands, that heaven, as it has made this marriage, may bless it, that the scepter may be swayed with the help of heaven that gave it, and that these crowns may long be worn by these two, and may at length be worn by their son's son and their descendants thereafter.

Letter 5c

KING HENRY VIII TO KING FERDINAND II

Shortly after his coronation in June 1509, the young King Henry wrote to Catherine's father, Ferdinand II of Spain, about the recent events in England, in particular his marriage to Catherine and his affection for his new wife. The source of this letter is volume one of *Letters of the Kings of England*, edited by James Orchard Halliwell-Phillipps (London: Henry Colburn, 1848).

GREENWICH PALACE
26 JULY 1509

To the most serene and most excellent Prince Lord Don Ferdinand, by the grace of God, king of Aragon, of the two Sicilies and Jerusalem, our very dear father, Henry, by the same grace, king of England and France, and lord of Ireland, health and prosperous success.

We have the letters of your serene highness, dated to us on the fourth of this month from Turre de Gylles, whereby we have been affected with violent joy, beyond what can be expressed; in the first place, as your majesty, having read our letters and having learnt the consummation of our marriage with the most serene lady the queen, your daughter, hath yourself conceived no little delight at that event, and hath in consequence made a public demonstration and festival in your own person: the past delay of which long tormented your majesty's mind. In the second place, as your serene highness greatly commends ourself, in having completed this marriage so liberally, and in having rejected all other ladies in the world that have been offered to us; showing hereby our singular love, which we bear towards your majesty and the most illustrious house of Aragon, as well as to the most serene lady herself the queen our very beloved consort.

From this cause, your majesty, just like a most excellent and true father, forming a most true judgment of our inward and cordial feeling towards yourself, most generously offers to us yourself and all yours. Wherefore, for so singular and such paternal affection wherewith you honor us, we owe undoubtedly to your serene highness boundless thanks, (and greater than these, if possible) accepting most willing your paternal offers, and confidently intending to avail ourself of them when opportunity happen; offering equally and in like manner to you ourself, and ours, and whatever shall ever possibly proceed from us, inasmuch as this our strict alliance and bond so requires and demands: so that all things may be common, both ours with you and yours with us.

And, as regards that sincere love, which we have to the most serene queen our consort,—her eminent virtues daily more and more shine forth, blossom, and increase so much, that, if we were still free, her we would yet choose for our wife before all other. And, we will so strive to answer your majesty's expectation and fatherly love to ourself, that you may be convinced we neither omit, nor neglect, in any particular, our filial duty; but in all points repay the reciprocal debt of love and attention to our utmost power. All these things, of course, you will be pleased to relate, in our name, to the most illustrious lady, the queen of Castile, your daughter, our very dear kinswoman, and to commend ourself to her in singular degree.

However, as regards the ambassador, whom your majesty purposes to send, to sojourn with us, we shall see him very cheerfully; both that from him we may be assured at length of your majesty's happy state, (which we earnestly desire to know) and likewise that he may be able, from time to time, to acquaint you of our daily proceedings.

May the God Almighty preserve you long, happy, prosperous, and safe, with daily increase of auspicious events!

From our palace at Greenwich, 26th of July, 1509, and in the first year of our reign.

H. Rex

Letter 5d

THOMAS MORE'S "PETITION FOR FREEDOM OF SPEECH"

MADE AS SPEAKER OF THE HOUSE OF COMMONS
TO KING HENRY VIII, 1523

In 1523, Thomas More was chosen to be Speaker of the House of
Commons of Parliament. Hesitant to accept the post, he asked King
Henry VIII to release him from the duty. The king refused his request
and, accepting the position, More made a second request to King
Henry: a request for free speech, the first such request known to
be made. Like the *Coronation Ode,* this petition is a fascinating and
important example of communication between More and Henry,
and so is included in this volume of letters. The text is from William
Roper's *Life of Sir Thomas More,* modernized by Mary Gottschalk.

<18 APRIL 1523>

My other humble request, most excellent Prince, is this. Of your
commoners here assembled by your high command for your Parliament, a great number have been, in accord with the customary
procedure, appointed in the House of Commons to treat and
advise on the common affairs among themselves, as a separate
group. And, most dear liege Lord, in accord with your prudent
advice communicated everywhere by your honorable commands,
due diligence has been exercised in sending up to your Highness's
court of Parliament the most discreet persons out of every area
who were deemed worthy of this office; hence, there can be no
doubt that the assembly is a very substantial one, of very wise
and politic persons. And yet, most victorious Prince, among so
many wise men, not all will be equally wise, and of those who
are equally wise, not all will be equally well-spoken. And often it

happens that just as a lot of foolishness is uttered with ornate and polished speech, so, too, many coarse and rough-spoken men see deep indeed and give very substantial counsel. Also, in matters of great importance the mind is often so preoccupied with the subject matter that one thinks more about what to say than about how to say it, for which reason the wisest and best-spoken man in the country may now and then, when his mind is engrossed in the subject matter, say something in such a way that he will later wish he had said it differently, and yet he had no less good will when he spoke it than he has when he would so gladly change it. And therefore, most gracious Sovereign, considering that in your high court of Parliament nothing is discussed but weighty and important matters concerning your realm and your own royal estate, many of your discreet commoners will be hindered from giving their advice and counsel, to the great hindrance of the common affairs, unless every one of your commoners is utterly discharged of all doubt and fear as to how anything that he happens to say may happen to be taken by your Highness. And although your well known and proven kindness gives every man hope, yet such is the seriousness of the matter, such is the reverent dread that the timorous hearts of your natural-born subjects conceive toward your high Majesty, our most illustrious King and Sovereign, that they cannot be satisfied on this point unless you, in your gracious bounty, remove the misgivings of their timorous minds and animate and encourage and reassure them.

It may therefore please your most abundant Grace, our most benign and godly King, to give to all your commoners here assembled your most gracious permission and allowance for every man freely, without fear of your dreaded displeasure, to speak his conscience and boldly declare his advice concerning everything that comes up among us. Whatever any man may happen to say, may it please your noble Majesty, in your inestimable goodness, to take it all with no offense, interpreting every man's words, however badly they may be phrased, to proceed nonetheless from a good zeal toward the profit of your realm and honor of your royal person, the prosperous condition and preservation of which, most excellent Sovereign, is the thing which we all, your most humble and loving subjects, according to that most binding duty of our heartfelt allegiance, most highly desire and pray for.

Letter 6

To John Colet [8]

In this letter, More encourages Colet to press on at St. Paul's, where the "new learning" of Christian humanism was meeting some opposition. More's understanding of humanism has its roots in both classical texts and the biblical and patristic writings on the subject. For example, the Roman philosopher and statesman Cicero wrote in *De Oratore* that the liberal arts "were devised for the purpose of fashioning the minds of the young according to *humanitas* and virtue" (3.58). Another Roman author, Seneca, the moral philosopher and tragic playwright, defined *humanitas* as "the idea of man, according to which man is fashioned" (*Letter* 65). In Cicero's judgment, one's sense of *humanitas* was so important that he counseled his young reader: "Work out your own ideas and sift your thoughts so as to see what conception of a good person they contain," unless one wants to become another "Caesar, [who] overturned all the laws, human and divine, to achieve for himself a principate fashioned according to his own erroneous opinion" (*De Officiis* 3.81, 1.26). Scripture and tradition bring *humanitas* further to light in the person of Christ, "fully God and fully man" according to the Nicene Creed. As St. Irenaeus of Lyons remarked, "The glory of God is man fully alive, and the life of man is the vision of God. If the revelation of God through creation already brings life to all living beings on the earth, how much more will the manifestation of the Father by the Word bring life to those who see God?" (*Adversus Haereses* IV.20). See letter 19 below for more on Thomas More's distinctive humanism, and see especially the first three chapters of *Young Thomas More*, for a full discussion of More's understanding of the liberal arts, *humanitas*, and liberty.

<LONDON

c. 1512>

I don't much wonder if they are bursting with jealousy of your excellent school [i.e., St. Paul's in London]. For they see that, just as the Greeks who destroyed barbarian Troy came out of the Trojan horse, so from your school come those who reprove and overthrow their ignorance.

Letter 7

TO ERASMUS [16]

The young Thomas More first became friends with the Dutch humanist, Desiderius Erasmus (1467–1536), when Erasmus traveled to England in 1499. Later, in 1505–1506, Erasmus visited England again, this time staying with Thomas More. In 1509, Erasmus composed his satire *Praise of Folly* (*Moriae Encomium*) while staying with More's family at Bucklersbury. In the prefatory letter addressed to Thomas More, Erasmus explains the origin of the satire and its relation and dedication to his friend: "I chose to amuse myself composing an encomium of Folly. 'How did you ever get that idea?' you will say. First of all, it was suggested to me by your family name 'More,' which comes as close to the Greek word for folly (*Moria*) as

you yourself are far removed from the fact of folly. . . . Then too,
I suspected that this *jeu d'esprit* of mine would be especially acceptable to you because you ordinarily take great pleasure in jokes of this
sort . . . and because you habitually play the role of Democritus
[the laughing philosopher] by making fun of the ordinary lives of
mortals. On the other hand, though your extraordinarily keen intelligence places you worlds apart from the common herd, still the
incredible sweetness and gentleness of your character makes you
able and willing to be a man for all seasons with all men" (1–2).

In 1516, the year of this letter, Erasmus would publish his influen-
tial edition of the Greek New Testament with his own Latin translation, and he also would supervise the publication of Thomas More's
Utopia (see letter 8). Notable among Erasmus' later writings are his
Complaint of Peace (1521) and *On Free Will* (1524), a diatribe against
Martin Luther in defense of free will, understood by Erasmus as "the
power of the human will whereby man can apply to or turn away
from that which leads to eternal salvation" (*Discourse on Free Will*,
20). Like Thomas More, Erasmus would go on to critique Luther's
rhetorical fire as well: "Luther . . . who had previously allowed
something to free choice, is now carried so far in the heat of his
defense as to destroy it entirely. But I believe it was Lycurgus, who
was rebuked by the Greeks because, in his hatred of drunkenness, he
gave the orders for the vines to be cut down, when he should rather,
by giving access to the fountains, have excluded drunkenness without destroying the use of wine" (90). King Henry VIII also critiqued
Luther's new theology in his *Defense of the Seven Sacraments* (1521),
for which he was given the title "Defender of the Faith," and in his
later epistle to Luther as well (1526).

In this letter, More reflects on the sweetness of friendship and
the difficult life of a diplomat and public servant; he also discusses
the doings of the English humanists Richard Pace, William Warham, Archbishop of Canterbury, and Cuthbert Tunstall, as well as
the continental humanists, Jerome de Busleyden, Beatus Rhenanus,

and especially Peter Giles, praised by More for his "genuine friendliness." Martin Dorp, a theologian from Louvain, was embroiled in a
controversy with Erasmus, in which Thomas More intervened (see
letters 27a–b below). William Warham's successor as Archbishop of
Canterbury is Thomas Wolsey (1470–1529), first butcher's son and
later Cardinal of York, who would exert such great influence over
King Henry and England as he pursued his ambitions and rose to
the office of Lord Chancellor before his fall from power and death in
1529. Thomas More succeeded Wolsey as Lord Chancellor, an office
More held until his resignation in 1532. In the later history play, *King
Henry VIII* (1613), Shakespeare presents the freshly fallen Wolsey as
a man who "out of his wrack" tries to teach Thomas Cromwell, his
young protégé, "a way . . . to rise" (3.2.516). Shakespeare's Wolsey
comments on Sir Thomas More as well: "He's a learned man. May
he continue / Long in his highness' favor, and do justice / For truth's
sake and his conscience; that his bones, / When he has run his course
and sleeps in blessings, / May have a tomb of orphans' tears wept
on 'em!" (3.2.471–75). Earlier in his career, Shakespeare also collabo-
rated on a rather mysterious and apparently never produced play, *Sir
Thomas More* (ca. 1593), with a group of London playwrights. For
the full text of *Sir Thomas More*, a manuscript containing the only
surviving example of dramatic writing in Shakespeare's own hand,
see *A Thomas More Sourcebook* (Catholic University of America
Press, 2004), and John Jowett's new Arden edition of the play.

<LONDON
c. 17 FEBRUARY 1516>

Since your departure, my dearest Erasmus, I have received altogether three letters from you. If I claimed to have answered all
of them I do not suppose you would believe me, no matter how
solemnly I lied; especially since you know me very well as a lazy
correspondent and not so scrupulously truthful as to shrink from

a little white lie as if it were parricide. Our friend Pace is on an embassy in your locality, although not exactly in the same place as you. He can converse with me by letter, but not with you face to face. May he come home soon with his business happily concluded, so that at least one half of me can be with me. For I do not know when to expect you, since you intend to move on to Italy, where, I fear, you will meet people who will not let you get away. For the present, I shall be missing one half of me, while he is gone; and the other half, while you are gone. . . .

. . . The Archbishop of Canterbury has finally been relieved of the office of chancellor, a burden, which, as you know, he had tried extremely hard to shake off for several years; at long last he has attained his heart's desire, a life of privacy, and if having wonderful leisure amid his books and his memories of duties well done. He has been replaced, at the appointment of the King, by the Cardinal of York [i.e., Thomas Wolsey], who as an administrator is far exceeding everyone's expectations, which were very high in virtue of his other qualities; it is no easy thing to be the successor of an extraordinary person, and yet to give complete satisfaction.

. . . Our embassy, which like everything else I do is a matter of interest to you, was quite successful, though it dragged on much longer than I had hoped or wanted. When I left home, I expected to be gone at the most two months; but the embassy lasted more than six. However, those long months were crowned by rather gratifying results. So, when I say that my mission was accomplished and also that further complications were arising which, apparently, would lead to greater delay (as regularly happens with administrators), I wrote to the Cardinal and received permission to return, thanks to the assistance of my friends, especially Pace, who had not as yet gone. But on my return trip I unexpectedly met him at Gravelines; he was in such a hurry that he hardly had time to stop and exchange greetings. Tunstall came back recently, but was here barely ten days, without spending a single one of them pleasantly as he wanted, for his entire stay was squandered on a bothersome, disgusting review of all the details entrusted to him on his mission, and then, without warning, he has been promptly shoved back again on another embassy. It is very much against his will, I am sure, but he cannot refuse.

The office of ambassador has never held a great attraction for me. It does not suit us laymen as it does you clergy, for you either have no wives and children at home, or you find them wherever you travel. Whenever we are away for a short while, our hearts quickly go back to our wives and children.

Then too, when a priest goes on an embassy, he can take along with him wherever he wishes, his entire household and, for the time being, can support them at the expense of the king, while at home he would have to support them at his own expense. But when I am on leave, I must support two households, one at home, the other abroad. A rather generous allowance was granted to me by the King for the benefit of my retinue, but no consideration was made for those whom I had to leave at home; and although I am, as you know, a kindly husband and an indulgent father and a gentle master, still I have never had the least success in persuading the members of my family to do without food, for my sake, until I came home. Finally, it is easy for sovereigns, without any cost to themselves, to reimburse clergymen for their work and expenditures by means of ecclesiastical preferments; but no such generous and handy provisions are made for us, though the King, it is true, marked me out, on my return, for an annual pension, which, because of the distinction or the revenue involved, is not to be scorned. However, I have not as yet accepted it, and I do not think I ever shall; for its acceptance would mean that I either would have to leave my present post in London, which I do prefer even to a higher one, or, what is not at all to my liking, I would have to retain it and thereby occasion resentment among the townsfolk. If any dispute over privileges arises between them and the King, as sometimes happens, they would be skeptical about my sincerity and loyalty to them and consider me under obligation to the King as his pensioner.

However, certain aspects of that embassy gave me great pleasure; first of all, the extended and constant association with Tunstall, who is second to none in literary attainments [*bonis literis*] and strictness in life and morals [*vita moribusque seuerior*], and yet is a genial companion [*ita nemo est usquam in conuictu iucundior*]; secondly, the friendship which I formed with Busleiden, who is extremely wealthy and very generous, and therefore a magnificent and gracious host. He gave me a tour of his home, which is very artistically decorated and fitted with exquisite appointments; he also showed me his large collection of antiquities, in which, as you know, I am very interested. Finally, he displayed to me his remarkable well-stocked library and a mind even more so than any library, so that he completely filled me with amazement. I understand that he will very soon be sent on an embassy to our King. However, the most pleasant experience of my entire trip was my personal relationship with your host, Peter Gilles of Antwerp; his learning, his wit, his modesty, his genuine friendliness [*vere amici*] are such that, bless my soul, I would be happy to pay a good part of my wealth to purchase the companionship of that one man. He sent me your *Apology* and also your commentary on the Psalm *Beatus Vir* [Ps 1], which you dedicated to Beatus Rhenanus, a man truly blessed with this wonderful, lasting memorial of a friend. Dorp has had his letter printed and included as a preface to your *Apology*. I had hoped to meet him, if I had the chance. Since I did not, I sent him my greetings by letter,

Thomas More

Letter 8

TO ERASMUS [20]

With this letter, More alludes to his efforts to secure Erasmus patronage in England and entrusts his masterwork of humanism, *Utopia*, to Erasmus for publication. Also mentioned in the letter are Thomas More's *Epigrams*, his provocative—and occasionally revolutionary—collection of Latin poetry. Included in that collection are poems such as *The Coronation Ode* as well as others with arresting titles such *The Consent of the People Both Bestows and Withdraws Sovereignty* (#121), *What Is the Best Form of Government?* (#198), and *On Lust for Power* (#243). There are verses devoted to friendship, imagined as the active love that unites the work of a blind man and a lame man, as they learn the wisdom of helping one another, and still others that are comical, such as *On a Man Who Was a Philosopher Only by Reason of his Beard* (#157). The *Epigrams* would not be published until 1518, when they were included with the third edition of *Utopia*, a work upon which they cast helpful light.

The request for advice on whether or not to publish "my remarks about Brixius" refers to the imminent, explosive controversy between More and the French humanist, Germain de Brie (1490–1538). In the *Epigrams*, More wrote satirical verses on an epic poem Brixius had published valorizing a French victory over the English in the war of 1512–1513; despite some reservations, the verses were included in the 1518 edition of the *Epigrams*. Later in 1519, the incensed Brixius responded by publishing the *Antimorus*, a work that maliciously accused More of disloyalty to the King and stirred up trouble during a time of peace between England and France. The *Antimorus* prompted More's spirited defense of himself in the *Epistola ad Germanum Brixium* in 1520. The letter was never published, and the quarrel ended with an uneasy peace worked by Erasmus. For an account and analysis of the

Brixius controversy, see Gerard Wegemer's *Thomas More: A Portrait in Courage* (pp. 64, 75–76). For the complete text of More's response to Brixius, see volume 3.2 of More's *Complete Works*.

LONDON
3 SEPTEMBER <1516>

MORE SENDS HIS VERY BEST GREETINGS
TO MASTER ERASMUS:

I am sending you my *"Nowhere"* [i.e., *Utopia*] which is nowhere well written. I have added a prefatory epistle to my friend, Peter Giles. I know from experience that I do not have to tell you to give proper attention to everything else. I have delivered your letter to the Venetian ambassador, who, it appears, was very well disposed to receive your New Testament, which was intercepted by a Carmelite. He is completely devoted to sacred learning and has finished reading almost all the authors who treat of petty questions; he attributes so much importance to them that not even Dorp could outdo him in that. We conferred with one another like candidates campaigning for votes; we tickled one another with set speeches and lengthy encomia. But, to be honest, I like him very much. Apparently, he is very sincere and very competent in the things of man, and now he is completely dedicating himself to learning the things of God; and last, but not least, he is very interested in you.

I have no news as yet from the Archbishop of Canterbury about the situation. Colet has not had a conference with him about that business of yours, but he did have one with the Archbishop of York and says that he found him so much in your favor and so lavish in his praises of you that all he wants now is to have the Archbishop match his brilliant words with deeds. I expect him to do that soon, with openhanded generosity. The money you left with me will be delivered to Gilles by my John, at Michaelmas; he will not reach Antwerp before that feast. If you publish my *Epigrams,* give some thought to the propriety of printing my remarks about Brixius, some of them are rather caustic, although it might well seem that I had provocation from his insulting comments about my country. In any case, as I said, examine those expressions carefully and, in general, anything else that seems to you spiteful. As for any silly remarks, handle them all as you know will be for my own good. Quintilian regrets that Seneca did not follow someone else's judgment in using his own ability as a writer; however, it were better for me, when writing, not only to follow someone else's judgment, but also to use someone else's ability. Farewell, and give my regards to Master Tunstall and Master Busleiden. Hurriedly, from London, September 3.

Thomas More.

Letter 9

To PETER GILES [25]

Published as a kind of introduction to More's satirical-philosophical masterpiece *Utopia,* this letter is addressed to More's friend, Peter Giles, both a fellow humanist and a "character" in the playful fiction that is *Utopia.* More introduces Giles with high praise at the beginning of book one: "He was a native of Antwerp, a man of high reputation, already appointed to a good position and worthy of the very best: I hardly know whether the young man is distinguished more in learning or in character. Apart from being cultured, virtuous, and courteous to all, with his intimates he is so open-hearted, affectionate, loyal, and sincere that you would be hard-pressed to find another man anywhere whom you would think comparable to him in all points of friendship. No one is more modest or more frank; no one better combines simplicity with wisdom" (9).

In this letter, More first paradoxically claims that he has aimed at "truth" in the highly imaginative *Utopia,* and then he discusses the claims of Raphael Hythloday, the philosopher-wanderer who speaks on behalf of Utopia in books one and two, while More and Giles listen and occasionally attempt to cross-examine him. The letter is also valuable for the portrait it offers of More as a father, worker, and writer, and for its pointed critique of safe readers who stay "out of shot" and yet pontificate upon the work of writers who suffer the slings and arrows of outrageous criticisms. The young man mentioned, John Clement, would go on to become a reader in rhetoric and humanity at Corpus Christi College, Oxford, in 1518, and then a physician and the husband of More's adopted daughter, Margaret Giggs; he would also be imprisoned in the Tower of London with More in 1535, though he was later released (*ODNB*). See *www.thomasmorestudies.org* for a comprehensive study guide to More's *Utopia.* More's roughly contemporary—and considerably darker—study of tyranny, *The History of King Richard the Third*, makes an intriguing companion piece to the *Utopia.*

<London
c. October 1516>

Thomas More to Peter Giles, Greeting:

I am almost ashamed, my dear Peter Giles, to send you this little book about the state of *Utopia* after almost a year, when I am sure you looked for it within a month and a half. Certainly you know that I was relieved of all the labor of gathering materials for the work and that I had to give no thought at all to their arrangement. I had only to repeat what in your company I heard

Raphael relate. Hence there was no reason for me to take trouble
about the style of the narrative, seeing that his language could
not be polished. It was, first of all, hurried and impromptu and,
secondly, the product of a person who, as you know, was not so
well acquainted with Latin as with Greek. Therefore the nearer
my style came to his careless simplicity the closer it would be to
the truth, for which alone I am bound to care under the circumstances and actually do care.

I confess, my dear Peter, that all these preparations relieved
me of so much trouble that scarcely anything remained for me
to do. Otherwise the gathering or the arrangement of the materials could have required a good deal of both time and application
even from a talent neither the meanest nor the most ignorant. If
it had been required that the matter be written down not only
accurately but eloquently, I could not have performed the task
with any amount of time or application. But, as it was, those
cares over which I should have had to perspire so hard had been
removed. Since it remained for me only to write out simply what
I had heard, there was no difficulty about it.

Yet even to carry through this trifling task, my other tasks left
me practically no leisure at all. I am constantly engaged in legal
business, either pleading or hearing, either giving an award as
arbiter or deciding a case as judge. I pay a visit of courtesy to one
man and go on business to another. I devote almost the whole
day in public to other men's affairs and the remainder to my own.
I leave to myself, that is to learning, nothing at all.

When I have returned home, I must talk with my wife, chat
with my children, and confer with my servants. All this activity
I count as business when it must be done—and it must be unless
you want to be a stranger in your own home. Besides, one must
take care to be as agreeable as possible to those whom nature
has supplied, or chance has made, or you yourself have chosen,
to be the companions of your life, provided you do not spoil

them by kindness, or through indulgence make masters out of your servants.

Amid these occupations that I have named, the day, the month, the year slip away. When, then, can we find time to write? Nor have I spoken a word about sleep, nor even of food, which for many people takes up as much time as sleep—and sleep takes up almost half a man's life! So I get for myself only the time I filch from sleep and food. Slowly, therefore, because this time is but little, yet finally, because this time is something, I have finished *Utopia* and sent it to you, my dear Peter to read—and to remind me of anything that has escaped me.

In this respect I do not entirely distrust myself. (I only wish I were as good in intelligence and learning as I am not altogether deficient in memory!) Nevertheless, I am not so confident as to believe that I have forgotten nothing. As you know, John Clement, my pupil-servant, was also present at the conversation. Indeed I do not allow him to absent himself from any talk which can be somewhat profitable, for from this young plant, seeing that it has begun to put forth green shoots in Greek and Latin literature, I expect no mean harvest some day. He has caused me to feel very doubtful on one point.

According to my own recollection, Hythlodaeus declared that the bridge which spans the river Anydrus at Amaurotum is five hundred paces in length. But my John says that two hundred must be taken off, for the river there is not more than three hundred paces in breadth. Please recall the matter to mind. If you agree with him, I shall adopt the same view and think myself mistaken. If you do not remember, I shall put down, as I have actually done, what I myself seem to remember. Just as I shall take great pains to have nothing incorrect in the book, so, if there is doubt about anything, I shall rather tell an objective falsehood than an intentional lie—for I would rather be honest than wise.

Nevertheless, it would be easy for you to remedy this defect if you ask Raphael himself by word of mouth or by letter. You must do so on account of another doubt which has cropped up, whether more through my fault or through yours or Raphael's I do not know. We forgot to ask, and he forgot to say, in what part of the new world Utopia lies. I am sorry that point was omitted, and I would be willing to pay a considerable sum to purchase that information, partly because I am rather ashamed to be ignorant in what sea lies the island of which I am saying so much, partly because there are several among us, and one in particular, a devout man and a theologian by profession, burning with an extraordinary desire to visit Utopia. He does so not from an idle and curious lust for sight-seeing in new places but for the purpose of fostering and promoting our religion, begun there so felicitously.

To carry out his plan properly, he has made up his mind to arrange to be sent by the pope and, what is more, to be named bishop for the Utopians. He is in no way deterred by any scruple that he must sue for this prelacy, for he considers it a holy suit which proceeds not from any consideration of honor or gain but from motives of piety.

Therefore I beg you, my dear Peter, either by word of mouth if you conveniently can or by letter if he has gone, to reach Hythlodaeus and to make sure that my work includes nothing false and omits nothing true. I am inclined to think that it would be better to show him the book itself. No one else is so well able to correct any mistake, nor can he do this favor at all unless he reads through what I have written. In addition, in this way you will find out whether he accepts with pleasure or suffers with annoyance the fact that I have composed this work. If he himself has decided to put down in writing his own adventures, perhaps he may not want me to do so. By making known the commonwealth of Utopia, I should certainly dislike to forestall him and to rob his narrative of the flower and charm of novelty.

Nevertheless, to tell the truth, I myself have not yet made up my mind whether I shall publish it at all. So varied are the tastes of mortals, so peevish the characters of some, so ungrateful their dispositions, so wrongheaded their judgments, that those persons who pleasantly and blithely indulge their inclinations seem to be very much better off than those who torment themselves with anxiety in order to publish something that may bring profit or pleasure to others, who nevertheless receive it with disdain or ingratitude.

Very many men are ignorant of learning; many despise it. The barbarian rejects as harsh whatever is not positively barbarian. The smatterers despise as trite whatever is not packed with obsolete expressions. Some persons approve only of what is old; very many admire only their own work. This fellow is so grim that he will not hear of a joke; that fellow is so insipid that he cannot endure wit. Some are so dull-minded that they fear all satire as much as a man bitten by a mad dog fears water. Others are so fickle that sitting they praise one thing and standing another thing.

These persons sit in taverns, and over their cups criticize the talents of authors. With much pontificating, just as they please, they condemn each author by his writings, plucking each one, as it were, by the hair. They themselves remain under cover and, as the proverb goes, out of shot. They are so smooth and shaven that they present not even a hair of an honest man by which they might be caught.

Besides, others are so ungrateful that, though extremely delighted with the work, they do not love the author any the more. They are not unlike discourteous guests who, after they have been freely entertained at a rich banquet, finally go home well filled without thanking the host who invited them. Go now and provide a feast at your own expense for men of such dainty palate, of such varied taste, and of such unforgetful and grateful natures!

At any rate, my dear Peter, conduct with Hythlodaeus the business which I mentioned. Afterwards I shall be fully free to take fresh counsel on the subject. However, since I have gone through the labor of writing, it is too late for me to be wise now. Therefore, provided it be done with the consent of Hythlodaeus, in the matter of publishing which remains I shall follow my friends' advice, and yours first and foremost. Good-by, my sweetest friend, with your excellent wife. Love me as you have ever done, for I love you even more than I have ever done.

Letter 10

TO ERASMUS [26]

In these hurried lines composed sometime before dawn, More writes to Erasmus about a variety of matters, including the attempt to get his Dutch friend a new horse from Christopher Urswick, the priest who had given Erasmus a horse in 1506 in return for a copy of Erasmus' *Sommium*; unfortunately, the horse died in 1516, and Erasmus sent Urswick more books in an ultimately unsuccessful attempt to curry himself a new steed (*ODNB*). The popular *Epistolae Obscurorum Virorum, or Letters of Obscure Men,* were satires on later Scholasticism, religious practices, and ecclesial matters, written by Crotus Rubianus and Ulrich von Hutten in 1515, and although More writes that the learned took them in jest, the *Oxford Dictionary of the Christian Church* points out they "contributed much to the discredit the old theological learning and its representatives" (559), much as the *Praise of Folly* did despite the designs and even protests of its author and his friends.

LONDON

31 OCTOBER <1516>

THOMAS MORE SENDS HIS GREETINGS TO HIS FRIEND,
MASTER ERASMUS.

My answer, dear Erasmus, is a little tardy, because I was anxious
to get some definite information to send on to you from Urswick
about that horse for you; but that has been impossible, since he is
gone on a business trip several miles from London and has not as
yet returned. I expect him any day now, and as soon as he gets back,
the matter will be taken care of. The money you had left with me, I
am sure, has been paid over to our friend, Gilles, as I have received
a communication from my agent in Antwerp, saying that he would
make prompt payment. I could not entrust this bearer with the letters from Basel, which you sent me some time ago to peruse; but
I will send them shortly, as soon as I hit upon someone to burden
with a large bundle. Bedill showed me the letter from the Bishop of
Basel to the Archbishop of Canterbury, and also the Archbishop's
response; both were the original copies. The latter, however, was
much too much the original; it was so smeared with words struck
out or written in as to be not at all legible except to the one who
wrote it, and perhaps not even to him.

Our two letters encouraging Latimer to spend a month or
two with the Bishop of Rochester reached him too late; he had
already made up his mind to go to Oxford and could not possibly
be persuaded to postpone his trip for the time being. You know
how these philosophers regard their own decisions as immutable
laws; I suppose from a love of consistency. He does like your rendering of the New Testament very much, although you are too
punctilious to suit him. He does not like the fact that you have
retained the word "Sabbath," and other similar points, which you
did not think necessary to change, or did not dare to do so. However, he does not admit of any word at all that would be foreign

to Roman ears. I approved of his criticism insofar as Hebrew customs and practices would permit. However, I urged him to note down the various words for which he prefers a different rendering and to send them on to you, along with his criticism; and I think he will do that. This interest of his, I know, will make you very happy.

There are other people, though, my dearest Erasmus, who have formed a conspiracy here in our country to read through your writings from quite a different point of view; and I find their dreadful plot disturbing. Therefore, do not be in a rush to publish a second edition of your works, as the time is ripe to take stock. Out of my loyalty and my anxiety for you I urge you, and I beg you to do at least this much—to revise and correct everything promptly so as to leave the very least opportunity for slander in any passage. Some very sharp-minded men have set their hearts upon making a careful search for such opportunities and will snap them up greedily. You want to know who these people are? I am reluctant, of course, to mention any names, for fear that your spirit be crushed by the frightening thought of such powerful enemies. However, I shall tell you anyhow, to put you more on your guard. The top-ranking Franciscan theologian, whom you know and to whom you gave honorable mention in your edition of Jerome, has picked a group of men who are of the same Order and made of the same stuff, and has hatched a plot with them, aimed at refuting any errors of yours he can find. To make this operation easier and more effective, they devised a scheme whereby they would divide up your works among themselves, read through each one with a critical eye, and then understand absolutely nothing of it all. So you see what a crisis is hanging over your head! You have got to work hard to condition your troops for facing this monstrous peril. You can be sure, Erasmus, this decision was reached at a council meeting of the elders, late at night, when they were well soaked. But the morning after, as I am told, with the effects of the wine slept off, they forgot, I guess, all about their resolution; since the decree was written in wine, it was now blotted out of their memory, and so they abandoned their proposal, and instead of reading, they went back to their begging, which experience had taught them to be a far more profitable enterprise.

It is worth noting how much everybody enjoys the *Epistolae Obscurorum Virorum;* the educated take it as a joke, while the uneducated take it seriously and think that our laughter is caused by the style alone. While not defending the style, they do maintain that it is offset by the weighty contents, and under the crude scabbard lies a very handsome blade. It is unfortunate that the work does not have a different title! Then not even in a hundred years would the silly fools realize that the authors were sneering at them with a snout more obtrusive than that of a rhinoceros.

I am happy that my *Nowhere* [i.e., *Utopia*] meets the approval of my friend, Peter; if such men like it, I shall begin to like it myself. I am anxious to find out if it meets with the approval of Tunstall, and Busleiden, and your Chancellor; but their approval is more than I could wish for, since they are so fortunate as to be top-ranking officials in their own governments, although they might be won over by the fact that in this commonwealth of mine the ruling class would be completely made up of such men as are distinguished for learning and virtue. No matter how powerful those men are in their present governments—and, true, they are very powerful—still they have some high and mighty clowns as their equals, if not their superiors, in authority and influence. I do not think that men of this caliber are swayed by the fact that they would not have many under them as subjects, as the term is now used by kings to refer to their people, who are really worse off than slaves; for it is a much higher honor to rule over free people; and good men, such as they, are far removed from that spiteful feeling which desires others to suffer while they are well off themselves. I expect, therefore, that those men will also give their approval to my work, and I am very anxious to have it. However, if a deep conviction to the contrary has been implanted in their minds by satisfaction with their present good fortune, then your one vote will be more than adequate to influence my decision. To my way of thinking, we two are a crowd, and I think I could be happy with you in any forsaken spot.

Farewell, dearest Erasmus, more precious to me than my own eyes!

I have succeeded in getting a more favorable letter from Maruffo; that seemed to me to be more convenient and more prudent than to bother the Bishop again about the same matter. Not that he would be unwilling to listen to anything, as long as it concerned you; but I do prefer to approach him with matters of greater import.

Hurriedly, from London, before dawn, All Hallows Eve.

Thomas More

Letter 11

TO REV. CUTHBERT TUNSTALL [28]

Cuthbert Tunstall (1474–1559), diplomat and bishop, was educated at Oxford, Cambridge, and Padua before his ordination in 1511. First serving under Cardinal Wolsey and with Thomas More in 1515, he became the friend and benefactor of many humanists; he was made bishop of London in 1522, and Queen Catherine chose him as one of her defenders in the controversy over her marriage, though Tunstall eventually sided with Henry and accepted the new queen, Anne Boleyn, whom Henry wedded in 1533 and then beheaded in 1536 (*ODNB*).

<LONDON
c. November 1516>

Although all the letters I receive from you, my honored friend,
are pleasing to me, yet the one you last wrote is the most pleasing
of all; for besides its eloquence and its expressions of friendship—
merits which are shared by all your letters and render them highly
agreeable to me—it gave me especial satisfaction by its praise of
my Commonwealth (would that it were as true as it is flattering).
I asked our friend Erasmus to describe to you in conversation my
views on that subject, but forbade him to urge you to read the
book. Not that I did not wish you to read it—nothing would
have pleased me more—but I was mindful of your wise resolution not to take into your hands any modern authors until you
had finished with the ancients—a task which, measured by the
profit you have derived from them, is fully accomplished, but,
measured by the love you bear them, can never come to an end.
I feared that when the learned works of so many other authors
could not engage your attention, you would never willingly
descend to my trifles. Nor would you have done so, unless you
had been moved rather by your love of me than by the subject
of the book. Wherefore, for having so carefully read through the
Utopia, for having undertaken so heavy a labor for friendship's
sake, I owe you the deepest gratitude; and my gratitude is no less
deep for your having found pleasure in the work. For this, too, I
attribute to your friendship which has obviously influenced your
judgment more than strict rules of criticism. However that may
be, I cannot express my delight that your judgment is so favorable. For I have almost succeeded in convincing myself that you
say what you think, for I know that all deceit is hateful to you,
whilst you can gain no advantage by flattering me, and you love
me too much to play a trick upon me. So that if you have seen the
truth without any distortion, I am overjoyed at your verdict; or if

in reading you were blinded by your affection for me, I am no less delighted with your love, for vehement indeed must that love be if it can deprive a Tunstall of his judgment.

Letter 12

To Erasmus [29]

In this letter, More provides another update on Erasmus' equine request and playfully imagines himself as king of the Utopians. More's praise for his friend's work in "advancing the intellectual life of all men" is repeated in letter 54. In the twentieth century, A.G. Sertillanges in his famous book, *The Intellectual Life*, likewise emphasizes the need to renew and foster the intellectual life of the culture and the world: "Here I am, a man of the twentieth century, living in a time of permanent drama, witnessing upheavals such as perhaps the globe never saw since the mountains rose and the seas were driven into their caverns. What have I to do for this panting, palpitating century? More than ever before thought is waiting for men, and men for thought. The world is in danger for lack of life-giving maxims" (14–15).

In this letter, "Lily" is William Lily (1468–1522/23), grammarian and first schoolmaster of St. Paul's School in London, and "Palsgrave" is John Palsgrave (d. 1554), another teacher and schoolmaster of Princess Mary, the sister of Henry the Eighth (*ODNB*). Both men were friends of More and the other humanists. An "attic talent" is an ancient Greek weight and money; one talent weighed approximately 55 pounds and was worth that weight in gold or silver (*Oxford Classical Dictionary*).

<LONDON
c. 4 DECEMBER 1516>

MORE SENDS HIS SPECIAL GREETINGS TO ERASMUS.

I have conferred with Urswick about that horse for you. He insists that he still does not have a horse which he considers suitable to send to you, but is definitely going to send you one by the next market day, if not before. I recently dispatched to you Maruffo's money draft, along with his letter containing more favorable terms. At least, so he says; but I was unable to decipher it; neither could our friend, Lily, although he knows Italian very well. The money you had left with me has been in the hands of our friend Gilles for some time now; my agent, who has returned, told me he had made the payment to him.

Our friend Master Palsgrave, who, as you are aware, has long been very much attached to you, is going to Louvain to study law. But he will retain his devotion to the classics of Latin and Greek literature. He has heard that you will be living there, and while he might expect absolutely anything from you since he is an old friend of yours, still he earnestly begged me for a letter of recommendation to increase the favor which, he believes, he by himself already enjoys with you. Notice how people think I have great influence with you; for me this is as much a triumph as is the friendship of kings, which is the boast of other men. Palsgrave would like to have your advice and assistance, so as to make progress in his studies. I realize, my dear Erasmus, that there is no need of many words when one asks you to help in his studies a person who has a love for intellectual things, who is already a well-known scholar, with a great future before him, whose great progress is also known to you, and who, moreover, is your friend and my friend, which means, he is twice your friend. Years ago, you took upon yourself the special task of spending the days and nights of your whole life in advancing the intellectual life of all men. And, if this involves even a further request, I also ask you to be openhanded in bestowing upon our friend, Palsgrave, that which you refuse to no man. I have given him to deliver to you all the letters which you received long ago from your friends in Basel and which I had in my possession for some time. This is a fortunate coincidence; you could not find a more reliable letter carrier, nor could he want anything that would assure him a warmer reception than a large bundle of erudite letters written by dear friends of yours, letters which you had missed a long time and had almost despaired of recovering. I have told him, however, not to hand them over to you until you sign the contract and agree to receive him as if every single one of them were a letter of recommendation for him.

Each day I stand by, waiting with eager ears, for news about that business of yours in Sicily. Please God, it may have a happy ending. Master Tunstall recently wrote me a most friendly letter. Bless my soul, but his frank and complimentary criticism of my commonwealth has given me more cheer than would an Attic talent. You have no idea how thrilled I am; I feel so expanded, and I hold my head high. For in my daydreams I have been marked out by my Utopians to be their king forever; I can see myself now marching along, crowned with a diadem of wheat, very striking in my Franciscan frock, carrying a handful of wheat as my sacred scepter, thronged by a distinguished retinue of Amaurotians, and, with this huge entourage, giving audience to foreign ambassadors and sovereigns; wretched creatures they are, in comparison with us, as they stupidly pride themselves on appearing in childish garb and feminine finery, laced with that despicable gold, and ludicrous in their purple and jewels and other empty baubles. Yet, I would not want either you or our friend, Tunstall, to judge me by other men, whose character shifts with fortune. Even if heaven has decreed to waft me from my lowly estate to this soaring pinnacle which, I think, defies comparison with that of kings, still you will never find me forgetful of that old friendship I had with you when I was but a private citizen. And if you do not mind making the short trip to visit me in Utopia, I shall definitely see to it that all mortals governed by my kindly rule will show you the honor due to those who, they know, are very dear to the heart of their king.

I was going to continue with this fascinating vision, but the rising Dawn has shattered my dream—poor me!—and shaken me off my throne and summons me back to the drudgery of the courts. But at least this thought gives me consolation: real kingdoms do not last much longer.

Farewell, dearest Erasmus.

Letter 13

To Archbishop William Warham [31]

More offers his congratulations to William Warham (1450–1532), Archbishop of Canterbury and Lord Chancellor of England, who resigned from the office of Lord Chancellor on 22 December 1515 and was replaced by Thomas Wolsey. A friend and patron of Erasmus, Warham would later play a part in Henry's "great matter," his eventual divorce from Queen Catherine of Aragon (*ODNB*). More was the first English author, according to the *OED*, to use the word "integrity," which here comes up ironically in More's discussion of Warham's resignation as Lord Chancellor. See letter 56 on More's own resignation years later, and his desire to "protect the integrity of his reputation."

<London
January 1517>

I ever judged your paternity happy in the way you exercised your office of Chancellor, but I esteem you much happier now that you have laid it down and entered on that most desirable leisure, in which you can live for yourself and for God. Such leisure, in my opinion, is not only more pleasant than the labor you have forsaken, but more honorable than all your honors. To be a judge is the lot of many, and sometimes of very bad men. But you possessed that supreme office which, when relinquished, is as much exposed to calumny as it formerly conferred authority and independence; and to give up this willingly is what none but a moderate-minded man would care, and none but an innocent man dare, to do.

I do not know which to admire the most, your modesty in willingly laying down an office of such dignity and power, your unworldliness in being able to despise it, or your integrity in having no fear of resignation; but together with many other men I give to your act my most cordial approval as certainly most excellent and wise. Indeed I can hardly say how heartily I congratulate you on your singular good fortune and how I rejoice in it for your sake, for I see your paternity retiring far away from the affairs of the world and the bustle of the courts, raised to a rare eminence of fame both on account of the honorable manner in which you have held your office and the honorable way in which you have resigned it. Happy in the consciousness of duty well done, you will pass your time gently and peacefully in literature and philosophy. Whilst daily I appreciate more and more the happiness of your lot, I realize my own misery; for although I have no business worth mentioning yet my attention is fully occupied, for poor talents find even trivial things as much as they can manage. I have so little free time that I can rarely visit your paternity or excuse my remissness in writing—indeed I have scarcely been able to get ready this present letter.

Herewith I would beg your grace to accept a little book [*Utopia*]. It was written in undue haste, and I fear it is lacking in wit, but a friend of mine, a citizen of Antwerp [Peter Gilles] allowed his affection to outweigh his judgment, thought it worthy of publication and without my knowledge had it printed. Although I know it is unworthy of your high rank, your wide experience and your learning, yet I venture to send it, relying on the ready kindness with which you welcome all works of fancy, and trusting to the favor I have always experienced from you. Thus I hope that even if the book pleases you but little, yet your good-will may be extended to the author.

Farewell, my Lord Archbishop.

Letter 14

To Antonio ⟨Bonvisi⟩ [34]

Antonio Bonvisi (1475–1558), an Italian merchant and banker, was a lifelong friend of Thomas More, as More attests in one of his last letters from the Tower of London (see Letter 80). Specializing in cloth and jewels, Bonvisi moved within the most prominent and powerful political and literary circles in London, where he lived and worked most of his life. He was friendly with Wolsey, Cromwell, and others in the King's court, but after More and Bishop John Fisher were imprisoned in the Tower of London, Bonvisi stepped forward to provide them with wine, food, and other such necessaries as helped to provide a little warmth and to preserve at least their good spirits during the long imprisonment. Though Bonvisi himself was not harmed during Henry's lifetime despite his continuing and well-known allegiance to the "old faith," he was forced to flee England during Edward VI's reign; he opened his home in Louvain to other exiled English Catholics, including Nicholas Harpsfield, one of More's earliest biographers (*ODNB*).

<LONDON
JANUARY 1517>

That you have such esteem of me issues, I suspect, from affection rather than judgment. For love, generally, when it settles deep in men, spreads darkness over their thinking. Which I see has happened to you, especially since my *Utopia* has pleased you so much, a book which I think clearly deserves to hide itself away forever on its own island.

Letter 15

TO PETER GILES [41A]

Like letter 9 above, this letter was included with the publication of *Utopia*. Placed after the main text, it casts intriguing light not only on the earlier letter and the work itself, but also on More's continuing interest in good reading, as seen in his praise of the "unusually sharp person" who has raised pointed questions about the meaning of *Utopia* and Raphael's large claims. This "sharp-eyed" reader stands in contrast to the safe and "pontificating" reader critiqued in the earlier letter to Peter Giles. Terence (195/185–159 BC) was a classical comic playwright who lived during the time of the Roman Republic. Mysis is the name of a servant girl in his comedy *Andria*.

< LONDON
1517>

THOMAS MORE TO PETER GILES, HIS FRIEND, GREETINGS.

I was extremely delighted, my dearest Peter, with a criticism already known to you, made by an unusually sharp person who put this dilemma about our *Utopia*: If the facts are reported as true, I see some rather absurd elements in them, but if as fictitious, then I find More's finished judgment wanting in some matters. Whoever this fellow was, I am very much obliged to him, my dear Peter. I suspect him to be learned, and I see him to be friendly. By this very frank criticism of his, he has gratified me more than anyone else since the publication of my little volume.

In the first place, attracted either by devotion to me or by interest in the work, he seems not to have wearied of the labor but read it through. This feat he has accomplished not perfunctorily and hastily, as priests are wont to read the hours—at any rate, those who are wont to do so at all—but slowly and carefully so as to weigh all the details intelligently. Secondly, having marked for criticism certain points, and that quite sparingly, he declares that he has given his approval to the rest not thoughtlessly but discreetly. Finally, in the very words in which he censures me, he gives me more praise than all who have praised me of set purpose. For he shows plainly how highly he thinks of me when he complains of being cheated of his hope whenever he read something not precise enough, whereas for me it would be more than I could hope if I happened to be able to write at least a few things—even among so many—that were not altogether absurd.

Nevertheless, if I may in my turn deal no less frankly with him, I do not see why he should appear to himself so open-eyed, or, as the Greeks say, "sharp-sighted," because he has detected that some little absurdities exist in the institutions of Utopia or that I have devised some things not expedient enough in the framing of a commonwealth. Why should he be so minded as if there were nothing absurd elsewhere in the world or as if any of all the philosophers had ever ordered the commonwealth, the ruler, or even the private home without instituting some feature that had better be changed? Why, if the memory of the greatest men, hallowed by time, were not sacred to me, I could in each of them quote points in the condemnation of which I should indubitably get a unanimous vote.

Now, when he doubts whether Utopia is real or fictitious, then I find his finished judgment wanting. I do not pretend that if I had determined to write about the commonwealth and had remembered such a story as I have recounted, I should have perhaps shrunk from a fiction whereby the truth, as if smeared with honey, might a little more pleasantly slide into men's minds. But I should certainly have tempered the fiction so that, if I wanted to abuse the ignorance of common folk, I should have prefixed some indications at least for the more learned to see through our purpose.

Thus, if I had done nothing else than impose names on ruler, river, city, and island such as might suggest to the more learned that the island was nowhere, the city a phantom, the river without water, and the ruler without a people, it would not have been hard to do and would have been much wittier than what I actually did. Unless the faithfulness of an historian had been binding on me, I am not so stupid as to have preferred to use those barbarous and meaningless names, Utopia [i.e., "no place" or "good place"], Anydrus [i.e., river "without water"], Amaurotum [i.e., city "made dark"], and Ademus [i.e., "without form or idea" or "without people"].

In spite of all, my dear Giles, I see some persons are so wary that they can hardly be induced to believe what we simple and credulous folk have written down of Hythlodaeus' account. Lest my trustworthiness, as well as Historical veracity, be equally in danger with these persons, I am glad that I may say on behalf of my offspring what Terence's Mysis says about Glycerium's boy lest he be regarded as supposititious: "Truly I thank the gods that some free women were present when I gave birth." For this also has happened to me very conveniently: Raphael told his tale not merely to you and to me but to many other respectable and worthy men. I do not know whether he told them more numerous and important details, but certainly no fewer and no less weighty, than he did to ourselves.

If these unbelievers will not believe them either, let them go to Hythlodaeus himself, for he is not yet dead. I heard lately from travelers coming from Portugal that on last March first he was as hale and spirited as ever. Let them inquire the truth from him or, if they like, dig it out of him with questions. I would only have them understand that I am responsible for my own work alone and not also for the credit of another.

Farewell, dearest Peter, to you and your charming wife and pretty little daughter. My wife wishes them long life.

Letter 16

To Rev. Cuthbert Tunstall [37]

More writes a quick note of thanks to Tunstall for a gift of amber he has received.

<LONDON
1517?>

That in your letter you thank me so carefully for my services on behalf of your friends, is a mark of your great courtesy. What I did was quite trifling: it is only your goodness that exaggerates it. But you scarcely do justice to our friendship, for you seem to think that what I may do puts you under an obligation, whereas you should rather claim it as due to you and yours by right, etc. . . . The amber which you sent me—a rich and noble tomb for flies—was most acceptable on many grounds. As for the material, in color and brightness it can challenge comparison with any precious stone, and as for the form, it is all the more excellent in that it represents a heart—a symbol of your love for me. For thus do I interpret your meaning: As the fly, winged like Cupid and as fickle as he, is so shut up and enclosed in the substance of the amber that it cannot fly away, so embalmed in the aromatic juice that it cannot perish, so your love will always remain constant and unchanged. That I have nothing to give you in return does not greatly trouble me. For I know you do not look for gifts in exchange, and moreover, I am willing to remain under an obligation to you. But yet I am somewhat distressed that my capabilities are so poor, for do what I will, I must ever seem unworthy of such proofs of your friendship. Wherefore, since I cannot hope to win the approval of others, I must be content that you know, as well as I do myself, the depth of my affection for you.

Letter 17

TO HIS DAUGHTERS [43]

Many of More's letters address the subject of education, and his letters to his children are particularly revealing of his keen interest, as a father, in the careful education and formation of his children. More was first married to Jane Colt (1489–1511), and with her he had three daughters, Margaret, Elizabeth, and Cecily, and one son, John. After Jane's death in 1511, More married the plain yet virtuous widow Alice Middleton, and together they raised the growing family. Margaret Giggs was More's foster daughter. In the letters to his children, he makes a special point of encouraging and complimenting their efforts at diligent composition and careful writing.

<1517?>

Thomas More to Margaret, Elizabeth, Cecily his dearest daughters, and to Margaret Giggs as dear as though she were a daughter:

I cannot express, my dearest children, the very deep pleasure your eloquent letters gave me, especially as I see that although traveling and frequently changing your abode you have not allowed your customary studies to be interfered with, but have continued your exercises in logic, rhetoric and poetry. I am now fully convinced that you love me as you should since I see that, although I am absent, yet you do with the greatest eagerness what you know gives me pleasure when I am present. When I return you shall see that I am not ungrateful for the delight your loving affection has given me. I assure you that I have no greater solace in all the vexatious business in which I am immersed than to read your letters. They prove to me the truth of the laudatory reports your kind tutor sends of your work, for if your own letters did not bear witness to your zealous study of literature, it might be suspected that he had been influenced by his good-nature rather than by the truth. But now by what you write you support his credit, so that I am ready to believe what would otherwise be his incredible reports upon the eloquence and wit of your essays.

So I am longing to return home that I may place my pupil by your side and compare his progress with yours. He is, I fear, a little lazy, for he cannot help hoping that you are not really quite so advanced as your teacher's praise would imply. Knowing how persevering you are, I have a great hope that soon you will be able to overcome your tutor himself, if not by force of argument, at any rate by never confessing yourselves beaten. Farewell, my most dear children.

Letter 18

TO BISHOP JOHN FISHER [57]

Bishop John Fisher, martyr and saint (1469–1535), took a B.A. and M.A. at Cambridge before he was elected chancellor of Cambridge University in 1501 and then named Bishop of Rochester in 1504 at the request of Henry VII. As bishop and writer, he delivered the sermon at Henry VII's funeral in 1509; he also extensively opposed the theological opinions of Martin Luther in sermons and in print. Later, he would serve as chaplain to the King and confessor to Queen Catherine, and he defended the Queen in public against Henry's attempts to declare their marriage null and void in 1527. To the further rankling of the King's brows, Fisher preached against the divorce in public in 1532, and later was arrested and imprisoned, where he wrote *The Ways to Perfect Religion* and *Spiritual Consolations* (*ODNB*). He was tried by jury, condemned for treason, and put to death on 22 June 1535, two weeks before Thomas More's execution on July the sixth. In the month before his execution, Fisher was appointed Cardinal by Rome, but King Henry famously remarked that he would send Fisher's severed head to Rome before any "red hat" ever arrived for Fisher to wear in England. The lives and falls of More and Fisher, layman and bishop, are distinctive of course, and yet similar in some striking ways: both men believed there was legal safety in silence; both were betrayed by Richard Rich; both were condemned on the charge of malicious treason for denying Henry the title of Supreme

Head of the Church in England; both bodies were laid to rest in St. Peter ad Vincula, in the same pit; both heads were displayed for a time on Tower Bridge as a warning to all; and both men were canonized together in 1935. This letter supports the claims made by and about More on the subject of his reluctant entrance into King Henry VIII's service in 1518. See letter 28 for Erasmus' testimony on the same subject. For an excellent contemporary edition of Fisher's English writings, see Cecilia Hatt's *English Works of John Fisher, Bishop of Rochester: Sermons and Other Writings, 1520–1535* (Oxford University Press, 2002).

<c.1517–1518>

It was with the greatest unwillingness that I came to Court, as everyone knows, and as the King himself in joke often throws up in my face. I am as uncomfortable there as a bad rider is in the saddle. I am far from enjoying the special favor of the King, but he is so courteous and kindly to all that everyone who is in any way hopeful finds a ground for imagining that he is in the King's good graces; like the London wives who, as they pray before the image of the Virgin Mother of God which stands near the Tower, gaze upon it so fixedly that they imagine it smiles upon them. But I am not so happy as to perceive signs of favor or so hopeful as to imagine them. But the King has virtue and learning, and makes great progress in both with daily renewed zeal, so that the more I see His Majesty advance in all the qualities that befit a good monarch, the less burdensome do I feel this life of the Court.

Letter 19

TO OXFORD UNIVERSITY [60]

In this letter, Thomas More intervenes in a scholarly controversy at Oxford University, where the faculty had fomented an academic "Trojan War" between those supportive of the new study of Greek, and those hostile to such study on various grounds. The letter is a good example of More's rhetorical gifts—note the skillful use of all the classical means of persuasion in the letter, *ethos*, *pathos*, and *logos*—yet more important is the light the letter sheds on More's understanding of liberal education as the secular learning that *animam ad virtutem praeparat*, that is, "prepares the soul for virtue," in Daniel Kinney's recent translation (*CW* 15, p. 139).

As discussed above (see letter 6), More's understanding of education has its roots in the classical Roman writers Cicero and Seneca, who are singled out by More as offering the reader something distinct from the teachings and wisdom of the Greek philosophers. Though More does not explain the unique contribution of Cicero and Seneca in this letter, these two authors were prized by the earlier humanists, especially More and Erasmus, for their articulation of the ideal of civic humanism and the art of forming leading citizens, devoted to serving the common good and the cause of peace. Erasmus, for example, recommended that the young "spend long hours in reading [Cicero] and even in learning him by heart" (*CWE* 10, Letter 1390), while Thomas More was known as a "Christian English Cicero" according to the early biographer, Nicholas Harpsfield (see Appendix III).

<Abingdon
29 March 1518>

Thomas More to the Reverend Fathers, the Commissary, Proctors, and Others of the Guild of Masters of Oxford University, Greetings.

I have been wondering, gentlemen, whether I might be permitted to communicate to scholars of your distinction certain conclusions to which I have recently come. Yet I have hesitated in approaching so brilliant a group, not so much on the ground of my style as on that of seeming to give an exhibition of pride and arrogance. Who am I, the possessor of little prudence and less practice, a scholar of mediocre proportions, to arrogate to myself the right to advise you in anything? And how can I dare to offer advice in the field of letters especially, when any one of you is fitted by his wisdom and erudition to give advice in that field to thousands?

At first sight, Venerable Fathers, I was therefore deterred by your unique wisdom. But, on second thought, I was encouraged; for it occurred to me that only ignorant and arrogant fools would disdain to give a man a hearing, and that the wiser and more learned you were, the less likely you would be to think highly of yourselves or to scorn the advice of others. I was further emboldened by the thought that no one was ever harmed by just judges, such as you are above all, simply on the ground that he offered advice without thinking of the consequences. On the contrary, loyal and affectionate advice, even if imprudent, has always deserved praise and thanks.

Finally, when I consider that, with God's help, I ought to offer you whatever slight learning I have acquired, since it was at your University that my education began, it seems the duty of a loyal friend not to pass over in silence what I deem it serviceable to bring to your attention. Since, then, the only danger in putting my pen to paper seemed to lie in the fact that a few might deem me too audacious, while I know that my silence would be condemned by many as ingratitude, I have preferred that the whole world should condemn my audacity rather than that anyone should have the chance to say that I showed myself ungrateful to your University, the honor of which I feel myself bound to defend to the uttermost. Moreover, no situation has, I believe, arisen in recent years, which, if you desire to maintain the honor of that institution, more urgently requires your serious attention.

The matter is as follows: when I was in London recently, I rather frequently heard that some members of your teaching body, either because they despised Greek or were simply devoted to other disciplines, or most likely because they possessed a perverse sense of humor, had proceeded to form a society named after the Trojans. The senior sage christened himself Priam; others called themselves Hector, Paris, and so forth; the idea, whether as a joke or a piece of anti-Greek academic politics, being to pour ridicule on those devoted to the study of Greek. And I hear that things have come to such a pass that no one can admit in public or private that he enjoys Greek, without being subjected to the jeers of these ludicrous "Trojans," who think Greek is a joke for the simple reason that they don't know what good literature is. To these modern "Trojans" applies the old saw, "Trojans always learn too late."

The affair aroused much comment, all very critical; and I myself felt somewhat bitter that even a few academics among you had nothing better to do in their spare time than to cast slurs on their colleagues' subjects. But I kept in mind that one could not expect the whole crowd of academics to possess wisdom, temperance, and humility; and so I began to dismiss the matter as a triviality. However, since I have been here in Abingdon in attendance at the court of His Victorious Majesty [Henry VIII], I have found that the silliness is developing into a form of insanity. For one of the "Trojans," a scholar in his own estimation, a wit of the first water in that of his friends, though slightly deranged in that of anyone observing his actions, has chosen during Lent to babble in a sermon against not only Greek but Roman literature, and finally against all polite learning, liberally berating all the liberal arts.

His whole performance was of a piece. Perhaps such a body of nonsense could not be preached on the basis of any sensible text; in any case, he followed neither the old custom of elucidating a whole passage of Scripture, nor the recent one of expounding some few words of Scripture; instead he elaborated on some stupid British proverbs. So I have no doubt that his frivolous sermon very deeply disturbed those who heard it; since I see that all who have heard fragmentary reports of it are unfavorably impressed.

What man in the audience, in whose breast burned even a spark of Christianity, would not groan at the degradation of the royal office of sacred preaching, which gained the world for Christ—above all at the hands of those whose supreme duty it was to protect it with the authority of their office? Who could possibly have devised a more outrageous insult than for an avowed preacher, during the most solemn season of the Church's year, in the presence of a large Christian congregation, in the sanctuary itself, from the elevation of the pulpit (as it were from the throne of Christ), and in view of the Sacred Body of Christ, to turn a Lenten sermon into Bacchanalian ravings? What a look must have been on the faces of the audience, who had come to hear spiritual wisdom, and saw the laughable pantomime he put on in the pulpit! They had expected to listen in reverence to the Word of Life; when they departed, all they could record they had heard was an attack on humane letters and a defamation of the preaching office by a fatuous preacher.

It would have been no reproach to secular learning if some good man, who had retired from the world to monastic life, suddenly returned and used this speaker's phrases: "much in watchings, much in prayer," or "the path to be trod by those who seek for heaven" or "other matters, like humanistic education, trivial if not a positive hindrance to the spiritual life," or "simple country folk, and the unlettered, flying quicker to heaven," etc., etc. All this could have been borne from such a man. His simplicity would have been pardoned by his audience. They would have generously admitted his saintliness, and given serious consideration to his piety, devotion, and righteousness. But when they saw a man with the academic ermine over his shoulders, step on to the platform in the midst of a gathering composed solely of academics, and calmly proceed to rant against all humane learning, one would have had to be stone blind not to notice a signal pride and wickedness, a positive hatred of the higher arts. Many must have wondered indeed how such a man could get the idea that he had to preach either about Latin, of which he did not know much, or about the liberal arts, of which he knew less, or about Greek—in which he could not even grunt that it was "all Greek" to him!

If such an abundance of material had been supplied by the seven deadly sins, an altogether suitable theme for sermons, who would have believed him totally inexperienced therein! Though, as a matter of fact, what is it but sloth, when one is in the habit of denouncing rather than of learning that of which one is ignorant? And what is it but hatred, when one defames those who know what one deprecates but does not comprehend? And what is it but supreme pride, when he wishes no kind of knowledge to be prized save what he has falsely persuaded himself that he knows, and when he even—not from modesty, as might be the case with other people—arrogates more praise to himself for his ignorance than for his knowledge?

Now as to the question of humanistic education being secular. No one has ever claimed that a man needed Greek and Latin, or indeed any education in order to be saved. Still, this education which he calls secular does train the soul in virtue [literally: prepare the soul for virtue]. In any event, few will question that humanistic education is the chief, almost the sole reason why men come to Oxford; children can receive a good education at home from their mothers, all except cultivation and book learning. Moreover, even if men come to Oxford to study theology, they do not start with that discipline. They must first study the laws of human nature and conduct, a thing not useless to theologians; without such study they might possibly preach a sermon acceptable to an academic group, without it they would certainly fail to reach the common man. And from whom could they acquire such skill better than from the poets, orators, and historians?

Moreover, there are some who through knowledge of things natural construct a ladder by which to rise to the contemplation of things supernatural; they build a path to theology through philosophy and the liberal arts, which this man condemns as secular; they adorn the queen of heaven with the spoils of the Egyptians! This fellow declares that only theology should be studied; but if he admits even that, I don't see how he can accomplish his aim without some knowledge of languages, whether Hebrew or Greek or Latin; unless, of course, the elegant gentleman has convinced himself that there is enough theology written in English or that all theology can be squeezed into the limits of those [late scholastic] "questions" which he likes to pose and answer, for which a modicum of Latin would, I admit, suffice.

But really, I cannot admit that theology, that august queen of heaven, can be thus confined. Does she not dwell and abide in Holy Scripture? Does she not pursue her pilgrim way through the cells of the holy Fathers: Augustine and Jerome; Ambrose and Cyprian; Chrysostom, Gregory, Basil, and their like? The study of theology has been solidly based on these now despised expositors of fundamental truth during all the Christian centuries until the invention of these petty and meretricious "questions" which alone are today glibly tossed back and forth. Anyone who boasts that he can understand the works of the Fathers without an uncommon acquaintance with the languages of each and all of them will in his ignorance boast for a long time before the learned trust his judgment.

But if this foolish preacher pretends that he was not condemning humanistic education in general but only an immoderate thirst for it, I can't see that this desire was such a sin that he had to deal with it in a public assembly, as if it were causing society to rush headlong to ruin. I haven't heard that many have gone so far in such studies that they will soon be overstepping the golden mean. Further, this fellow, just to show how immoderate he could be in a sermon, specifically called students of Greek "heretics," teachers of Greek "chief devils," and pupils in Greek "lesser devils" or, more modestly and facetiously as he thought, "little devils"; and the zeal of this holy man drove him to call by the name of devil one whom everybody knows the Devil himself could hardly bear to see occupy a pulpit. He did everything but name that one [Erasmus], as everybody realized just as clearly as they realized the folly of the speaker.

Joking aside—I have no desire to pose as the sole defender of Greek learning; for I know how obvious it must be to scholars of your eminence that the study of Greek is tried and true. To whom is it not obvious that to the Greeks we owe all our precision in the liberal arts generally and in theology particularly; for the Greeks either made the great discoveries themselves or passed them on as part of their heritage. Take philosophy, for example. If you leave out Cicero and Seneca, the Romans wrote their philosophy in Greek or translated it from Greek.

I need hardly mention that the New Testament is in Greek, or that the best New Testament scholars were Greeks and wrote in Greek. I am but repeating the consensus of scholarship when

I say: however much was translated of old from Greek, and however much more has been recently and better translated, not half of Greek learning has yet been made available to the West; and, however good the translations have been, the text of the original still remains a surer and more convincing presentation. For that very reason all the Doctors of the Latin Church—Jerome, Augustine, Bede, and a host of others—assiduously gave themselves to learning Greek; and even though many works had already been translated, they were much more accustomed to reading them in the original than are many of our contemporaries who claim to be erudite; nor did they merely learn it themselves, but counseled those among their successors who wanted to be theologians above all to do the same.

So it is not as if I were just giving your Worships good advice about preserving the study of Greek. I am rather exhorting you to do your duty. You should not allow anyone in your university to be frightened away from the study of Greek, either by public assemblies or private inanities, since Greek is a subject required in every place of learning by the Church Universal. Common sense is surely enough to convince you that not all of your number who give themselves to the study of Greek can be blockheads; in fact, it is in part from these studies that your university had acquired its pedagogical prestige both at home and abroad.

There seems to be an increasing number of cases where Oxford has benefited from the presence of men nominally studying Greek only, but really taking the whole liberal arts course. It will be a wonder if their enthusiasm for you does not evaporate when they realize that so serious an enterprise is held in such contempt. Just think, too, what they are doing at Cambridge, which you have always outshone; those who are not studying Greek are so moved by common interest in their university that they are actually making large individual contributions to the salary of the Greek professor!

You see what I mean; and much more could be said to the point by men with better minds than mine. All I am doing is warning you of what others are saying and thinking, not telling you what it behooves you to do. You see much better than I that, if wicked factions are not suppressed at birth, a contagious disease will spread, and the better half be slowly absorbed by the worse, and that outsiders will be forced to take a hand in helping the good and wise among you. Any former student of the university takes its welfare as much to heart as you who are its living members. And I am sure that the Reverend Father in Christ who occupies the See of Canterbury [William Warham], who is the Primate of all our Clergy, and who is also the Chancellor of your university will not fail to do his part. Whether for the clergy's sake or yours, he rightly feels interested in preventing the decay of learning; and learning will perish if the university continues to suffer from the contentions of lazy idiots, and the liberal arts are allowed to be made sport of with impunity. And what about the Reverend Father in Christ, the Cardinal of York [Thomas Wolsey], who is both a patron of learning and himself the most learned of the episcopate? Would he endure patiently if aspersions were cast in your university on the liberal arts and the study of languages? Will he not rather aim the shafts of his learning, virtue, and authority at these witless detractors from the arts?

Last but not least: what of our most Christian King? His sacred Majesty has cultivated all the liberal arts as much as ever a king did; indeed, he possesses greater erudition and judgment than any previous monarch. Will his wisdom and piety suffer him to allow the liberal arts to fail—through the interests of evil and lazy men—in a place where his most illustrious ancestors wished that there be an illustrious seat of letters, a place which is an ancient nursery of learning, whose products have been an ornament not only to England but to the whole Church, a place which possesses so many colleges that have perpetual endowments specially designated for the support of students (in which respect there is no university outside the kingdom that can compare with Oxford), a place in which the aim of all its colleges and the purpose of all its endowments is none other than that a great body of academics, delivered from the necessity of earning their daily bread, might there pursue the liberal arts?

I have no doubt that you yourselves will easily in your wisdom find a way to end this dispute and quiet these stupid factions; that you will see to it not only that all the liberal arts may be free from derision and contempt but that they shall be held in dignity and honor. By such diligence in intellectual pursuits you will reap benefit for yourselves; and it can hardly be said how much you will gain favor with our Illustrious Prince and with the above-mentioned Reverend Fathers in Christ. You will forge an almost miraculous bond between yourselves and myself, who have thought that all this had to be written now in my own hand out of my deep personal affection for you. You know that my services are at the disposal of each and all of you. May God preserve your glorious seat of learning unharmed; and may He grant that it flourish continually in virtue and in all the liberal arts.

Thomas More.

Letter 20

To William Gonell [63]

Schoolmaster and friend of Erasmus, William Gonell (d. 1560) succeeded John Clement as the tutor of More's children from 1518–1525, and then returned to Cambridge as a professor; in a later biography of More, he is praised as a man "whose memory is yet fresh in Cambridge for his learning and works of piety" (*ODNB*, 723). More's counsel to the teacher of his children reveals his understanding of the ends of learning and education, more valuable than the riches of Croesus, fabled king of Lydia, or the beauties of Helen of Troy, whose "face launched a thousand ships / and burnt the topless towers of Ilium" in Christopher Marlowe's fine lines before midnight's toll in *Doctor Faustus*. More's warning to Gonell on the perils of fostering pride through education is an example of More's lifelong concern with recognizing and struggling against even the first motions of the "pest of pride," or what Raphael Hythloday describes as the "one single monster, the prime plague and begetter of all others" at the end of his account of Utopia's founding and development in book two (106). See More's later *Dialogue of Heresies, Treatise on the Passion,* and *Dialogue of Comfort against Tribulation* for his most extensive considerations of pride. More's claim in this letter that the whole fruit of learning consists in "the testimony of God and a good conscience" anticipates the later, famous discussion of conscience with his daughter, Margaret Roper, in the Tower of London (see letters 68–69). For an examination of the fortitude of More's conscience throughout his life, see Peter Berglar's *Thomas More* (Scepter, 2009). The ages of More's children ranged from nine to thirteen at the time of this letter in 1518.

AT COURT
22 MAY <1518?>

I have received, my dear Gonell, your letter, elegant, as your letters always are, and full of affection. From your letter I perceive your devotion to my children; I argue their diligence from their own. Every one of their letters pleased me, but I was particularly pleased, because I notice that Elizabeth shows a gentleness and self-command in the absence of her mother, which some children would not show in her presence. Let her understand that such conduct delights me more than all possible letters I could receive from anyone. Though I prefer learning joined with virtue to all the treasures of kings, yet renown for learning, when it is not united with a good life, is nothing else than splendid and notorious infamy: this would be specially the case in a woman. Since erudition in women is a new thing and a reproach to the sloth of men, many will gladly assail it, and impute to literature what is really the fault of nature, thinking from the vices of the learned to get their own ignorance esteemed as virtue. On the other hand, if a woman (and this I desire and hope with you as their teacher for all my daughters) to eminent virtue should add an outwork of even moderate skill in literature, I think she will have more real profit than if she had obtained the riches of Croesus and the beauty of Helen. I do not say this because of the glory which will be hers, though glory follows virtue as a shadow follows a body, but because the reward of wisdom is too solid to be lost like riches or to decay like beauty, since it depends on the intimate conscience of what is right, not on the talk of men, than which nothing is more foolish or mischievous.

It belongs to a good man, no doubt, to avoid infamy, but to lay himself out for renown is the conduct of a man who is not only proud, but ridiculous and miserable. A soul must be without peace which is ever fluctuating between elation and disappointment from the opinions of men. Among all the benefits that learning bestows on men, there is none more excellent than this, that by the study of books we are taught in that very study to seek not praise, but utility. Such has been the teaching of the most learned men, especially of philosophers, who are the guides of human life, although some may have abused learning, like other good things, simply to court empty glory and popular renown. I have dwelt so much on this matter, my dear Gonell, because of what you say in your letter, that Margaret's lofty character should not be abased. In this judgment I quite agree with you; but to me, and, no doubt, to you also, that man would seem to abase a generous character who should accustom it to admire what is vain and low. He, on the contrary, raises the character who rises to virtue and true goods, and who looks down with contempt from the contemplation of what is sublime, on those shadows of good things which almost all mortals, through ignorance of truth, greedily snatch at as if they were true goods.

Therefore, my dear Gonell, since we must walk by this road, I have often begged not you only, who, out of your affection for my children, would do it of your own accord, nor my wife, who is sufficiently urged by her maternal love for them, which has been proved to me in so many ways, but all my friends, to warn my children to avoid the precipices of pride and haughtiness, and to walk in the pleasant meadows of modesty; not to be dazzled at the sight of gold; not to lament that they do not possess what they erroneously admire in others; not to think more of themselves for gaudy trappings, nor less for the want of them; neither to deform the beauty that nature has given them by neglect, nor to try to heighten it by artifice; to put virtue in the first place, learning in the second; and in their studies to esteem most whatever may teach them piety towards God, charity to all, and Christian humility in themselves. By such means they will receive from God the reward of an innocent life, and in the assured expectation of it, will view death without horror, and meanwhile possessing solid joy, will neither be puffed up by the empty praise of men, nor dejected by evil tongues. These I consider the genuine fruits of learning, and though I admit that all literary men do not possess them, I would maintain that those who give themselves to study with such views, will easily attain their end and become perfect.

Nor do I think that the harvest will be much affected whether it is a man or a woman who sows the field. They both have the same human nature, which reason differentiates from that of beasts; both, therefore, are equally suited for those studies by which reason is cultivated, and becomes fruitful like a ploughed land on which the seed of good lessons has been sown. If it be true that the soil of woman's brain be bad, and apter to bear bracken than corn, by which saying many keep women from study, I think, on the contrary, that a woman's wit is on that account all the more diligently to be cultivated, that nature's defect may be redressed by industry. This was the opinion of the ancients, of those who were most prudent as well as most holy. Not to speak of the rest, St Jerome and St Augustine not only exhorted excellent matrons and most noble virgins to study, but also, in order to assist them, diligently explained the abstruse meanings of Holy Scripture, and wrote for tender girls letters replete with so much erudition, that now-a-days old men, who call themselves professors of sacred science, can scarcely read them correctly, much less understand them. Do you, my learned Gonell, have the kindness to see that my daughters thoroughly learn these works of those holy men? From them they will learn in particular what end they should propose to themselves in their studies and what is the fruit of their endeavors, namely the testimony of God and a good conscience. Thus peace and calm will abide in their hearts and they will be disturbed neither by fulsome flattery nor by the stupidity of those illiterate men who despise learning.

I fancy that I hear you object that these precepts, though true, are beyond the capacity of my young children, since you will scarcely find a man, however old and advanced, whose mind is so firmly set as not to be tickled sometimes with desire of glory. But, dear Gonell, the more I see the difficulty of getting rid of this pest of pride, the more do I see the necessity of getting to work at it from childhood. For I find no other reason why this evil clings so to our hearts, than because almost as soon as we are born, it is sown in the tender minds of children by their nurses, it is cultivated by their teachers, and brought to its full growth by their parents; no one teaching even what is good without, at the same time, awakening the expectation of praise, as of the proper reward of virtue. Thus we grow accustomed to make so much of praise, that while we study how to please the greater number (who will always be the worst) we grow ashamed of being good (with the few). That this plague of vainglory may be banished far from my children, I do desire that you, my dear Gonell, and their mother and all their friends, would sing this song to them, and repeat it, and beat it into their heads, that vainglory is a thing despicable, and to be spit upon; and that there is nothing more sublime than that humble modesty so often praised by Christ; and this your prudent charity will so enforce as to teach virtue rather than reprove vice, and make them love good advice instead of hating it. To this purpose nothing will more conduce than to read to them the lessons of the ancient Fathers, who, they know, cannot be angry with them; and, as they honor them for their sanctity, they must needs be much moved by their authority. If you will teach something of this sort, in addition to their lesson in Sallust—to Margaret and Elizabeth, as being more advanced than John and Cecily—you will bind me and them still more to you. And thus you will bring about that my children, who are dear to me by nature, and still more dear by learning and virtue, will become most dear by that advance in knowledge and good conduct. Adieu.

From the Court on the Vigil of Pentecost.

Thomas More

Letter 21

To William Budé [65]

The leading French humanist, William Budé (1468–1540) contributed a prefatory letter to More's *Utopia*, which Budé praised as an "extremely profitable and amusing book" fashioned by "a man of the keenest wit, the most agreeable temper, and the most profound experience in judging human affairs" (111, 112, trans. Logan). He corresponded with More beginning in 1518, and the two men met one another at the Field of the Cloth of Gold in 1520; Budé would later become a member of the French parliament, the provost of Paris merchants, and royal librarian of Francis I for good measure (*CE* 1, pp. 212–14).[4] Like More, Budé was a married humanist.

<c. August 1518>

I never skim any of your works, but study them seriously as works of the first importance. To your treatise, however, on Roman money I gave a very special attention such as I have given to no ancient author. You have made it necessary for your readers to give a sustained attention by your careful choice of words, your well-balanced sentences, the studied gravity of your diction, and not least by the serious and difficult nature of the matters you treat of—matters almost lost in antiquity, and requiring the deepest research. But yet if any one will turn his eyes to what you have written and give it careful and continued attention, he will find that the light you have thrown upon your subject brings the dead past to life again. Whilst he ponders your words, he will live

---

4. Here and throughout "CE" refers to *Contemporaries of Erasmus: A Biographical Register of the Renaissance and Reformation*, ed. Peter G. Bietenholz and Thomas B. Deutscher, 3 vols. (University of Toronto Press, 1985–1987).

in imagination through all the past ages, and will be able to gaze upon, to count and almost to take into his hands, the hoarded wealth of all kings, all tyrants and all nations, which is more than any misers have been able to do. I can hardly enumerate the multitude of reasons for which I am attached to you, my dear Budé. You are so exceedingly good to me; whomsoever I may love, you, by good fortune, love also; you possess so many excellent virtues; you are, as I judge, to some extent at least, fond of me; you have earned the gratitude of all men for your useful literary labors; though a married man you have happily acquired a degree of learning that was once the exclusive possession of the clergy. Indeed I am hardly content to call you a layman when by your many splendid gifts you are so highly raised beyond the level of the laity.

Letter 22

To Margaret More [69]

More enjoyed a particularly close relationship with his daughter Margaret, or "Meg" (1505–1544), who married the lawyer William Roper in 1521. Like her father, Margaret was a gifted thinker, speaker, and writer; she went on to publish her own translation of Erasmus' *Devout Treatise on the Paternoster* in 1525. After Meg sent Erasmus a sketch of Holbein's famous More family portrait in 1528, Erasmus wrote in return: "I'm scarcely able to express in words, my dear Margaret Roper, ornament of Britain, the pleasure I felt in my heart when the painter Holbein depicted for me your entire family like this, so skillfully that even if I'd been present among you, I could hardly have seen you all more clearly. How often I've found myself privately wishing that, just once more before I die, I could have the pleasure of seeing that little circle of friends that is so dear to me, and to whom I owe a good part of my fame and reputation" (quoted in John Guy, *A Daughter's Love*, 176). When More was later imprisoned in the Tower, she visited him, and she is More's prime interlocutor in the so-called *Dialogue of Conscience* (1534), a work she may have co-authored with her father, who ever had an eye to posterity and history (see letters 68–69). After More's death, Meg daringly recovered his head from Tower Bridge. The head is now buried in St. Dunstan's Church, Canterbury, where the Ropers lived out their lives after the death of More in 1535. After his death, Meg's determination would prove instrumental in eventually bringing about the publication of her father's written works, as John Guy conjectures: "With the last of her children, Anthony, safely delivered and baptized, she decided to devote all her energy to preparing a collected edition of her father's works, a monument to learning in which each item would be memorialized by a short explanation putting it into context, making his life and example a beacon for others. She also meant to include a carefully chosen selection of her father's letters, knowing from Erasmus that not only are letters a cherished way of reuniting friends and family whom fate has parted, they are in themselves the original, pristine source for biography. No longer did she worry about decorum, since no longer had she any interest in gaining recognition for herself. All that mattered was that her father's name should never perish" (*A Daughter's Love*, 266). More than twenty years later—and more than a decade after Meg's own death—her "project" came to fruition with the publication of *The Works of Sir Thomas More, Knight*, published in 1557 by More's nephew, William Rastell.

<1518>

I was delighted to receive your letter, my dearest Margaret, informing me of Shaw's condition. I should have been still more delighted if you had told me of the studies you and your brother are engaged in, of your daily reading, your pleasant discussions, your essays, of the swift passage of the days made joyous by literary pursuits. For although everything you write gives me pleasure, yet the most exquisite delight of all comes from reading what none but you and your brother could have written. . . .

I beg you, Margaret, tell me about the progress you are all making in your studies. For I assure you that, rather than allow my children to be idle and slothful, I would make a sacrifice of wealth, and bid adieu to other cares and business, to attend to my children and my family, amongst whom none is more dear to me than yourself, my beloved daughter.

Letter 23

TO MARGARET MORE [70]

More again takes the time to encourage his daughter's learning and writing. "Choerilos" was an epic poet, or perhaps hack thereof, from Iasus; he traveled with Alexander the Great and was paid gold coins ("philippines") to celebrate and immortalize the conqueror (*ODCC*).

<1518>

You ask, my dear Margaret, for money, with too much bashfulness and timidity, since you are asking from a father who is eager to give, and since you have written to me a letter such that I would not only repay each line of it with a golden philippine, as Alexander did the verses of Choerilos, but, if my means were as great as my desire, I would reward each syllable with two gold ounces. As it is, I send only what you have asked, but would have added more, only that as I am eager to give, so am I desirous to be asked and coaxed by my daughter, especially by you, whom virtue and learning have made so dear to my soul. So the sooner you spend this money well, as you are wont to do, and the sooner you ask for more, the more you will be sure of pleasing your father. Good-bye, my dearest child.

Letter 24

To Erasmus [72]

<1518>

My Clement lectures at Oxford to an audience larger than has ever gathered to any other lecturer. It is astonishing how universal is the approbation and the love he gains. Even those to whom classical literature was almost anathema now show attachment to him, attend his lectures and gradually modify their opposition. Linacre, who, as you know, never praises anyone extravagantly, cannot contain his admiration for his letters, so that, although I love Clement so much, I am almost tempted to envy him for the high praises heaped upon him.

Letter 25

To John Fisher [74]

<1519>

I cannot express in words my delight, both for your own sake and for the sake of our country, that your Lordship writes in a style that might well pass for Erasmus'. As for the subject-matter, ten Erasmuses could not be more convincing. . . .

Farewell, my Lord Bishop, most highly esteemed for virtue and learning.

Letter 26

To His Beloved Children: More's Letter in Verse [76]

More composed this letter, originally written in Latin verse, to his "little troop of children" while he was in the midst of unpleasant travels on a road made difficult by "mud" and "miserably stormy weather."

<c. 1518>

Thomas More Greets His Beloved Children, Margaret, Elizabeth, Cecilia and John:

I hope that a single letter to all four of you may find my children in good health and that your father's good wishes may keep you so. In the meantime, while I am making a long journey, drenched by a soaking rain, and while my mount, too frequently, is bogged down in the mud, I compose these verses for you in the hope that, although unpolished, they may give you pleasure. From these verses you may gather an indication of your father's feelings for you—how much more than his own eyes he loves you; for the mud, the miserably stormy weather, and having to urge a small horse through deep waters have not been able to distract his thoughts from you or to prevent his proving that, wherever he is, he thinks of you. For instance, when—and it is often—his horse stumbles and threatens to fall, your father is not interrupted in the composition of his verses. Many people can hardly write poetry even when their hearts are at ease, but a father's love duly provides verses even when he is in distress. It is not so strange that I love you with my whole heart, for being a father is not a tie which can be ignored. Nature in her wisdom has attached the parent to the child and bound their minds together with a Herculean knot. Thence comes that tenderness of a loving heart that accustoms me to take you so often into my arms. That is why I regularly fed you cake and gave you ripe apples and fancy pears. That is why I used to dress you in silken garments and why I never could endure to hear you cry. You know, for example, how often I kissed you, how seldom I whipped you.

My whip was never anything but a peacock's tail. Even this I wielded hesitantly and gently so as not to mark your tender backsides with painful welts. Ah, brutal and unworthy to be called father is he who does not himself weep at the tears of his child. How other fathers act I do not know, but you know well how soft and kind I am by temperament, for I have always intensely loved the children I begot, and I have always been (as a father should be) easy to win over. But now my love has grown so much that it seems to me I did not love you at all before. This is because you combine the wise behavior of old age with the years of childhood, because your hearts have been informed with genuine learning, because you have learned to speak with grace and eloquence, weighing each word carefully. These accomplishments tug at my heart so wonderfully, they bind me to my children so closely, that what, for many fathers, is the only reason for their affection—I mean the fact that they begot their children—has almost nothing to do with my love for you. Therefore, most dear little troop of children, continue to endear yourselves to your father and, by those same accomplishments, which make me think that I had not loved you before, make me think hereafter (for you can do it) that I do not love you now.

Letter 27a

TO MARTIN DORP [15]

Martin Dorp (1485–1525), a humanist from Louvain, was both a friend and critic of Erasmus. In 1515, Dorp sharply criticized Erasmus' *Praise of Folly* and his edition of the New Testament in particular. Thomas More wrote two letters to Martin Dorp, the first in 1515 and the second in 1519. The first letter was one of More's long "humanist letters," and the selection below reprints the beginning and ending of this lengthy letter (see Yale *CW* 15 for the full text of that letter, as well as the Letter to Lee and Letter to a Monk). More's artful candor and intervention in this controversy eventually won Dorp over. The second letter, written four years later, refers to the change that More's letter—and correction—worked in Dorp's thought over time. As John Olin explains in his edition of Erasmus' letters, Dorp and Erasmus did indeed resume friendly relations after the controversy subsided, and Erasmus would later write Dorp's epitaph (67). Martin Dorp died 31 May 1525.

<BRUGES
21 OCTOBER 1515>

THOMAS MORE SENDS HIS GREETINGS TO MARTIN DORP.

If I were as free to visit you as I strongly desire to do, my dear
Dorp, I could then discuss with you personally and more
appropriately these matters which I now put down, quite inap-
propriately, in writing. Then too for the time being I would be
enjoying your actual company—the sweetest pleasure I could
have enjoyed; for Erasmus has implanted in my heart an extraordinary longing to see you, to get acquainted with you and to love
you; he is very fond of both of us and, I hope, dear to both of us
alike. His greatest pleasure is to praise absent friends to friends
present. Since he is greatly loved by so many men and that too
in different parts of the world, because of his learning and most
charming character, he tries earnestly to bind all men together
with that same affection which all have for him alone. And so he
constantly mentions each one of his friends individually to them
all, and, to insinuate them into the friendship of all the others, he
constantly talks about those qualities each one has that deserve
affection. Now while he constantly deals in this manner with all
his friends, with no one, my dear Dorp, does he do so more often,
more effusively, and more readily than with you. He has sung
your praises in England for so long a time that every scholar there
knows and respects the name of Dorp as much as do the scholars
of Louvain, who most respect him (as they should). When we
were alone, he described you in such accurate terms that long ago
I conceived a very beautiful picture of you, one that conformed
exactly to the picture I received from the reading of your splendid
writings, after I came here.

So, as soon as I got word from our Invincible King that I
was to serve in the embassy to this country, rest assured, my dear
Dorp, the possibility of my being offered a chance to meet with

you somehow was not, in my opinion, the least reward for my lengthy journey. But the transaction of the business entrusted to me has deprived me of this opportunity, which I had hoped was offered to me, and has detained me at Bruges, for a previous agreement had been made with the noble representatives of our Illustrious Prince Charles to discuss our business here. Consequently, now, though my mission may be successful for many other reasons, I am very unhappy, because my luck has completely abandoned me just where I had hoped I was particularly lucky. But—to get down to the point which has compelled me to at the present moment—while I have been staying I have chanced upon some persons who, to my way of thinking, are not unacquainted with the world of letters. In conversation with them, I have introduced Erasmus' name, and yours too. Erasmus they knew from his writings and reputation; you too they knew, but also for other reasons. They told me a story that was not only unpleasant, but quite unbelievable. They said that you are acting in a rather unfriendly manner toward Erasmus, and that this attitude is obvious from your letters to him. They promised to bring those letters the next day, as they were aware I was not inclined to accept their word. They came back the next day, bringing me three letters; one was addressed by you to Erasmus. This letter, as I gather from his answer, he had not received; but he had read through a copy of it, just as I have done, given him by somebody. In this letter you make some charges against the *Folly,* and you suggest that he write a "Praise of Wisdom"; and as for his plan to emend the text of the New Testament with the aid of Greek manuscripts, you give such little approval of it and encourage him to restrict it within such narrow limits that you practically oppose the entire plan. The second was a letter of his in which he apologized to you briefly, because he was travel-weary and still very much occupied with the same trip, but promising to write at greater length after reaching Basel. And then there was a third letter containing your answer to this letter of Erasmus.

I read through this letter in their presence. There was nothing in it to convince me of any hostile intent on your part toward Erasmus; nor could there be anything to convince me of that. There was, however, some evidence that you were confused beyond my expectations. But as I desired rather to uproot this view from their minds than corroborate it, I claimed I read nothing in the letter which might not proceed from a friendly heart. "But," one of the group remarked, "I am not criticizing what he wrote, rather the fact that he did write; for that reason, in my view, he by no means acted as a friend." For if the *Folly* gives so much offense to any person—and I have never heard of that happening, not even at Louvain, although I have often been there since the *Folly* has been published, and for long periods of time—except from one or the other person, and they were soured old men in their second childhood, the object of derision even of children in that place—with this exception the work has met with universal approval, here at Bruges and at Louvain, so much so that many people even memorize several passages of the work.

But as I started to say—if the *Folly* gives so much offense to any person that it seemed necessary to challenge Erasmus to write a retraction, still since Dorp was summoned to the side of Erasmus not so very long ago, and, on his own evidence, all by himself, what was the purpose of writing a letter? If he thought he ought to deliver some admonition, why did he not give it when present personally with Erasmus? Why did he not give his orders face to face (to quote from Terence) as to what was to be done instead of departing and shouting them out in the middle of the street, while Erasmus was so far away that he was the only one not to know for some time and finally heard only from others a matter which he should have been the first or even the only one to hear? "Consider," he said, "the sincerity of his action in this matter.

First, he makes a pretense of defending before the public a man against whom no one brings any charges; then the reasons for his defense are read openly by everybody, though I have my doubts whether anybody, except the one who ought to, listens to his objections." After he finished, different remarks were passed by the others, not necessary to retail here. My rejoinders and my manner of dismissing them were such that they readily grasped the idea that I would not listen to any untoward remarks about you and that I was almost as well disposed toward you as toward Erasmus, and I could not possibly be better disposed toward him. For as to the fact that you preferred to discuss the matter with him by letter rather than by word of mouth, no matter what your intention was in so doing, I am convinced, in keeping with my opinion of you, that you definitely did not act out of ill will; and he too entertains no doubts in the matter, knowing full well your attitude toward him.

As for your second letter, now widely read with unhappy consequences, I am inclined to believe it was no deliberate action of yours but merely an accident that it reached the public. I am forced to this point of view especially because in this letter there are some things which I am fully convinced you would have changed had you wished to publish it, as they are not quite the sort of thing to be written either to him or by you. You would not have written such harsh words to so important a friend, or in such an off-hand fashion to a man as learned as he; as a matter of fact, I am positive, you would have written in a more kindly vein, in keeping with your temperate character, and with greater care, in keeping with your extraordinary learning. Furthermore, as for the jests and jeers with which your whole letter abounds immoderately, I have no doubt you would have employed them much more sparingly, or at least, my dear Dorp, more cleverly. I do not make much of the fact that you attack the *Folly,* that you inveigh against the poets, that you deride all the grammarians, that you do not approve of the annotations on Holy Scripture, that you are of the opinion a thorough knowledge of Greek literature is not pertinent—all of these points I do not make much of, since they are views each man is free to hold without offending anybody; and they have been discussed by you up to now in such a fashion that I do not have any doubt that several answers, which ought to be given to your objections, will occur to anyone reading them. Besides, by no means do I think you have said too much against anyone of these points; and in certain instances even I miss many points with which I should like to have seen your letter better equipped as it advanced against Erasmus, so that he could have a finer opportunity to fortify his camp with more powerful siege works to oppose you.

But I am definitely very much disturbed because, in your work, you give the impression of attacking Erasmus in a manner not at all becoming to you or him. You treat him sometimes as if you despise him, sometimes as if you looked down upon him in derision, sometimes not as one giving him an admonition, but scolding him like a stern reprover or a harsh censor; and lastly, by twisting the meaning of his words, as if you were stirring up all the theologians and even the universities against him. I do not want this letter of mine to be interpreted as being in opposition to you, for I thoroughly believe that you have done none of these things out of any ill will toward him. While I should need a defender myself, I shall take up the defense of one who, I know, is definitely considered in the eyes of all, and in reality is, too outstanding a man to have to be reduced to their level. Out of love for you and my interest in your reputation. I have wanted to warn you of those matters which men, not fully understanding your temperate character and utter sincerity, are using as an opportunity to think that you are extremely greedy for your own reputation and making sneak attacks on the reputation of another. I wish, Dorp—just as in Virgil, Aeneas, enveloped in a mist, mingled with Carthaginians and viewed the portrayal of the tapestries of himself and his exploits—so I wish you could view, without being seen, the facial expression of those reading this last letter of yours. I am quite sure you would consider me much more worthy of gratitude for frankly advising you to make corrections than you would consider those people who, when by themselves, criticize the very things they fawningly praise in your presence; for by making corrections you can get everybody to think—as I am doing myself—that the letter was not sent by you, but escaped from you.

However, I am certainly surprised if any person should take it into his head to be so flattering as to extol such matters even in your presence; and, as I began to say, I wish you could watch through a window and see the facial expression, the tone of voice, the emotion with which those matters are read. In the letter to Erasmus more than once you ride roughshod over our theologians, over Erasmus, and over your grammarians, as if, while occupying a throne high up among the ranks of the theologians, you were shoving him down among the poor grammarians. You take your place among the theologians, and rightly so, and not just a place, but the first place. Still he should not be shoved from the throne of the theologians down to the benches of the grammarians. Though I do not think Erasmus will scorn the title of grammarian, which you laugh at with more frequency than wit. As a matter of fact, he deserves that title most of all perhaps. But he is so modest, he does not admit it, since he realizes that the name "grammarian" is synonymous with learned; the function of the grammarian penetrates all types of letters—that is, all the arts. Consequently, a person who has made a thorough study of dialectics can be called a dialectician, of arithmetic, an arithmetician; likewise in the other arts. But it is my definite opinion that only the man who has investigated all the branches of knowledge has the right to be called learned. Otherwise you could attach the name of grammarian even to little children who have learned the alphabet. But you mean by grammarian only those men who, as you put it, with whip in hand instead of a scepter play the king in the cave of flogging and, though more stupid than Self-love and Folly, think they understand all branches of learning, just because they know feeble words and the structure of clauses. I would admit, my dear Dorp, that such men are far from being learned. Yet, I really believe that they are much closer to learning than are those theologians who do not know the structure of clauses and feeble words. I can think of several, and you, I suppose, of even more, who belong to that class, although we both keep it a deep secret. Erasmus definitely does not belong to that group of grammarians who have learned only feeble words, nor to that group of theologians who know absolutely nothing but a confused labyrinth of petty problems. He does belong to the group of grammarians such as Yarra and Aristarchus, and to the group of theologians such as yourself, my dear Dorp, and that is to the very best. He is not ignorant of those petty problems; yet, just as you in a thorough way have done, he has acquired what is much more useful, a competent knowledge of good literature, primarily sacred, but also of other kinds.

All of this then, my dear Dorp, is my view on Folly. It is without reason that you warn me, since there is no warning that has to be given; and if there were any, you are giving it to me too late, after so many years. Your suggestion at the conclusion of your former letter—namely, that Erasmus would be reconciled with those theologians who were disturbed by the Folly, if he were to write a praise of Wisdom in answer to the praise of Folly—that suggestion really brought a slight smile to my lips. They are indeed wise men, if they think that by this *Praise of Folly* Folly has been so lauded as to want wisdom lauded in the same manner! If that is what they think, why are they angry? They too have been copiously lauded by Folly that has been so lauded. Besides, I do not see how Erasmus could appease the ill-will of such men towards himself; rather he would only aggravate it, whether he wants to or not, because he would be forced to expel them from the coterie of Wisdom, just as now he has been forced to admit them into the company of the most gifted priests of the secret rites of Folly.

While I have been writing this, a letter has reached me from my Prince, recalling me. Though I desire to continue, I am forced at last to stop and, even though unwilling, to put an end to this letter; it is so lengthy, perhaps it might have been shorter, an *"Orestes* written also on the back of the pages, and still not finished" [Juvenal, *Satires* 1.6]. Because of some vague longing to talk with you, it still wanted to go on and on.

Although I have now left nothing untouched, certainly, as far as I know, I have omitted nothing deliberately. I do not think that anyone will expect me to defend *The Folly* from even a suspicion of blasphemy or lack of piety, as if, because of that book, Christ's Religion has been in bad repute. You have so represented these men in your former letter as to show plainly that you were giving someone else's view, contrary to your own personal opinion; and in your later letter, though much of it was not your own true thoughts, everything you wrote was adorned splendidly and fully, especially in those passages where there was an opportunity for the brilliant style that is typical of your genius and learning; and yet you purposely omitted any mention of this slanderous charge of lack of piety, as if that charge itself were impious and sacrilegious, and not only flagrant, but also idle and absurd. Therefore, I did not have to say anything about that subject; I think I have spoken about everything else. And so there is nothing left of the subjects I wanted to discuss. If I had not been interrupted by the letter from my Prince, I would probably have written more fully about the same matters.

I am not displeased by having to fold up this letter, as I am afraid that, because of its length, it could be bothersome to you.

Yet I am not happy to be deprived of the opportunity to revise this letter, and give shape to this crude and ugly offspring of mine by frequently retouching it. I had definitely decided to do that, so it would reach you, most learned Dorp, in a more finished state; for I want myself and all I am to meet your approval. Please, pardon the lack of finish, due to the fact that I cannot even reread it because of my hasty departure, but also to the fact that I had no library here while writing, in fact, almost no books at all. However, your kindness first of all, gives me hope that this letter, no matter what it is like, will not even as it is cause you displeasure; and, secondly, the pains I have taken in writing it, for I trust that I have carefully avoided saying anything that could justifiably offend your ears, unless it be, since I am human, that self-love has deceived me. If that should happen, upon being reminded of my fault, I shall admit it frankly, and not defend it. Just as I am not unwilling to admonish those I love, if it is of any importance to them, so too I am certainly very happy to be admonished by my friends. I am aware also of this fact, that some of the reproaches you made against Erasmus were not the result of your own irritation, but rather you were repeating what you had gotten from others. I say this, so you may in turn realize that many of the answers I have made in this letter are directed through you against them, rather than against you. For I not only love you as being a most affectionate person, and regard you as most learned, but I also respect you as an excellent man.

Goodbye, my dearest Dorp, and be truly convinced that no one, even in your native Holland, is more interested in you than is More among the British, sundered from all the world; and you are no less dear to him than you are to Erasmus. For you cannot be any dearer, not even to me. Again, goodbye.

Letter 27b

TO MARTIN DORP [82]

<LONDON
1519>

It was not difficult for me to foresee that you would one day think otherwise than then you thought. But that you would not only become wiser, but even in a most eloquent address proclaim that you had changed, openly, sincerely and straightforwardly, this indeed went far beyond my expectation, and indeed almost beyond the hopes and desires of all, for it seemed vain to look for such transparent honesty and want of affectation. Nothing indeed is more sad than that men should form varying judgments about identical problems; but nothing is more rare than that after they have published their views, argued strongly for them and defended them against attack, they then, acknowledging the truth, should change their course, and, as if their voyage had been in vain, sail back into the port from which they came. Believe me, my dear Dorp, what you have done with such great humility, it is almost impossible to demand even from those whom the world nowadays considers as most humble. Men are commonly so wrong-headed in their folly that they prefer to proclaim aloud that they still are fools rather than own that they ever were. How much more virtuously have you not acted, my dear Dorp. Although you are so keen-witted, so learned and so eloquent that whatever be the thesis you may desire to defend, improbable as it may be, or even purely paradoxical, you are able to win the agreement of your readers, yet in your love of truth rather than shams you have preferred publicly to acknowledge that once you were deceived, rather than go on deceiving.

But what am I to say of a further act of modesty which throws into the shade even that singular modesty which I have been praising? Although it was due to the clearness and sincerity of your mind that you saw the truth, yet you chose to ascribe it to the admonitions of others, and even to mine. Thus, although the first rank in wisdom is yours by right, and is given to you by common consent, yet you deliberately put yourself in the second rank. It is certainly the duty of the learned to raise you again to your rightful position. For that letter of mine was wordy rather than convincing; and when I compare it with your address, so eloquent, so full of cogent arguments, I feel quite ashamed, my dear Dorp, to see what little power my words could have had to win your assent, although your modesty or your courtesy leads you now to ascribe such power to them. But the praise that you seek to avoid is yours all the more surely. So, my dear Dorp, you must understand that this act of yours, of such rare virtue, has procured for you glory of the noblest kind, which will never die.

Letter 28

FROM ERASMUS TO ULRICH VON HUTTEN

This famous letter offers Erasmus' "full-length portrait" of his friend, Thomas More. In addition to describing More's person in detail, Erasmus also discusses More's education, his sense of duty, his habits of friendship, his hatred of tyranny, and his decision to enter into King Henry VIII's service in 1518. This translation of the letter is taken from *The Epistles of Erasmus,* Vol. 3, ed., Francis M. Nichols (New York: Russell and Russell, 1962), pp. 387–401. A later letter from Erasmus to William Budé (1521) describes in detail More's understanding of education and the education of his daughters. See *A Thomas More Sourcebook*, pp. 221–226 for the text of that letter.

ANTWERP
23 JULY 1519

Most illustrious Hutten, your love, I had almost said your passion for the genius of Thomas More, kindled as it is by his writings, which, as you truly say, are as learned and witty as anything can possibly be, is, I assure you, shared by many others; and moreover the feeling in this case is mutual; since More is so delighted with what you have written, that I am myself almost jealous of you. It is an example of what Plato says of that sweetest wisdom, which excites much more ardent love among men than the most admirable beauty of form. It is not discerned by the eye of sense, but the mind has eyes of its own, so that even here the Greek saying holds true, that out of Looking grows Liking; and so it comes to pass that people are sometimes united in the warmest affection, who have never seen or spoken to each other. And, as it is a common experience, that for some unexplained reason different people are attracted by different kinds of beauty, so between one mind and another, there seems to be a sort of latent kindred, which causes us to be specially delighted with some minds, and not with others.

As to your asking me to paint you a full-length portrait of More, I only wish my power of satisfying your request were equal to your earnestness in pressing it. For to me too, it will be no unpleasant task to linger awhile in the contemplation of a friend, who is the most delightful character in the world. But, in the first place, it is not given to every man to be aware of all More's accomplishments; and in the next place, I know not whether he will himself like to have his portrait painted by any artist that chooses to do so. For indeed I do not think it more easy to make a likeness of More than of Alexander the Great, or of Achilles; neither were those heroes more worthy of immortality. The hand of an Apelles is required for such a subject, and I am afraid I am more like a Fulvius or a Rutuba than an Apelles. Nevertheless I will try to draw you a sketch, rather than a portrait, of the entire man, so far as daily and domestic intercourse has enabled me to observe his likeness and retain it in my memory. But if some diplomatic employment should ever bring you together, you will find out, how poor an artist you have chosen for this commission; and I am afraid you will think me guilty of envy or of wilful blindness in taking note of so few out the many good points of his character.

To begin with that part of him which is least known to you, in shape and stature More is not a tall man, but not remarkably short, all his limbs being so symmetrical, that no deficiency is observed in this respect. His complexion is fair, his face being rather blonde than pale, but with no approach to redness, except a very delicate flush, which lights up the whole. His hair is auburn inclining to black, or if you like it better, black inclining to auburn; his beard thin, his eyes a bluish grey with some sort of tinting upon them. This kind of eye is thought to be a sign of the happiest character, and is regarded with favor in England, whereas with us black eyes are rather preferred. It is said, that no kind of eye is so free from defects of sight. His countenance answers to his character, having an expression of kind and friendly cheerfulness with a little air of raillery. To speak candidly, it is a face more expressive of pleasantry than of gravity or dignity, though very far removed from folly or buffoonery. His right shoulder seems a little higher than his left, especially when he is walking, a peculiarity that is not innate, but the result of habit, like many tricks of the kind. In the rest of his body there is nothing displeasing, only his hands are a little coarse, or appear so, as compared with the rest of his figure. He has always from his boyhood been very negligent of his toilet, so as not to give much attention even to the things, which according to Ovid are all that men need care about. What a charm there was in his looks when young, may even now be inferred from what remains; although I knew him myself when he was not more than three and-twenty years old; for he has not yet passed much beyond his fortieth year. His health is sound rather than robust, but sufficient for any labors suitable to an honorable citizen; and we may fairly hope, that his life may be long, as he has a father living of a great age, but an age full of freshness and vigor.

I have never seen any person less fastidious in his choice of food. As a young man, he was by preference a water-drinker, a practice he derived from his father. But, not to give annoyance to others, he used at table to conceal this habit from his guests by drinking, out of a pewter vessel, either small beer almost as weak as water, or plain water. As to wine, it being the custom, where he was, for the company to invite each other to drink in turn out of the same cup, he used sometimes to sip a little of it, to avoid appearing to shrink from it altogether, and to habituate himself to the common practice. For his eating he has been accustomed to prefer beef and salt meats, and household bread thoroughly fermented, to those articles of diet, which are commonly regarded as delicacies. But he does not shrink from things that impart an innocent pleasure, even of a bodily kind, and has always a good appetite for milk-puddings and for fruit, and eats a dish of eggs with the greatest relish.

His voice is neither loud nor excessively low, but of a penetrating tone. It has nothing in it melodious or soft, but is simply suitable for speech, as he does not seem to have any natural talent for singing, though he takes pleasure in music of every kind. His articulation is wonderfully distinct, being equally free from hurry and from hesitation.

He likes to be dressed simply, and does not wear silk, or purple, or gold chains, except when it is not allowable to dispense with them. He cares marvelously little for those formalities, which with ordinary people are the test of politeness; and as he does not exact these ceremonies from others, so he is not scrupulous in observing them himself, either on occasions of meeting or at entertainments, though he understands how to use them, if he thinks proper to do so; but he hold it to be effeminate and unworthy of a man to waste much of his time on such trifles.

He was formerly rather disinclined to Court life and to any intimacy with princes, having always special hatred of tyranny and a great fancy for equality; whereas you will scarcely find any Court so well-ordered, as not to have much bustle and ambition and pretence and luxury, or to be free from tyranny in some form or other. He could not even be tempted to Henry the Eighth's Court without great trouble, although nothing could be desired more courteous or less exacting than this Prince. He is naturally fond of liberty and leisure; but as he enjoys a holiday when he has it, so whenever business requires it, no one is more vigilant or more patient.

He seems to be born and made for friendship, of which he is the sincerest and most persistent devotee. Neither is he afraid of that multiplicity of friends, of which Hesiod disapproves. Accessible to every tender of intimacy, he is by no means fastidious in choosing his acquaintance, while he is most accommodating in keeping it on foot, and constant in retaining it. If he has fallen in with anyone whose faults he cannot cure, he finds some opportunity of parting with him, untying the knot of intimacy without tearing it; but when he has found any sincere friends, whose characters are suited to his own, he is so delighted with their society and conversation, that he seems to find in these the chief pleasure of life, having an absolute distaste for tennis and dice and cards, and the other games with which the mass of gentlemen beguile the tediousness of Time. It should be added that, while he is somewhat neglectful of his own interest, no one takes more pains in attending to the concerns of his friends. What more need I say? If anyone requires a perfect example of true friendship, it is in More that he will best find it.

In company his extraordinary kindness and sweetness of temper are such as to cheer the dullest spirit, and alleviate the annoyance of the most trying circumstances. From boyhood he was always so pleased with a joke, that it might seem that jesting was the main object of his life; but with all that, he did not go so far as buffoonery, nor had ever any inclination to bitterness. When quite a youth, he wrote farces and acted them. If a thing was facetiously said, even though it was aimed at himself, he was charmed with it, so much did he enjoy any witticism that had a flavor of subtlety or genius. This led to his amusing himself as a young man with epigrams, and taking great delight in Lucian. Indeed, it was he that suggested my writing the *Moria,* or Praise of Folly, which was much the same thing as setting a camel to dance.

There is nothing that occurs in human life, from which he does not seek to extract some pleasure, although the matter may be serious in itself. If he has to do with the learned and intelligent, he is delighted with their cleverness, if with unlearned or stupid people, he finds amusement in their folly. He is not offended even by professed clowns, as he adapts himself with marvelous dexterity to the tastes of all; while with ladies generally, and even with his wife, his conversation is made up of humor and playfulness. You would say it was a second Democritus [i.e., "the laughing philosopher], or rather that Pythagorean philosopher, who strolls in leisurely mood through the market-place, contemplating the turmoil of those who buy and sell. There is no one less guided by the opinion of the multitude, but on the other hand no one sticks more closely to common sense.

One of his amusements is in observing the forms, characters and instincts of different animals. Accordingly there is scarcely any kind of bird, that he does not keep about his residence, and the same of other animals not quite so common, as monkeys, foxes, ferrets, weasels and the like. Beside these, if he meets with any strange object, imported from abroad or otherwise remarkable, he is most eager to buy it, and has his house so well supplied with these objects, that there is something in every room which catches your eye, as you enter it; and his own pleasure is renewed every time that he sees others interested. When of a sentimental age, he was not a stranger to the emotions of love, but without loss of character, having no inclination to press his advantage, and being more attracted by a mutual liking than by any licentious object.

He had drunk deep of Good Letters from his earliest years; and when a young man, he applied himself to the study of Greek and of philosophy; but his father was so far from encouraging him in this pursuit, that he withdrew his allowance and almost disowned him, because he thought he was deserting his hereditary study, being himself an expert professor of English Law. For remote as that profession is from true learning, those who become masters of it have the highest rank and reputation among their countrymen; and it is difficult to find any readier way to acquire fortune and honor. Indeed a considerable part of the nobility of that island has had its origin in this profession, in which it is said that no one can be perfect, unless he has toiled at it for many years. It was natural, that in his younger days our friend's genius, born for better things, should shrink from this study; nevertheless, after he had had a taste of the learning of the Schools, he became so conversant with it, that there was no one more eagerly consulted by suitors; and the income that he made by it was not surpassed by any of those who did nothing else; such was the power and quickness of his intellect.

He also expended considerable labor in persuading the volumes of the orthodox Fathers; and when scarcely more than a youth, he lectured publicly on the *De Civitate Dei* [i.e., *The City of God*] of Augustine before a numerous audience, old men and priests not being ashamed to take a lesson in divinity from a young layman, and not at all sorry to have done so. Meantime he applied his whole mind to religion, having some thought of taking orders, for which he prepared himself by watchings and fastings and prayers and such like exercises; wherein he showed much more wisdom than the generality of the people who rashly engage in so arduous a profession without testing themselves beforehand. And indeed there was no obstacle to his adopting this kind of life, except the fact, that he could not shake off his wish to marry. Accordingly he resolved to be a chaste husband rather than a licentious priest.

When he married, he chose a very young girl, a lady by birth, with her character still unformed, having been always kept in the country with her parents and sisters,—so that he was all the better able to fashion her according to his own habits. Under his direction she was instructed in learning and in every kind of Music, and had almost completely become just such a person as would have been a delightful companion for his whole life, if an early death had not carried her away. She had however borne him several children, of whom three girls, Margaret, Alice and Cecily, and one boy, John, are still living.

More did not however long remain single, but contrary to his friends' advice, a few months after his wife's death, he married a widow, more for the sake of the management of his household, than to please his own fancy, as she is no great beauty, nor yet young, *nec bella admodum nec puella,* as he sometimes laughingly says, but a sharp and watchful housewife; with whom nevertheless he lives, on as sweet and pleasant terms as if she were as young and lovely as any one could desire ; and scarcely any husband obtains from his wife by masterfulness and severity as much compliance as he does by blandishments and jests. Indeed, what more compliance could he have, when he has induced a woman who is already elderly, who is not naturally of a yielding character, and whose mind is occupied with business, to learn to play on the harp, the viol, the spinet and the flute, and to give up every day a prescribed time to practice? With similar kindness he rules his whole household, in which there are no tragic incidents, and no quarrels. If anything of the kind should be likely, he either calms it down, or applies a remedy at once. And in parting with any member of his household he has never acted in a hostile spirit, or treated him as an enemy. Indeed his house seems to have a sort of fatal felicity, no one having lived in it without being advanced to higher fortune, no inmate having ever had a stain upon his character. It would be difficult to find any one living on such terms with a mother as he does with his step-mother. For his father had brought in one stepmother after another; and he has been as affectionate with each of them as with a mother. He has lately introduced a third, and More swears that he never saw anything better. His affection for his parents, children and sisters is such, that he neither wearies them with his love, nor ever fails in any kindly attention.

His character is entirely free from any touch of avarice. He has set aside out of his property what he thinks sufficient for his children, and spends the rest in a liberal fashion. When he was still dependent on his profession, he gave every client true and friendly counsel with an eye to their advantage rather than his own, generally advising them, that the cheapest thing they could do was to come to terms with their opponents. If he could not persuade them to do this, he pointed out how they might go to law at least expense; for there are some people whose character leads them to delight in litigation.

In the City of London, where he was born, he acted for some years as judge in civil causes. This office, which is by no means burdensome,—inasmuch as the Court sits only on Thursdays before dinner,—is considered highly honorable; and no judge ever disposed of more suits, or conducted himself with more perfect integrity. In most cases he remitted the fees which are due from the litigants, the practice being for the plaintiff to deposit three groats before the hearing, and the defendant a like sum, and no more being allowed to be exacted. By such conduct he made himself extremely popular in the City.

He had made up his mind to be contented with this position, which was sufficiently dignified without being exposed to serious dangers. He has been thrust more than once into an embassy, in the conduct of which he has shown great ability; and King Henry in consequence would never rest until he dragged him into his Court. 'Dragged him,' I say, and with reason; for no one was ever more ambitious of being admitted into a Court, than he was anxious to escape it. But as this excellent monarch was resolved to pack his household with learned, serious, intelligent and honest men, he especially insisted upon having More among them,— with whom he is on such terms of intimacy that he cannot bear to let him go. If serious affairs are in hand, no one gives wiser counsel; if it pleases the King to relax his mind with agreeable conversation, no man is better company. Difficult questions are often arising, which require a grave and prudent judge; and these questions are resolved by More in such a way, that both sides are satisfied. And yet no one has ever induced him to accept a present. What a blessing it would be for the world, if magistrates like More were everywhere put in office by sovereigns!

Meantime there is no assumption of superiority. In the midst of so great a pressure of business he remembers his humble friends; and from time to time he returns to his beloved studies. Whatever authority he derives from his rank, and whatever influence he enjoys by the favor of a powerful sovereign, are employed in the service of the public, or in that of his friends. It has always been part of his character to be most obliging to everybody, and marvelously ready with his sympathy; and this disposition is more conspicuous than ever, now that his power of doing good is greater. Some he relieves with money, some he protects by his authority, some he promotes by his recommendation, while those whom he cannot otherwise assist are benefited by his advice. No one is sent away in distress, and you might call him the general patron of all poor people. He counts it a great gain to himself, if he has relieved some oppressed person, made the path clear for one that was in difficulties, or brought back into favor one that was in disgrace. No man more readily confers a benefit, no man expects less in return. And successful as he is in so many ways,—while success is generally accompanied by self-conceit,—I have never seen any mortal being more free from this failing.

I now propose to turn to the subject of those studies, which have been the chief means of bringing More and me together. In his first youth his principal literary exercises were in verse. He afterwards wrestled for a long time to make his prose more smooth; practicing his pen in every kind of writing in order to form that style, the character of which there is no occasion for me to recall, especially to you, who have his books always in your hands. He took the greatest pleasure in declamations, choosing some disputable subject, as involving a keener exercise of mind. Hence, while still a youth, he attempted a dialogue, in which he carried the defense of Plato's community even to the matter of wives! He wrote an answer to Lucian's *Tyrannicide,* in which argument it was his wish to have me for a rival, in order to test his own proficiency in this kind of writing. He published his *Utopia* for the purpose of showing, what are the things that occasion mischief in commonwealths; having the English constitution especially in view, which he so thoroughly knows and understands. He had written the second book at his leisure, and afterwards, when he found it was required, added the first off-hand. Hence there is some inequality in the style.

It would be difficult to find any one more successful in speaking *ex tempore,* the happiest thoughts being attended by the happiest language; while a mind that catches and anticipates all that passes, and a ready memory, having everything as it were in stock, promptly supply whatever the time, or the occasion, demands. In disputations nothing can be imagined more acute, so that the most eminent theologians often find their match, when he meets them on their own ground. Hence John Colet, a man of keen and exact judgment, is wont to say in familiar conversation, that England has only one genius, whereas that island abounds in distinguished intellects.

However averse he may be from all superstition, he is a steady adherent of true piety; having regular hours for his prayers, which are not uttered by rote, but from the heart. He talks with his friends about a future life in such a way as to make you feel that he believes what he says, and does not speak without the best hope. Such is More, even at Court; and there are still people who think that Christians are only to be found in monasteries! Such are the persons, whom a wise King admits into his household, and into his chamber; and not only admits, but invites, nay, compels them to come in. These he has by him as the constant witnesses and judges of his life,— as his advisers and travelling companions. By these he rejoices to be accompanied, rather than by dissolute young men or by fops, or even by decorated grandees, or by crafty ministers, of whom one would lure him to silly amusements, another would incite him to tyranny, and a third would suggest some fresh schemes for plundering his people. If you had lived at this Court, you would, I am sure, give a new description of Court life, and cease to be Misaulos ; though you too live with such a prince, that you cannot wish for a better, and have some companions like Stromer and Copp, whose sympathies are on the right side. But what is that small number compared with such a swarm of distinguished men as Mountjoy, Linacre, Pace, Colet,

Stokesley, Latimer, More, Tunstall, Clerk, and others like them, any one of whose names signifies at once a world of virtues and accomplishments ? However, I have no mean hope, that Albert, who is at this time the one ornament of our Germany, will attach to his household a multitude of persons like himself, and set a notable example to other princes; so that they may exert themselves in their own circles to do the like.

You have now before you an ill-drawn portrait, by a poor artist, of an excellent original! You will be still less please with the portrait, if you come to have a closer acquaintance with More himself. But meantime I have made sure of this, that you will not be able to charge me with neglecting your command, nor continue to find fault with the shortness of my letters ; though even this one has not seemed too long to me in writing it, and will not, I am confident, appear prolix to you, as you read it ; our More's sweetness will secure that. . . .

Farewell.

Letter 29

To William Budé [96]

<CALAIS
c. June 1520>

If it were not for the vehemence of my desires, I would not dare to ask you to lessen the pain of your absence by writing to me. For I fear that engaged as you are in the affairs of the Most Christian King, you will not enjoy much leisure, and for my part I am only too conscious of my remissness in this kind of duty, when letters ought to be answered. It is not only my lack of eloquence, my dear Budé, that keeps me from writing to you, but still more my respect for your learning. Shame would even have forbidden me to write this letter, unless another kind of shame had wrung it from me. This is the fear lest the letters that you have received from me should be published along with yours. If they should go forth to the world alone, their defects would be abundantly clear, but if they were side by side with yours their shameful poverty would be exposed as by a light of fierce and unpitying brilliance. For I remember that in our conversation mention was made of the letters that I had formerly sent you, which you had it in your mind to publish if you thought I would raise no objection. It was only a passing suggestion, and I forget what reply I gave. But now, as I think the matter over, I see that it would be safer if you would wait awhile, at least until I revise my letters. It is not only that I fear there may be passages where the Latin is faulty, but also in my remarks upon peace and war, upon morality, marriage, the clergy, the people, etc., perhaps what I have written has not always been so cautious and guarded that it would be wise to expose it to captious critics.

Letter 30

To William Budé [97]

<Calais
c. June 1520>

I doubt, my dear Budé, whether it is advisable ever to possess what we dearly love unless we can retain possession of it. For I used to think that I would be perfectly happy if it should once be my lot to see Budé face to face, of whom by reading I had created a beautiful image in my mind. When at last my wish was fulfilled, I was happier than happiness itself. But, alas! our duties prevented us from meeting often enough to satisfy my desire of conversing with you, and within a few days, as our kings were obliged by affairs of state to separate, our intercourse was broken off when it had scarce begun; and as each of us had to follow his own prince, we were torn apart, perhaps never to see each other again. My sorrow at having to leave you can only be compared to my joy at meeting you. Yet you can assuage my grief a little, if you will deign from time to time by letter to make yourself present to me. This favor, however, I would not dare to ask, if an overwhelming desire did not urge me thereto.

Letter 31

To His School [101]

More encourages his children's astrological studies while reminding them to raise their minds to heaven and to "look up" with good hope during the Lenten season. The "beautiful and holy poem" of Boethius is his *Consolation of Philosophy,* composed in prison while Boethius awaited unjust execution and struggled with the despairing siren songs of the tragic muses. This work, a cornerstone of medieval and Renaissance thought on freedom, fortune, fate, evil, and providence, is an important precursor for the work More wrote while awaiting his own trial and death, *The Dialogue of Comfort against Tribulation,* a book which C.S. Lewis judges "the noblest of all his vernacular writings" and one that "should be on every man's shelf" (*English Literature in the Sixteenth Century,* pp. 177 and 178). For a modernized version of More's *Dialogue,* see the Scepter edition; for the complete text of the original *Dialogue,* see *CW* 12.

AT COURT
23 MARCH <1521>

THOMAS MORE TO HIS WHOLE SCHOOL, GREETING.

See what a compendious salutation I have found, to save both time and paper, which would otherwise have been wasted in reciting the names of each one of you, and my labor would have been to no purpose, since, though each of you is dear to me by some special title, of which I could have omitted none in a set and formal salutation, no one is dearer to me by any title than each of you by that of scholar. Your zeal for knowledge binds me to you almost more closely than the ties of blood. I rejoice that Master Drew has returned safe, for I was anxious, as you know, about him. If I did not love you so much I should be really envious of your happiness in having so many and such excellent tutors. But I think you have no longer any need of Master Nicholas, since you have learnt whatever he had to teach you about astronomy. I hear you are so far advanced in that science that you can not only point out the polar-star or the dog-star, or any of the constellations, but are able also—which requires a skilful and profound astrologer—among all those heavenly bodies, to distinguish the sun from the moon! Go forward then in that new and admirable science by which you ascend to the stars. But while you gaze on them assiduously, consider that this holy time of Lent warns you, and that beautiful and holy poem of Boethius keeps singing in your ears, to raise your mind also to heaven, lest the soul look downwards to the earth, after the manner of brutes, while the body looks upwards. Farewell, my dearest ones.

From Court, the 23rd March.

Letter 32

FROM JOHN FISHER [104]

After entering Henry's service in 1518, More was knighted in 1521. In this letter, Bishop John Fisher writes the new "Sir Thomas More" in the hope that More will help the advancement of a young Cambridge priest. Fisher's request is for a "prebend," that is, he is asking that a portion of the revenues of a cathedral or collegiate church be granted as a stipend of support to this young man (*OED*). More's response follows.

<1521?>

I beg that, through your good offices with our Most Gracious King, we at Cambridge may have some hope that our young men may receive encouragement to learning from the bounty of so noble a Prince. We have very few friends at Court who have the will and the power to commend our interests to the King's Majesty, and among them we reckon you the chief; for hitherto, even when you were of lower rank, you have always shown the greatest favor to us. We rejoice that now you are raised to the dignity of Knighthood and become so intimate with the King, and we offer you our heartiest congratulations, for we know that you will continue to show us the same favor. Please now give your help to this young man, who is well versed in theology and a zealous preacher to the people. He puts his hopes in your influence with our noble King and in your willingness to accept my recommendation.

Letter 33

TO JOHN FISHER [105]

As to this priest, Reverend Father, of whom you write that he will soon obtain a prebend if he can obtain a powerful advocate with the King, I think I have so wrought that our Prince will raise no obstacle. Whatever influence I have with the King—it is very little, but such as it is—is as freely at your disposal, for yourself or your scholar, as a house is to its owner. I owe your students constant gratitude for the heart-felt affection of which their letters to me are the token. Farewell, best and most courteous of Bishops, and continue your affection for me.

Letter 34

TO MARGARET ROPER [106]

In this letter, More mentions Margaret's teacher of astronomy, presumably Nicholas Kratzer, a German astronomer who joined Henry's court in 1517–18, taught in More's household, and is believed to be one of the first fellows at Corpus Christi College, Oxford (*ODNB*). "Momus" was the Greek god of ridicule and censure, who was banished from Olympus on account of his critical spirit; the word could also mean more generally a carping critic, or captious fault-finder (*OED*). Like Shakespeare's Iago, a Momus was "nothing, if not critical."

<1521?>

THOMAS MORE TO HIS MOST DEAR DAUGHTER, MARGARET:

There was no reason, my most sweet child, why you should have put off writing for a day, because in your great self-distrust you feared lest your letter should be such that I could not read it without distaste. Even had it not been perfect, yet the honor of your sex would have gained you pardon from any, while to a father even a blemish will seem beautiful in the face of a child. But indeed, my dear Margaret, your letter was so elegant and polished and gave so little cause for you to dread the judgment of an indulgent parent, that you might have despised the censorship even of an angry Momus.

You tell me that Nicholas [Kratzer], who is fond of you and so learned in astronomy, has begun again with you the system of the heavenly bodies. I am grateful to him, and I congratulate you on your good fortune; for in the space of one month, with only a slight labor, you will thus learn thoroughly these sublime wonders of the Eternal Workman, which so many men of illustrious and almost superhuman intellect have only discovered with hot toil and study, or rather with cold shiverings and nightly vigils in the open air in the course of many ages.

I am, therefore, delighted to read that you have made up your mind to give yourself diligently to philosophy, and to make up by your earnestness in future for what you have lost in the past by neglect. My darling Margaret, I indeed have never found you idling, and your unusual learning in almost every kind of literature shows that you have been making active progress. So I take your words as an example of the great modesty that makes you prefer to accuse yourself falsely of sloth, rather than to boast of your diligence; unless your meaning is that you will give yourself so earnestly to study, that your past industry will seem like indolence by comparison. If this is your meaning nothing could be more delightful to me, or more fortunate, my sweetest daughter, for you.

Though I earnestly hope that you will devote the rest of your life to medical science and sacred literature, so that you may be well furnished for the whole scope of human life, which is to have a healthy soul in a healthy body, and I know that you have already laid the foundations of these studies, and there will be always opportunity to continue the building; yet I am of opinion that you may with great advantage give some years of your yet flourishing youth to humane letters and liberal studies. And this both because youth is more fitted for a struggle with difficulties; and because it is uncertain whether you will ever in future have the benefit of so sedulous, affectionate and learned a teacher. I need not say that by such studies a good judgment is formed or perfected.

It would be a delight, my dear Margaret, to me to converse long with you on these matters: but I have just been interrupted and called away by the servants, who have brought in supper. I must have regard to others, else to sup is not so sweet as to talk with you. Farewell, my dearest child, and salute for me my most gentle son, your husband. I am extremely glad that he is following the same course of study as yourself. I am ever wont to persuade you to yield in everything to your husband; now, on the contrary, I give you full leave to strive to get before him in the knowledge of the celestial system. Farewell again. Salute your whole company, but especially your tutor.

Letter 35

To Francis Cranevelt [Ep. 41]

A Dutch scholar and doctor of canon and civil law, Francis Cranevelt (1485–1564) was first friends with Erasmus and later became friends with More in 1520. Two mutual friends mentioned at the end of the letter—"Feuijn" and "Laurijn"—are likely Jan van Feviijn (1490–1555), a Dutch priest and friend of Cranevelt, and Marcus Laurinus (1488–1540), a Belgian priest (*CE*). "Master Nicholas Bonvisi" is presumably an alternate name for More's dear friend, Antonio Bonvisi, or less probably another member of the Bonvisi household.

At Court

13 February <1521>

Cordial greetings from T. More
to his friend Cranevelt:

I who would not bear that you should be silent have myself been silent for a long time now, in order to provide something for you to write about, so that you could take your turn at reproaching me—which you have a perfect right to do, since for such a long time I have not repaid the copious letters I received from you. But right after Easter, unless something unforeseen happens, I will be with you and will repay everything in person with the loquacity which you have so often and so wearily been forced to put up with. In the meantime, farewell, together with your most delightful wife, a lady of the highest prudence and honor. From the court, on the 13th day of February.

Please give some thought to a house, and perhaps the one that I had before would not be the worst, but the price was the worst.

Find out at what price it could be rented for two months from May 1 and thereafter by the week. And also what it would cost to rent eight or ten beds, together with the rest of the suitable furnishings. And at your leisure let me know about these things. You can also discuss the matter with the friend who is the dearest of all my friends, Master Nicholas Bonviso.

If the candlesticks have not yet been sent, do not send them but keep them there till I arrive. Give my regards to Laurijn, Feuijn, all and our other friends.

Letter 36

TO FRANCIS CRANEVELT [EP. 50]

LONDON
9 APRIL <1521>

GREETINGS FROM T. MORE TO HIS FRIEND
FRANS CRANEVELT:

I have received two letters from you, my dear Cranevelt. From each of them I have perceived that most honest heart of yours and a certain, almost incredible love for me, to which if I should not respond with equal good will, I would certainly be an ungrateful wretch. As for my mistress your wife, or rather your mistress my wife, since I betrothed myself to her there long since—and seriously she is a woman of the highest dignity, completely adorned with the ornaments of all the feminine virtues—I am delighted that she has been unburdened by giving birth and that your family has been increased by offspring. I owe you an immense debt of gratitude for the great effort you have made in looking for a house for me. And then, as for your very friendly offer to me of your own home, I find no thanks adequate to it. There is many a slip, my dear Cranevelt, between the cup and the lip, as they say. Thus it can happen that I myself will not go as a member of the embassy which will shortly be going there—a journey I could comfortably do without, were it not that I would see you friends of mine, to see whom I would willingly go anywhere. But in a few days I will know for certain and once I know I will write you on the spot. In the meanwhile I have almost made up my mind to stay in your home immediately after my arrival, not to burden you with my presence very long but in order to enjoy for a while the spontaneous kindness of you and my lady, your wife, until I have an opportunity to consider in person what house I could most conveniently move into. In the meantime, my most delightful Cranevelt, farewell, together with your most charming wife, to whom give my warmest regards.

London, in haste, April 9. Give my regards to Master Laurijn, Feuijn.

Letter 37

TO FRANCIS CRANEVELT [EP. 81]

<LONDON?
SEPTEMBER 1521>

See, my dear Cranevelt [of the leaves there are no more but] indeed a decent scrap of paper is left. Even now I am mounting my horse. I am returning your book. Together with it you will receive a bundle of letters which Erasmus sent me to read. He

neither wants them published nor is there any need or useful-
ness in doing so, unless his adversary continues his insane antics
in some way or other. For which eventuality I deposit them with
you for safekeeping, just as Erasmus himself told me to do. Share
them with Master Laurijn, if he wants to read any of them. Give
my regards to that most excellent lady, your wife. For her and you
and your delightful children I pray for lasting health and happiness. I am now being called to my horse. Once more, farewell.
Completely at your service, T. M.

Letter 38

TO FRANCIS CRANEVELT [EP. 95]

<CHELSEA?>
12 NOVEMBER <1521>

I recently received a letter from you, my dear Cranevelt. It is just
like you: very fine, most affectionate, and thoroughly learned. I
got back safe and sound and found my dear ones safe and sound,
even though the plague is raging everywhere. I pray that, God
willing, they may long remain so. I myself lapsed into a tertian
fever immediately after my return; but now I am beginning to
get better and am almost well again. My whole school sends you
their regards. Give my regards to our mistress and wife. That
warfare of yours, I see, does not do very much for your welfare. I
pray that someday princes will become of sound mind, at least to
the point where some one of them will be willing to be content
with a realm more than sufficient for ten of them. But the very
weariness of war, I hope, will shortly bring peace. Farewell, my
dear Cranevelt—I have never come upon any companion more

dear than you. At my little country place not far from London, the 12th of November.

Your servant as much as his own,
Thomas More

Letter 39

To His Children and Margaret Giggs [107]

Margaret Giggs was More's adopted daughter, who would marry John Clement in 1526.

At Court
3 September <1522?>

Thomas More to his dearest children and to Margaret Giggs, whom he numbers amongst his own:

The Bristol merchant brought me your letters the day after he left you, with which I was extremely delighted. Nothing can come from your workshop, however rude and unfinished, that will not give me more pleasure than the most accurate thing another can write. So much does my affection for you recommend whatever you write to me. Indeed, without any recommendation, your letters are capable of pleasing by their own merits, their wit and pure Latinity. There was not one of your letters that did not please me extremely; but, to confess ingenuously what I feel, the letter of my son John pleased me best, both because it was longer than the others, and because he seems to have given to it more labor and study. For he not only put out his matter prettily and composed in fairly polished language, but he plays with me both pleasantly and cleverly, and turns my jokes on myself wittily enough. And this he does not only merrily, but with due moderation, showing that he does not forget that he is joking with his father, and that he is cautious not to give offence at the same time that he is eager to give delight.

Now I expect from each of you a letter almost every day. I will not admit excuses—John makes none—such as want of time, sudden departure of the letter-carrier, or want of something to write about. No one hinders you from writing, but, on the contrary, all are urging you to do it. And that you may not keep the letter-carrier waiting, why not anticipate his coming, and have your letters written and sealed, ready for anyone to take? How can a subject be wanting when you write to me, since I am glad to hear of your studies or of your games, and you will please me most if, when there is nothing to write about, you write about that nothing at great length. Nothing can be easier for you, since you are girls, loquacious by nature, who have always a world to say about nothing at all.

One thing, however, I admonish you, whether you write serious matters or the merest trifles, it is my wish that you write everything diligently and thoughtfully. It will be no harm, if you first write the whole in English, for then you will have much less trouble in turning it into Latin; not having to look for the matter, your mind will be intent only on the language. That, however, I leave to your own choice, whereas I strictly enjoin you that whatever you have composed you carefully examine before writing it out clean; and in this examination first scrutinize the whole sentence and then every part of it. Thus, if any solecisms have escaped you, you will easily detect them. Correct these, write out the whole letter again, and even then examine it once more, for sometimes, in rewriting, faults slip in again that one had expunged. By this diligence your little trifles will become serious matters; for while there is nothing so neat and witty that will not be made insipid by silly and inconsiderate loquacity, so also there is nothing in itself so insipid, that you cannot season it with grace and wit, if you give a little thought to it. Farewell, my dear children.

From the Court, the 3rd September.

Letter 40

To Margaret ⟨Roper⟩ [108]

AT COURT
11 SEPTEMBER ⟨1522?⟩

THOMAS MORE TO HIS DEAREST DAUGHTER MARGARET:

I forbear to express the extreme pleasure your letter gave me, my sweet child. You will be able to judge better how much it pleased your father when you learn what delight it caused to a stranger. I happened this evening to be in the company of his Lordship, John, Bishop of Exeter, a man of deep learning and of a wide reputation for holiness. Whilst we were talking I took out from my desk a paper that bore on our business and by accident your letter appeared. He took it into his hand with pleasure and examined it. When he saw from the signature that it was the letter of a lady, he was induced by the novelty of the thing to read it more eagerly. When he had finished he said he would never have believed it to have been your work unless I had assured him of the fact, and he began to praise it in the highest terms (why should I hide what he said?) for its pure Latinity, its correctness, its erudition, and its expressions of tender affection. Seeing how delighted he was, I showed him your declamation. He read it, as also your poems, with a pleasure so far beyond what he had hoped, that although he praised you most effusively, yet his countenance showed that his words were all too poor to express what he felt. He took out at once from his pocket a portague [i.e., a Portuguese gold coin] which you will find enclosed in this letter. I tried in every possible way to decline it, but was unable to refuse to take it to send to you as a pledge and token of his good-will towards you. This hindered me from showing him the letters of your sisters, for I feared that it would seem as though I had shown them to obtain for the others too a gift which it annoyed me to have to accept for you. But, as I have said, he is so good that it is a happiness to be able to please him. Write to thank him with the greatest care and delicacy. You will one day be glad to have given pleasure to such a man. Farewell.

From the Court, just before mid-night, September 11th.

Letter 41

To Francis Cranevelt [Ep. 111]

<Chelsea?>
<March? 1522>

I received your letter, my dearest Cranevelt, which delighted me very much, as everything of yours does. I thank you for taking care of my picture. The Virgin herself will thank you, since at your insistence she was finished with greater care. The remaining three crowns which were owed to the craftsman upon completion of the work I had thought I left with one of my friends there, but now I have arranged it that he will receive from Jan van Porter a half crown as a gift of my own over and above our agreement, if he shows that his work deserves it. As for the people of Bruges, my dear Cranevelt, I was disturbed by such meanness in the midst of such extravagance: when they have consumed immense wealth in such a way that whatever is spent is lost, they are forced to set things right by bits and pieces, snatching away precisely where it would be appropriate to add something. But these vices are theirs and let them come to a bad end. But as for you, my dear Cranevelt, your virtue and [diligence] are such that your circumstances will never be found to be anything but honorable. I pray that they may very happily remain so, and if you see anything that could contribute to that on my part I will strive to see to it as if all the resources of all my connections and my own also would be advanced in support of your standing. Farewell, my dearest Cranevelt, together with your wife, the best and most delightful of ladies. Regards from my wife and my whole family.

Letter 42

To Margaret Roper [128]

Reginald Pole (1500–1558) studied at Magdalen College, Oxford, and Padua, before becoming involved in political and theological controversy over Henry's "great matter," the king's desire to end his marriage with Queen Catherine of Aragon and marry Anne Boleyn. Pole left England in 1532 and published *De Unitate* in defense of the unity of the Church and against Henry the Eighth's position; he returned to England in 1554 and became the archbishop of Canterbury, when England returned to Catholicism briefly during the reign of Henry's daughter, Mary (*ODNB*). See Appendix III for an excerpt from Pole's *De Unitate*, addressed as a direct appeal to Henry the Eighth in 1536, on the significance of Thomas More's death.

<AUTUMN 1523>

I cannot put down on paper, indeed I can hardly express in my own mind, the deep pleasure that I received from your most charming letter, my dearest Margaret. As I read it there was with me a young man of the noblest rank and of the widest attainments in literature, one, too, who is as conspicuous for his piety as he is for his learning—Reginald Pole. He thought your letter nothing short of miraculous, even before he understood how you were pressed for time and distracted by ill-health, whilst you managed to write so long a letter. I could scarce make him believe that you had not been helped by a master until I told him in all good faith that there was no master at our house, and that it would not be possible to find a man who would not need your help in composing letters rather than be able to give any assistance to you.

Meanwhile, something I once said to you in joke came back to my mind, and I realized how true it was. It was to the effect that you were to be pitied, because the incredulity of men would rob you of the praise you so richly deserved for your laborious vigils, as they would never believe, when they read what you had written, that you had not often availed yourself of another's help: whereas of all writers you least deserved to be thus suspected. Even when a tiny child you could never endure to be decked out in another's finery. But, my sweetest Margaret, you are all the more deserving of praise on that account. Although you cannot hope for an adequate reward for your labor, yet nevertheless you continue to unite to your singular love of virtue the pursuit of literature and art. Content with the approbation of your conscience, in your modesty you do not seek for the praise of the public, nor value it over much even if you receive it, but because of the great love you bear us, you regard us—i.e., your husband and myself—as a sufficiently large circle of readers for all that you write.

In your letter you speak of your approaching confinement. We pray most earnestly that all may go happily and successfully with you. May God and our Blessed Lady grant you happily and safely a little one like to his mother in everything except sex. Yet let it by all means be a girl, if only she will make up for the inferiority of her sex by her zeal to imitate her mother's virtue and learning. Such a girl I should prefer to three boys. Good-bye, my dearest child.

Letter 43

To Francis Cranevelt [135, Ep. 115]

"Vives" is Juan Luis Vives (1492–1540), the great Spanish humanist, who was educated in Valencia and Paris before moving to Bruges in 1512. He taught at Louvain, and later, through the graces of Cardinal Wolsey, he taught Greek at Oxford. He enjoyed friendship with all the prominent humanists of the day, including More, Erasmus, Fisher, Linacre, and Cranevelt, and during Henry's "great matter," he served as Queen Catherine's legal advisor; after opposing the divorce and finding himself in the crown's frown, he left the country and returned to Bruges, across the water and safely away from England (*CE* 3). Letters 43–46 were first published by Henry de Vocht in *Literae Virorum Eruditorum ad Franciscum Craneveldium, 1522–1528* (Louvain, 1928).

LONDON
10 August <1524>

Cordial greetings! I see and I recognize, my dear Cranevelt, how deeply I am in your debt, so unceasingly do you do what to my mind is the most pleasant thing of all—writing about what is happening with you and our friends. For to Thomas More what either should or could be more agreeable in adversity or more pleasant in prosperity than to receive letters from Cranevelt, the dearest of all men? Unless someone could provide the opportunity to speak with the Tan himself in person—although whenever I read what you have written, I am so affected by it that while I am reading I seem to be talking with you face to face. Therefore nothing grieves me more distinctly than that your letter is not longer, although for that defect I could also find a sort of remedy: I read the ones I receive over and over, and slowly at that, so that quick reading does not take away the pleasure too quickly. So much for that! As for what you write about our friend Vives, and I say it in a discussion of bad women, I agree with your opinion so completely that I think it is not possible to live even with the best of them without any inconvenience at all. For if you happen to have a wife you will not be free of care, and, so far as I can tell, Metellus Numidicus [the Roman consul] told the truth about wives. But I would say it all the more emphatically if we were not to blame for causing many women to become worse. Nevertheless, Vives has such character and prudence, and has acquired such a wife, that he will not only avoid all the vexation of marriage, in so far as that is possible, but he will even find great pleasure from it. In fact everyone's mind is now so totally caught up in concern for the welfare of the public, while everywhere war rages and burns in such a way, that no one is free to pay attention to private worries. Hence whatever domestic concerns once vexed anyone are obscured by the collective disasters. But enough of such matters. I come back to you: whenever I think of your kindness and your friendship toward me (and I do so very often), I shake off all sadness. I am grateful for the little book you sent me. And I offer hearty congratulations that your family has been increased by new offspring, and indeed I do so not only for your sake but

also on behalf of the commonwealth, to which it is very important which parents enlarge it with the most numerous progeny,
for from you only the best can be born. Farewell, and greet your
most excellent wife from me most diligently and obligingly. From
the bottom of my heart I pray for her a happy state of health and
well-being. My wife and children also pray for your well-being,
for through my eulogies you are no less known and dear to them
than to me myself. Once more, farewell. At London, August 10.

 Yours with all my heart and more,

 Thomas More

Letter 44

To Francis Cranevelt [138, Ep. 151]

London

16 May <1525>

I was pleased, my dear Cranevelt, to receive the quite delightful
letter which you sent me from Ghent, from which I understood
that both you and all of yours are well, and that news gave me
great joy. To let you know in turn about me, I, too, and all of my
people are in excellent health, thank heavens.

 When I got your letter, our friend Vives had departed to
rejoin his wife. For some time now we have had the booklet
you wrote about, the one published against our friend Erasmus.
To me and to many others it seems that it was put out with an
assignment to a false author. Hence I would like you to inquire
who the real author was, who brought it to the printers, for perhaps it can be learned from them. But if that can be found out,

please inform me, so that I too may know who that ass is that has covered himself with the hide of another beast. I am as glad to hear that Feuijn has recovered as I was sorry to learn that he had suffered an illness. Please give him, and your excellent wife, my best regards. As for me there is nothing new. I am sending you and your spouse a number of consecrated rings as a little gift and together with them my best regards. London May 14. Farewell, my good man and dearest friend.

Yours with all my heart and more,

Thomas More

To the very eminent gentleman, Frans Cranevelt, at Ghent.

Letter 45

To Francis Cranevelt [139, Ep. 156]

In this short letter to Cranevelt, the news "about Luther" is unclear, but given the date of the letter, More may be referring to the Peasants' War unfolding in Germany and the surrounding region in the spring and summer of 1525. In several later writings, More criticized Luther strongly for the part Luther's rhetoric played in that violent uprising, which left 50,000–60,000 dead before it ended, though estimates vary. More wrote of Luther: "You hurled a burning torch on all of Germany. You lit the wildfire that is now consuming the world" (*CW* 7, p. 25). Despite his sympathy for reform, Erasmus too charged that Luther's rhetoric had "shattered almost the whole world" (*EE* 1670, trans. Hillerbrand). The other possibility is that the letter refers to Luther's relationship with the former Cistercian nun Katharina von Bora; Luther would marry von Bora a week after this letter, on June 13, 1525 (*ODCC*). In any event, Luther's early approach contrasts with the Christian "humanist project advanced by More, Erasmus, and their fellow advocates of international unity, peace, and reform based on the development of law, virtue, public deliberation, and education" (*Young Thomas More*, 21).

LONDON

6 JUNE <1525>

Greetings, my dear Cranevelt. I received your short letter, to which I am compelled to respond in an even shorter one. What you heard about Luther is true. My arrival was delayed but I hope that I will be with you in August. In the meantime farewell, together with the wife who is mine by day and yours by night but the mistress of us both. London, in haste, June 6.

 Yours,

 Thomas More

Letter 46

TO FRANCIS CRANEVELT [142, EP. 177]

With a copy surviving in More's own hand, this letter provides evidence of More's lifelong desire to work for and secure the peace of England and Christendom. In a later letter written after his resignation as Lord Chancellor in 1532, More will single out, in the epitaph he wrote for himself, the treaty signed at Cambrai in 1529, a moment More praises as "the renewal of a peace treaty between the supreme monarchs of Christendom and the restoration of a long-desired peace to the world" (see letter 56). The "trumpery of Taxander" refers to a pseudonymous publication against Erasmus, written by four Dominicans (*CE* 1, p. 398).

LONDON

22 FEBRUARY <1526>

I was delighted, my dearest Cranevelt, with your letter, which Harst delivered to me. Comparing the pictures of the spouses with your description, I could clearly see (and I was glad to see, precisely for the sake of the mistress) that you are not yet growing old, since you are still such an outstanding judge of beauty. The monarchs have agreed on peace—God knows how long it will last. I wish it would last forever, and I do not entirely despair of that. For they have learned enough of the evils of war to see very well that to enter into it again is not to their advantage. I would hope with more confidence if the terms under which the agreement was concluded were a little gentler than they are said to be (how accurately I do not know). The scoundrels who conspired to produce the trumpery of Taxander, like serpents who have spit out their venom, have hidden themselves in darkness, but the infamy of buffoons comes to light. By the death of Dorp true learning has suffered a great loss indeed. I cannot praise you enough, indeed. I cannot praise you enough, my dear Cranevelt, for the very elegant poem in which you paid your last respects. On my behalf please give best regards to your mistress, and likewise mine. Farewell, Cranevelt, most learned and most dear to my heart.

London, February 22, in great haste.

Letter 47

To Erasmus [148]

In this letter, More is urging Erasmus to complete his *Hyperaspistes diatribae adversus servum arbitrium Martini Lutheri (A Warrior Shielding a Discussion of Free Will against the Enslaved Will of Martin Luther)*, Erasmus' response to Luther's *De Servo Arbitrio*, which Luther composed in response to Erasmus' *De Libero Arbitrio* earlier in 1524. More also mentions Erasmus' other work in hand, *Christiani matrimonii institutio*, on the institution of Christian marriage, with the encouragement that such a work is "of supreme importance" to Queen Catherine. "The heresy of Carlstadt" refers to the teachings of Andreas Karlstadt, the German reformer and sometime associate of Luther (*ODCD*). The "painter" mentioned by More is Hans Holbein the Younger (1497–1543), the great Northern Renaissance artist who traveled to England in 1526. He painted portraits not only of Erasmus, More, and the More family, but also of King Henry, Thomas Cromwell, Anne Boleyn, and many other English nobles and notables. His portrait of the Thomas More family is particularly revealing of More's family life and humanism. Although only Holbein's sketch of the original portrait survives—the painting was destroyed in a fire during the eighteenth century—later copies made by Rowland Lockey endure still. For an in-depth study of the Lockey portrait and its significance, see "The Un-Utopian Thomas More Family Portrait" in *Young Thomas More*, pp. 160–75.

Greenwich

18 December <1526>

Best greetings: I have received two letters from you, dearest Erasmus, and have also read the one you addressed to the Reverend

Father, the Bishop of London [i.e., Cuthburt Tunstall]. We, who are your dear little friends, are very much disturbed to hear that the stone disorder which gave you terrible pains for so long has now been followed by the disease which proved fatal to Linacre; though God's goodness and your own virtue are turning such evils into good for you, still our joy at your spiritual blessings does not preclude all concern, on our part, for the human frailty of your body; our uneasiness is caused not only by concern for you personally—for whom as for ourselves we do hope and pray for every blessing—but also, and more especially, by concern for all of Christendom; we are afraid that this illness will interrupt the brilliant works you have been writing to promote Christian piety.

I pray God that you may bring them to a speedy and happy conclusion, especially the remaining part of the *Hyperaspistes*; for you could have no other work in mind that would be more profitable for others, more satisfying to your friends, and more notable or more urgent for your own self. You would find it hard to believe the eagerness with which all good men are looking forward to that work; there are, on the other hand, some wicked persons, either partisans of Luther or your jealous rivals, who apparently are gleeful and growing in numbers as a result of your delayed response. However, I can sympathize with your delay, if the interruption has been caused by your desire to complete other writings first—as, for instance, your work on *Christian Marriage*, which her Majesty the Queen correctly regards as being of supreme importance—and I hope that fact will shortly be brought home to you in a concrete way. And I am very contented, too, if the delay has been caused by your desire to handle the subject in a leisurely, thoughtful fashion; for I am anxious to see that part handled with the utmost care. But if, according to some reports, the delay is due to the fact that you have been terrorized, and have lost all interest in the work, and have no courage to go on with it, then I am thoroughly bewildered and unable to restrain my grief. You have endured, dearest Erasmus, many, many struggles and perils and Herculean labors; you have spent all the best years of your life on exhausting work, through sleepless nights, for the profit of all the world; and God forbid that now you should so unhappily become enamored of your declining years as to be willing to abandon the cause of God rather than lose a decision.

I am not afraid that you will now throw up to me that quotation from the comic poet: "When we are well, everybody," etc., or, "If you were here, you might think differently." Indeed, I am incapable of making any such promises, nor is anybody else capable of offering such prospects as the whole world is waiting with expectation to receive from you, because you have given extraordinary proof of a heart that is valiant and trusting in God. It is impossible for me to doubt that you will continue bravely to exhibit such strength of spirit right up to your dying breath, even if there were a disastrous catastrophe. For you could never fail to trust that God in His merciful kindness would intervene to calm the disturbance. Right now, as far as I can see, you are far from being terrorized; in fact, there is little cause for fear at all. If the Lutherans planned to make any threatening moves, very likely they would have made them before your reply. Then they might have forestalled any answer from you; or if they wanted to gain vengeance on you for your writings, they would have given vent to their rage at the time you published your first volume; for, in that work, you drew such a vivid description of the monster, and you pointed out so accurately the spirit that goads it on, that you displayed, for all the world to see, that fuming, hellish demon, as if you had dragged Cerberus up from the infernal regions.

At present I certainly fail to see any peril beyond that which would threaten you even if you did not write another line. You have replied to the false charges he made against you; you have stabbed him with the point of your pen; all that remains for you is a discussion of Scripture, and, by issuing, like so many promissory notes, a thousand copies of the first volume, you have solemnly promised the whole world that you would faithfully go through with the second volume. Therefore, not even Luther is such a fool as to hope, or such a wretch as to dare to demand, that you would now not carry out God's cause, having accomplished your own, or that you would not fulfill the promise you made publicly, especially since that would be so easy for you to do. Luther, I am sure, would rather have you say nothing, even though, in his letter to you, he pretends to have a supreme contempt for you; it is hard to tell whether that letter is marked more by boastful exaggeration or stupidity. In any case, he is fully conscious that his worthless comments, which laboriously obscure the most obvious passages of Scripture while being frigid enough in themselves, would become, under your criticism, a mass of sheer ice.

Since you, however, are present at the scene of action, while I am some distance away, if you notice that your reply involves some danger which you cannot elude and which I cannot foresee, then, please, do at least this much: write me a confidential note and have it delivered to me by a reliable carrier. Not only the Bishop of London, an absolutely honest person, as you know, and extremely devoted to you, but also I myself will conscientiously see to it that the note will never be made public, unless that can be done safely. Your painter, dearest Erasmus, is a remarkable artist; but I am afraid he will not find England as fertile and fruitful as he expected. Still, I shall do my best to see that he does not find it altogether barren. Your pamphlet was a very neat refutation of the rumor spread abroad by some malicious persons that you favored the heresy of Carlstadt; you thus foiled the sly attempts of the clown who had planted that story in some German work. If God ever grants you the free time, I would like eventually to see a treatise in support of our Faith flow from that heart of yours, so perfect an instrument for defending the truth; however, right now I am very much concerned about the *Hyperaspistes* and I would not want you to become absorbed in anything that might turn your interests elsewhere and thus prevent you from completing this work at the earliest possible date.

Farewell, Erasmus, dearest of all men; from the Court at Greenwich, December 18.

Sincerely and more than wholeheartedly yours,

Thomas More

To the excellent and most learned Master Erasmus of Rotterdam.

Letter 48

To Francis Cranevelt [155, Ep. 242]

Written in haste, this letter survives in Thomas More's hand.

Calais

14 July <1527>

Cordial greeting from T. More to his very charming friend Cranevelt.

Indeed I would be utterly heartless, my very dear friend Cranevelt, if I refused to repay the many letters I have received from you with a single letter in return, especially at this time when I have obtained such a reliable letter-carrier that I am completely deprived of the excuse I usually take as a pretext for my laziness, namely that I lack someone to carry my letter. This carrier is a servant of Erasmus, now returning directly to him, highly commended by him as very loyal and close-mouthed. If you want to communicate to Erasmus anything that you do not wish to commit to a letter, you can very safely entrust it to this man. If there is anything else I wish you to know, you will learn it from this letter-carrier. Calais, in haste, July 14.

Give a thousand greetings from me to that pre-eminent lady, your mistress-wife. Farewell, my good man, most distinguished and most dear to your friend More.

Letter 49

TO FRANCIS CRANEVELT [155A, EP. 262]

CHELSEA

10 JUNE 1528

As surely as I hope God loves me, your enormous kindness toward me, my dear Cranevelt, makes me ashamed of myself, for you send me such frequent, loving, and elaborate greetings, though I reply so rarely, especially since you have no fewer occupations than I do which you could give as pretexts, nay rather as genuine reasons. But you are so open-minded, so steadfast that, though you forgive everything in your friends, you yourself are always so persevering in pursuing your undertakings that you have no faults to be forgiven. But be sure of this, my dear Cranevelt, if something should happen which would seriously require that the services of a friend should be manifested, in that matter you would never find me at fault. Please give my regards to my mistress, your wife (for I do not dare to reverse the order again) and also to your whole household, to which mine sends heartfelt greetings. From my little country place, June 10, 1528.

Letter 50

To Francis Cranevelt [155b, Ep. 48a]

LONDON
8 NOVEMBER <1528>

That most eminent gentleman Master Hacket, our most serene king's ambassador to your country, has sent me your letter, which was as pleasant to me as is proper for a letter from someone who is so dear to my heart that no one else could be dearer. I congratulate you heartily on the peace which has been restored among you, and would that someday I could offer congratulations on a general peace, for which Christendom has so long been miserably yearning. I am delighted you have become so Homeric that you can command such fitting verses from him for any occasion, which you have also translated into Latin that is in no way inferior to the Greek I pray that your spouse, a lady of the highest dignity, will have a happy journey, complete her business exactly as she wishes, and swiftly return, though I remember that you once wrote to me that the most pleasant sleep is in a bed without a wife, but these are the words of husbands on the first nights after their wives have been sent away, for on the remaining nights desire comes creeping back and, unless the wife has left a proxy, it makes sleep unpleasant. As for your wife, I think she is so prudent that she has taken away all her maidservants with her. Farewell, most delightful of all men. London, November 8.

Such as he is, yours with all his heart,
Thomas More, knight

Letter 51

To His Wife Lady Alice More [174]

In this letter, More writes to Lady Alice after the news reaches him that their family barns have burnt down, along with their neighbors' barns as well. At this time of famine in England, the loss of such barns and their corn could very well prove catastrophic to a family, and hence More's words of consolation and good cheer to his trusted wife and partner for all seasons. In places, the language of this letter is reminiscent of biblical texts on unexpected suffering, endurance, and trust, such as *Job*. "Heron" is Giles Heron, who married More's daughter, Cecily. After More's death, Heron served as foreman of the grand jury that recommended treason charges against Queen Anne Boleyn go forward to trial in 1536. He was later himself executed for treason on 4 August 1540 after it was reported to authorities that a former tenant had heard Heron "mumble" against the king.

WOODSTOCK
3 SEPTEMBER <1529>

MISTRESS ALICE, IN MY MOST HEARTY WISE I RECOMMEND
ME TO YOU.

And whereas I am informed by my son Heron of the loss [by fire] of our barns and our neighbors' also, with all the corn that was therein; albeit, saving God's pleasure, it is great pity of so much good corn lost, yet since it hath liked Him to send us such a chance, we must and are bound, not only to be content, but also to be glad of His visitation. He sent us all that we have lost, and since He hath by such a chance taken it away again, His pleasure be fulfilled. Let us never grudge thereat, but take it in good worth and heartily thank Him as well for adversity as for prosperity. And peradventure we have more cause to thank Him for our loss than for our winning. For His wisdom better sees what is good for us than we do ourselves. Therefore, I pray you be of good cheer, and take all the household with you to church, and there thank God both for that He hath given us and for that He hath taken away from us, and for that He hath left us, which, if it please Him, He can increase when He will. And if it please Him to leave us less yet, at His pleasure be it.

I pray you to make some good ensearch what my poor neighbors have lost, and bid them take no thought therefore; for, and I should not leave myself a spoon, there shall no poor neighbor of mine bear no loss happened by any chance in my house. I pray you be with my children and your household merry in God. And devise somewhat with your friends what way were best to take for provision to be made for corn for our household, and for seed this year coming, if you think it good that we keep the ground still in our hands. And whether you think it good that we shall do so or not, yet I think it were not best suddenly thus to leave it all up and to put away our folk off our farm, till we have somewhat advised us thereon. Howbeit if we have more now than you shall need, and which can get them other masters, you may then discharge us of them. But I would not that any man were suddenly sent away he know never whither.

At my coming hither I perceived none other but that I should tarry still with the King's Grace. But now I shall (I think) because of this chance, get leave this next week to come home and see you; and then shall we further devise together upon all things what order shall be best to take. And thus as heartily fare you well, with all our children, as you can wish.

At Woodstock the third day of September, by the hand of your loving husband,

Thomas More, Knight.

Letter 52

FROM BISHOP CUTHBERT TUNSTALL

As Stapleton explains in his biography, this short letter is from the mathematics book Cuthbert Tunstall wrote and then dedicated to Thomas More.

<LONDON
1529>

When I looked round to see to whom, from among all my friends, I might dedicate this composition, you seemed to me the most fitting of all both on account of our intimacy and on account of your frankness; for I know that you will be pleased at whatever good it may contain, warn me of whatever is imperfect, and forgive whatever is amiss.

Letter 53

TO ERASMUS [178]

In this letter, More discusses his recent promotion to Lord Chancellor of England, a position he sees as involving "the interests of Christendom" and requiring his "complete loyalty and utter devotedness." More would resign this office three years later on May 16, 1532, a decision he explains in the next letter.

<CHELSEA>
28 OCTOBER <1529>

Best Greetings. My thoughts and heart had long been set upon a life of retirement, when suddenly, without any warning, I was tossed into a mass of vital business affairs. The nature of these affairs you will discover from your man, Quirinus [i.e., Erasmus' messenger]. Some people here, friends of mine, are jubilant and heap congratulations upon me. But you are usually a prudent and shrewd judge of human affairs; perhaps you will sympathize with my lot. I am adapting myself to circumstances, and I am very happy at the extraordinary favor and kindness shown me by our excellent King; lacking the talent and other gifts required for this position, I intend to try seriously to meet his optimistic expectations by making every effort I am capable of, by complete loyalty, and by utter devotedness.

The rest of the details you will get from Quirinus, as I have given him thorough instructions. The more I realize that this post involves the interests of Christendom, my dearest Erasmus, the more I hope it all turns out successfully, for your sake rather than my own. Farewell, dearest Erasmus, more than half of my soul. From my country home, October 28.

More than wholeheartedly yours,
Thomas More
To the excellent and most learned Master Erasmus of Rotterdam, at Freiburg.

Letter 54

TO ERASMUS [188]

After a tumultuous tenure, More resigned as Lord Chancellor of England on May 16, 1532, one day after the "Submission of the Clergy" to Henry the Eighth. Earlier on May 11, Henry had publicly complained that the clergy needed to be full subjects of the crown, in a speech preserved by Tudor historian Edward Hall in his *Chronicle*: "Well beloved subjects, we thought that the clergy of our realm had been our subjects wholly, but now we have well perceived that they be but half our subjects, yea, and scarce our subjects; for all the prelates at their consecration make an oath to the Pope, clean contrary to the oath that they make to us, so that they seem to be his subjects, and not ours. The copy of both oaths I deliver here to you, requiring you to invent some order, that we be not thus deluded of our spiritual subjects." As the *Oxford Dictionary of the Christian Church* explains, through the resulting Act of Submission, the English Church agreed "to make no new canon without royal license" and to "submit the existing canons to a committee of 32, half lay and half clerical and chosen by the King, for revision" (1563). The 1532 Act of Submission was the work of the Convocation of Bishops; under More's leadership, the 1532 Parliament refused to pass this Act. The later Act of Supremacy, however, was official since Parliament passed it in 1534; any refusal to grant Henry the title "Supreme Head of the Church of England" was thereafter treated as malicious treason, and on this charge both More and Fisher were found guilty and lost their heads. In this letter, More also discusses the health problems that played a part in his decision to tender his resignation in 1532.

CHELSEA
14 JUNE 1532

THOMAS MORE SENDS HIS GREETINGS TO ERASMUS OF
ROTTERDAM.

It has been my constant wish almost since boyhood, dearest
Desiderius, that some day I might enjoy the opportunity which,
to my happiness, you have always had, namely, of being relieved
of all public duties and eventually being able to devote some time
to God alone and myself; at long last this wish has come true,
Erasmus, thanks to the goodness of the Supreme and Almighty
God and to the graciousness of a very understanding Sovereign.
I have not, however, attained exactly what I had wished for. My
prayer had been to reach the crowning point of my life healthy
and vigorous, no matter how old, or at least without sickness and
suffering, as far as one could expect at that age. Perhaps that was a
little too bold; in any case, the answer to that prayer is at present
in God's hands. For some sort of chest ailment has laid hold of
me; and the discomfort and pain it causes do not bother me as
much as the worry and fear over the possible consequences. After
being troubled with this ailment continually for several months,
I consulted the doctors, who said that such a lingering disease
could be dangerous; in their view there was no speedy cure possible; healing would be a long, slow process, requiring proper diet,
medicines, and rest. They did not predict the length of convales-
cence, nor did they even give me assurance of a complete cure.

So, while turning these thoughts over in my mind, I realized
that I would either have to resign my office or be inefficient in
discharging it, as I would be unable to carry out the responsibili-
ties which my position entailed, except at the risk of my life; and
in the case of death, I would have to give up office as well as life.
Therefore I decided to do without the one rather than without
both. Out of concern, then, for affairs of state, as well as for my

own health, I humbly prevailed upon the generosity of our most
noble and excellent Sovereign to condescend to have pity on me
and to relieve me of the overwhelming burden of that office, the
highest in the realm, with which, as you know, he had shown
favor for me and marked me with a distinction far beyond any
merit or even ambition or wish on my part. My prayer, then, to
all the saints of Heaven is that God, Who alone has the power,
may repay adequately these acts of fond affection shown me by
our most noble King, and, to prevent me from spending whatever
time He will add to my life in idleness and inactivity, that God
may also grant me both the spirit to employ those good hours
well and, in addition, strength of body to do so. For when my
health is weak, I am so listless that I accomplish nothing at all.

My dear Erasmus, we are not all Erasmuses; the gracious gift
which God has granted to you, practically alone of all mankind,
that gift all of us must wait to receive. With the exception of
yourself, who would dare to promise what you produce? Though
burdened by the weight of your years and constantly suffering
from illnesses that would prove exhausting and overwhelming
for a healthy young man, still never all through the years of your
entire life have you failed to give an account to all the world with
outstanding publications, as if neither the weight of years nor ill
health could in any way diminish that record. While this one fact
alone is, in the judgment of all men, like a miracle, still, amaz-
ingly, the miracle is magnified by the fact that the host of brawl-
ing critics surrounding and attacking you have in no way deterred
you from publishing, though apparently they had the power to
crush the heart of a Hercules. Such men are constantly stirred up
against you, because they are envious of your unparalleled gifts
and also of your learning, which outmatches even those gifts;
they readily realize that such unique qualities of native talent and
hard work are far beyond their reach; still, almost bursting with
envy, they cannot endure being far inferior to you; therefore, of

course, they contrive together and strive with might and main by incessant personal abuse to see if they can drag your high honor down to their own shameful level.

However, all during the many years that they have been shouldering this rock of Sisyphus, what have they accomplished by their fruitless and wicked efforts except to have the rock come tumbling down again and again upon their own heads? Meanwhile you have kept surging ever upwards. And does it really matter that on occasion even good men, with a certain amount of learning, have been unsettled because, in their view, you perhaps handled some point with too little restraint? After all, every author has been guilty of that, including your own critics, who, while branding your works, could not refrain from committing the same defect—a defect, in this instance, that was too obvious for men of their rank, and of too frequent occurrence for any type of writing. There is much less reason for excusing them, as they are surely aware of the open confession you made before the outbreak of these pestilential heresies, which are now spreading like wildfire and wreaking utter havoc; you admitted that you had handled some points with too little restraint, but, had you been able to foresee the eventual cropping up of these treacherous enemies of religion, you would have treated those same points more gently and more delicately. The rather strong statements you made in those days were evoked by the defects of certain people—defects which were quite the opposite of your own, and which those people hugged to their bosoms as if they were virtues. Anyone who would consider your vigorous spirit a defect will have a difficult time trying to justify the holiest of the ancient doctors of the Church; if those doctors had had the same view of the modern age as they had of their own, I am absolutely sure that some of the statements they made in their day would have been more guarded and more carefully modified. But they did not do that, because they were trying to cure current evils and did not have in mind future ones. To be sure, they suffered the same experience as you now are suffering, in being the target for the slanderous charges of those fellows, for the heretics that mushroomed in a later age have boasted of their borrowings from the works of the ancients; this experience you have in common not only with those very holy Fathers and most ancient guardians of the orthodox Faith, but also with the Apostles and Evangelists, and even with our own Savior, for their words have been used by all heretics as the chief, or almost the sole, basis upon which they have attempted to lay the foundation of teachings utterly false.

Congratulations, then, my dear Erasmus, on your outstanding virtuous qualities; however, if on occasion some good person is unsettled and disturbed by some point, even without a sufficiently serious reason, still do not be chagrined at making accommodations for the pious dispositions of such men. But as for those snapping, growling, malicious fellows, ignore them and, without faltering, quietly continue to devote your self to the promotion of intellectual things and the advancement of virtue.

Concerning the person whom you recommended to me for scholarly reasons, not for religious ones, I have been very prudently and politely warned by friends to be on my guard so as not to be taken in by him. I shall certainly do all I can to handle the situation. I am keenly aware of the risk involved in an open-door policy toward these newfangled erroneous sects. Even though they have been held in check up to now in our country, thanks to the vigilance of the bishops and the influence of our Sovereign, still it is remarkable what tricks they use in their first attempts to sneak into a place, and then the pertinacity with which they try to crash their way through. And one or two of our own fellow countrymen, with a steady stream of books written in our vernacular and containing mistranslations, and worse, misinterpretations of Scripture, have been sending into our land every brand of heresy from Belgium, where they have sought refuge. I have written replies to several of these books, not however out of any great worry for one who would examine the works of both men thoroughly, but because some people like to give an approving eye to novel ideas, out of superficial curiosity, and to dangerous ideas, out of deviltry; and in so doing, they assent to what they read, not because they believe it is true, but because they want it to be true. However, one will never in any way succeed in satisfying that breed of humans who have a passion for wickedness. All my efforts are directed toward the protection of those men who do not deliberately desert the truth, but are seduced by the enticements of clever fellows. Farewell, most learned Erasmus, you who have been of great service to genuine intellectual life.

From my home at Chelsea. June 14, 1532.

Letter 55

LETTER TO REV. JOHN FRITH [190]

John Frith (1503–1533) was educated at Cambridge and appointed junior canon at Cardinal College (Christ Church), Oxford, by Cardinal Wolsey; after being imprisoned on heresy charges in 1528, he escaped England and worked with the reformer William Tyndale on his biblical translations abroad before returning to England in 1532, when he was again arrested and eventually put to death for heresy at Smithfield on July 4, 1533 (*ODCC*). After Thomas More came into possession of Frith's writings against the traditional Catholic understanding of the Eucharist in 1532, More wrote this letter to the young Frith in defense of the doctrine of transubstantiation, among other things, and in the hope that Frith would amend his thinking on "this great matter" and mature in his faith, reason, and habits of reading and judging.

Throughout the letter on Frith, More reiterates that the beliefs he is defending are those that have been held and confirmed "this 1500 years together" in the church. As in his 1529 *Dialogue Concerning Heresies*, More here focuses on the connection between heretical thought and authorship and the doubtful habits of mind and reasoning—what More calls "fantasy"—that support such opinions, for example in the interpreting of scripture. "And surely if this manner of handling of Scripture may be received and brought in use," More warns Frith, "that because of allegories used in some places every man may at his pleasure draw every place to an allegory, and say the letter means no thing else, there is not any text in all the Scripture, but a willful person may find other texts against it, that may serve him to trifle out the truth of God's words, with cavillations grounded upon God's other words, in some other place . . . . If every man that can find out a newfound fantasy upon a text of Holy Scripture may have his own mind taken, and his own exposition believed, against the expositions of the old holy cunning doctors and saints; then may you surely see that no article of the Christian faith can stand and endure long."

In the letter, "Berengarius" is Berengar of Tours (c. 1010–1088), a pre-scholastic theologian who first fell into error regarding the Eucharist, and then spent the rest of his life, in More's account, freely performing penance (*ODCC*). Robert Barnes (c. 1495–1540) was first an Austin friar in Cambridge and then became an English reformer, a friend of Luther and Tyndale, and able helpmate in the King's great matter of divorce and remarriage (*ODNB*). The other reformers mentioned in the letter are John Wycliffe (1330–1384), begetter of the Lollards; Ulrich Zwingli (1484–1531), the Swiss reformer; and Johannes Oecolampadius of Basel (1482–1531), first a collaborator with Erasmus on the Greek-Latin New Testament and later a reformer beginning in 1522 (*ODCC*). More also refers to the heresy of Arianism, the denial of Christ's divinity, a heresy that threatened the early church before the Council of Nicaea articulated the Nicene Creed and the orthodox belief that Christ is "true God and true man" (*ODCC*, 100).

More's other late work on the Eucharist is his *A Treatise to Receive the Blessed Body*, composed in the Tower of London in 1534 (*CW* 13). More scholar Germain Marc'adhour sees More's "keen sense of human solidarity" as one key to his theological writings on the church and its sacraments, and Richard Marius adds that "it could well be said that for More the church is the general sacrament of Christ" (quoted in *CW* 13, cxl). For excellent discussions of the debate over More's theological writings on the reformation controversies, see Brendan Bradshaw, "The Controversial Thomas More," in *The Journal of Ecclesiastical History* 36 (1985): 535–69; Louis Martz's *Thomas More: The Search for the Inner Man* (Yale University Press, 1992); and Eamon Duffy's "'The comen knowen multytude of crysten men': A *Dialogue Concerning Heresies* and the Defence of Christendom," in the *Cambridge Companion to Thomas More* (191–215). For a complete overview of Thomas More's handling of heresy as Lord Chancellor, see John Guy's *Thomas More* (106–25) and Richard Rex's "Thomas More and the Heretics" in the *Cambridge Companion* (93–115).

A LETTER OF SIR THOMAS MORE, KNIGHT REFUTING
THE ERRONEOUS WRITING OF JOHN FRITH AGAINST THE
BLESSED SACRAMENT OF THE ALTAR

Most heartily do I commend myself to you as by this bearer I return the book that you lent me. Since then, and quite recently as you know, I've been offered several more copies. That should show people how eagerly these brethren, newly so called, have been copying it out by hand and secretly circulating it.

Moving to counteract these pestilential works that sow such poisonous heresies among his people, his gracious Highness the King has, like a most faithful Catholic Prince, altogether forbidden that printed books in English be brought into this land from overseas. Otherwise our English heretics lurking abroad will print their heresies along with other matter and so send them hither unsuspected and therefore unperceived till more harm has been done than can well be remedied later. Now, though, the devil has taught his disciples, the devisers of these heresies, to compose many short treatises so that their scholars can quickly copy them, inserting into them as much poison in a single page as they previously printed in fifteen. A case in point is the book by this young man—who has, I note, lately composed various other things kept so secretly and tightly among the brethren that no copies have gotten into general circulation.

But since nothing can prevent them from plotting the writing and production of such evil and graceless works, I just wish God in his mercy would let them keep them so secret that they'd never be seen by anyone except those already so far gone in corruption that the infection was beyond curing. For, as Scripture says, it does less harm for those already sunk in filth to become even filthier than for them to sling their filth onto the clean clothes of others.

But alas—that isn't going to happen. For, as Saint Paul says, the contagion of heresy spreads secretly, like a cancer. As cancer gradually corrupts the body and infects all its parts with the same deadly disease, so these heretics steal about among good, simple souls, and, holding out vain hope of some high, secret wisdom that others have either deliberately kept from them or else couldn't teach them, in hidden byways corrupt and destroy large numbers every day.

They do that by means of such abominable books before those writings even come to light, till finally the smoke of the secret fire begins to seep out at some crack. But sometimes the fire bursts out all at once, consuming whole towns and wasting entire countries before it can be brought under control. And even then it's not so well and thoroughly quenched but that it still lurks in old, rotten timbers down in cellars and under ceilings, ever ready, unless people keep a sharp eye, to blaze up anew as an open fire. (In recent years, that has happened—the one kind of fire or the other—in more places than one.) And therefore I'm both sure and sorry that those other books, as well as the young man's, will eventually come to light, and then it will be evident why they've been kept so much under wraps.

For although its words are smooth and fair, I swear the devil himself couldn't write a worse book than this one. Going way beyond Luther, he teaches in a few pages all the poison previously taught by Wycliffe, Hussgen, Tyndale, and Zwingli in all their heavy tomes about the Blessed Sacrament of the altar. They not only claim, as Luther does, that it remains bread, but they join those other beasts in saying that it's nothing else, so that here there is neither Christ's blessed body and blood, but only ordinary bread and wine to remind us of Christ's passion. In the end, he goes so far as to say that in a way it's all the same to us whether it be consecrated or unconsecrated. But in making so little of the consecration and treating it so lightly, he makes the Blessed Sacrament (which is, and in all Christendom has ever been held to be, the chief sacrament, and not just a sacrament but the very thing that the other sacraments signify and draw their effect and strength from) in a way to be no sort of sacrament at all. And in this manner he goes beyond Tyndale and all the heretics I can recall.

Considering how weighty the matter is, it's truly remarkable on what light and slight grounds he falls into these abominable, heinous heresies.

He doesn't deny, nor can he, that our Savior himself said, "My flesh is food indeed, and my blood is drink indeed" [Jn 6:55]. Nor does he deny that at the Last Supper Christ himself, taking the bread into his blessed hands, blessed it and said to his disciples, "Take you this and eat it, this is my body that shall be given for you." And in like manner, after blessing and consecrating it, he gave them the chalice, telling them, "This is the chalice of my blood of the New Testament, which shall be shed for many. Do this in remembrance of me" [Matt 26:26–29; Mk 14:22–24; Lk 22:19–20; 1 Cor 11:24–25]. The young man doesn't deny, nor can he, that our Savior himself said it was his own body and his own blood, and ordained that it be continually consecrated in remembrance of him. So he has to admit that all those who believe this really is his real body and real blood have the plain words of our Savior himself on their side as the grounding and foundation of their faith.

But against all this the young man now says that in other places in Scripture the Savior speaks of himself a vine and his disciples as branches [Jn 15:5], and calls himself a door as well [Jn 10:7–9]. He isn't really any of those things, but he speaks that way in reference to certain properties that lead him to liken himself to them.

Think of a man who, because of certain properties of his neighbor's horse, says of it, "The horse is mine from top to bottom", by which he means that in everything the horse is very much like his own. Or again: Jacob built an altar and called it the God of Israel; he called the place where he wrestled with the angel the face of God; the paschal lamb was called the passover of the Lord; and so on with many other expressions of which the young man says they don't mean what the words say but only call attention to likenesses in properties.

And so he maintains that although Christ's plain words were "This is my body" and "This is my blood", nevertheless he didn't mean his real body and blood, any more than he meant that he was a real vine or a real door. It was in virtue of certain properties in common that he called himself both. In like manner, the young man says, Christ didn't say this was or would be his own real body and blood, but that in his absence it would be a remembrance of him for them, quite as if it were his body and blood. It's much like the case of the paschal lamb, the token and remembrance of the Lord's passing over; or like a bridegroom who upon departing for a distant country gives his bride a ring as a remembrance of him while he's gone and as a sure sign that he'll stay faithful to her and not break his promise to her.

In truth, it troubles me deeply to see this young man so confused and beguiled by some old trash peddled by the devil as we find him now, anxious to flee in conclusion from the faith of plain and open Scripture for the sake of defending this error. So far has he fallen prey to the newfangled fantasies of foolish heretics, that for the sake of a figure of speech he'd destroy the true sense of the letter so as to uphold a new, false sect against the holy, true Catholic faith so fully confirmed and upheld in Christ's holy Catholic Church for, lo, these fifteen hundred years.

For these dregs he has drunk deeply of Wycliffe and Oecolampadius, Tyndale and Zwingli, drawing from them all his arguments as well. It's widely observed and well known what sort of people these four are, and God has made that plain by openly taking vengeance upon one of them. And so he always has and always will display his wrath and indignation toward all who lapse into such damnable views against the blessed Body and Blood of his only begotten Son. From this perilous opinion and all his other errors may our sweet Savior's mercy call this young man home and save him in time.

I have no difficulty with his allegorical readings and his figures of speech where they are appropriate, even though it may happen that he take one of his neighbor's horses for his while someone else takes take his cow for his own. But always on the condition that in choosing to say something is like something else, he doesn't misinterpret Scripture and deny what's real as he does in this instance.

As for his example of the bridegroom's ring, I readily allow it. For I take it that the Blessed Sacrament was indeed left with us as a true token and memorial of Christ. But I maintain the whole substance of this same token and memorial to be Christ's own blessed body, whereas this man would make it only bread.

Thus I say Christ has left us a better token than this man would have us think. In acting as he does, he acts like someone to whom a bridegroom gives a fine gold ring with a rich ruby to present to his bride as a token; instead, like a deceiving troublemaker, he withholds that gold ring and, rather than a ring, gives the bride a straw, telling her the bridegroom wouldn't send her anything better. Or else, when the bridegroom gives his bride a gold ring as a token, he tells her and convinces her that the ring is only copper or brass in order to lessen her gratitude to the bridegroom.

If he were to say that besides their literal sense, Christ's words can be understood in an allegorical sense, I'd entirely agree with him. For that's true of nearly every word in the whole of Scripture. When words can be understood in some other, spiritual sense besides the true, plain, open sense denoted by their first, literal meaning, ones says they have an allegorical meaning. But he is at fault in this: merely because some passages in Scripture have only an allegorical meaning, he isn't entitled to conclude that elsewhere in Scripture—as here—he's free to set aside the solid, true, literal sense by reading the passage as if the meaning were exclusively allegorical. If we must accept that, then whatever in Scripture touches on any point of our faith must be taken as having no effect or force at all. I find it truly remarkable, then, that he doesn't hesitate to declare that what Christ says about his body and blood should be understood as expressing only a likeness or allegorical resemblance in the same way 'vine' and 'door' do.

Now, he knows very well that although some things spoken by Christ and found in passages of Scripture are to be understood only as simile or allegory, it doesn't therefore necessarily follow that every such word spoken by Christ elsewhere should be taken as no more than a figure of speech.

The quibbling and equivocating of the wicked Arians was the same sort of sophistry in argumentation. As this young man now takes from the Blessed Sacrament its reality as true body and blood of Christ by giving Christ's plain words an allegorical meaning because of places where allegory is all that's meant; so the Arians took from Christ's blessed Person his omnipotent godhead and wouldn't grant that he was equal to almighty God his Father.

Wrongly and brazenly they expounded the plain texts of Scripture, not only by appealing to other texts that seemed to say something different but also, like the young man here, by invoking allegory. They declared it a manner of speech to call him God and Son of God or claimed, as the young man does, that this was a turn of speech according to which Scripture elsewhere refers to other persons as gods and the sons of gods on account of some common property. As where God says to Moses, "I shall make you the god of Pharaoh" and "You shall not backbite the gods" and "I say that you are gods and the sons of the high God are you all" [Ex 7:1; Ps. 82:6; Jn 10:34].

Thus, as the Arians' quibbles directed against Christ's being God and Son of God involved interpreting plain meanings by way of false allegories and likening these passages to others where allegory is indeed present; so also this young man appeals to the fact that Christ was obviously using allegory is speaking of vine and door. The Arians quibbled against Christ's godhead; he tears away the true, literal sense of Christ's words about the reality of his very body and blood present in the Blessed Sacrament.

If this way of treating Scripture be allowed and adopted widely (so that because allegory is used in some places, whoever wishes can take everything as allegory and say there's no other meaning), then there will be no scriptural text against which someone who

wants to do it can't find other, opposed texts allowing him to frit-
ter away the truth of God's words by quibbles based on what God
says elsewhere. If people are given leave to rattle on long enough,
then even a woman can find enough matter to chatter about for
a year on end. That's what those old Arians did. God forbid this
young man should follow their evil example.

But suppose anyone who is able to base some new fantasy
on a text of Holy Scripture must be taken seriously and must
have his interpretation approved in opposition to the interpre-
tations of the old, holy, learned doctors and saints. In that case,
you'll soon see that no article of Christian faith can long stand
and endure. Speaking of himself, holy St. Jerome says that if the
exposition of other interpreters and the consent of the Church
community counted for so little that every passerby deserved credence in expounding texts of Scripture just as he pleased, then,
says this holy man, I could invent a new sect too and declare that,
according to Scripture, nobody who had two coats could be a
true Christian or a member of the Church.

In fact, if that approach were allowed, I could myself spin fifteen new sects out of one, each as firmly grounded in Scripture as
this heresy. But besides the common faith of all regions of Catholic Christianity, the expositions of the old holy doctors and saints
are as clearly opposed to this young man's ideas in this matter as
to any heresy anyone has ever heard of up to now.

Even though he may find some old holy men expounding Christ's words about the Blessed Sacrament figuratively
as well as literally, he'll nevertheless find none who deny the
literal sense and say Christ didn't mean this was his real body
and blood (which is what the young man does as a follower of
Wycliffe, Oecolampadius, Tyndale, and Zwingli). Besides any
such allegorical meanings, the old holy doctors and interpreters
plainly declare that our Savior, in those words as he expressly
spoke them, also definitely and plainly meant that what he

gave his disciples in this sacrament was indeed his very flesh and blood. Never did those old interpreters of Scripture take the places where Christ is called vine or door in that way. Evidently, then, the manner of speaking in the one place was not like that in the other; or else the old interpreters would hardly have understood what is said *here* so differently from their way of understanding what's said *there*.

And over and above that, the very circumstances of the places in the Gospel where our Savior speaks of that sacrament should illustrate the difference between what he said about this and what he said about those other things. In the latter cases he spoke merely by way of allegory, but this was something he said clearly, thus making it clear that he was setting allegory aside and referring to his real body and real blood.

For no one thought it remarkable when our Lord said he was a true vine or a door. Why not? Because they understood perfectly well that he didn't mean he was literally a vine or a door. But when he said his flesh was real meat and his blood real drink, and that they wouldn't be saved without eating his flesh and drinking his blood, then all of them marveled so much that they could hardly bear it [Jn 6:52–69]. And again: why? Because both by what he said and by the circumstances surrounding his saying of it, it was clear to them that Christ was indeed speaking of his very flesh and very blood. Otherwise the strangeness of what he said would have caused them to take it for an allegory quite as much as much as they did his words about the vine and the door. And in that case they would have marveled no more at the one thing than at the other.

But now, having experienced no wonderment at vine and door, they nevertheless wondered so much at the notion of eating his flesh and blood, and were so deeply troubled, and found it so hard to take in and the marvel of it so great, that they asked: How could that be? And almost all of them went away. Thus it's clear that his manner of speech in saying these things was such that the listeners realized he wasn't speaking in parable or allegory but indeed spoke of his real flesh and real blood.

Someone might draw many other clear proofs from the circumstances of those texts where Scripture speaks about this. But it isn't my purpose to dwell now on arguing the question—clear as it is beyond any possible doubt—but only to touch lightly on it so that you can see how little supporting weight and substance can be found for his position in all those instances of allegory that Wycliffe, Oecolampadius, Tyndale, and Zwingli have cited against the Blessed Sacrament.

Those old troublemakers with their false parallels have thereby sadly exploited the naivete and shallowness of this silly young man. If shallowness hadn't moved him to get out of his depth or naivete deceived him or pride and the sense of his self-importance in putting forth heresies hadn't caused him to be willfully beguiled and blinded, he might easily have seen for himself that the more such allegories he found in Scripture in other such turns of phrase and figures of speech, the worse for him. For that only makes it more clear that those passages referring to the Blessed Sacrament meant just what they said, beyond all allegories. Otherwise, neither would those who heard them at the time, nor their expositors ever since, nor all Christian people these fifteen hundred years have taken in its plain, literal sense what was said in just this one matter, so strange and remarkable that it might seem impossible, while in all other cases (so much more numerous, as he says and as indeed they are) setting aside literal meaning in favor of allegory.

The young man himself has understood well enough that the use of allegory in one place isn't reason enough for men to abandon the proper significance of God's word everywhere else and look for an allegorical meaning while forsaking the plain, common sense, literal meaning. He admits he wouldn't do that except from necessity, inasmuch as—he says—he finds that the common, literal sense expresses something impossible. For what is meant thereby, he says, can't be true—Christ's real body can't be in the sacrament because the sacrament is in many different places at once, as it was at the Last Supper when it was in the hands of Christ and also in the mouths of all his apostles although his body wasn't glorified at the time.

Then he says Christ's body, not being glorified, could no more be in two places at once than his own can. Indeed, he goes still further, saying it can't be in two places even when glorified. And this he proves by what he declares to be a saying of St. Augustine: that the body with which Christ rose must be in one place, and that it continues to be in heaven, and that it shall so until he comes to judge both the living and the dead.

So in the end he proves that Christ's body can't be in many places at once. For if it might be in many places at once, then, he says, it might be in all places at once. But in all places at once, he says, it can't be, and so he reasons that it can't be in many places at once. Thus the impossibility of what is denoted by the common, literal sense of Christ's words obliges him of necessity to put aside that meaning in favor of some allegory, which he admits he wouldn't do if the plain, literal sense expressed something possible.

But alas for the dear mercy of God! Suppose we gave up the letter of the text and sought an allegorical meaning that destroyed the literal sense whenever we came up against something beyond reason's reach or whose possibility we couldn't fathom so that we therefore took it for impossible. In that case, I'd like to know, what single article of faith spoken of in Scripture could this young man show me whose demonstration by reason his reason wouldn't oblige him to reject. For even though he ought to believe the letter of the text and make reason obedient to faith, yet his reason would insist he abandon the literal sense—on which proof ought to rest—and would require him to seek an allegorical meaning that could stand the test of rationality even while driving away faith.

I find it very remarkable that the notion of what's impossible should compel this young man to abandon the plain, open, literal sense of what Christ says about the Blessed Sacrament. For these fifteen hundred years many good and holy men have well and firmly believed the literal sense and couldn't be forced to abandon it because of its supposed impossibility. These men have been as natural, wise, well-educated and studious in the matter as this young man, and older and more reliable, settled, and substantial in judgment as well—men at least as likely to grasp what's impossible and what isn't as is this good young man. Thus, regarding all his reasons based on impossibility, I make bold to think as all those holy men of old have thought and all wise men I believe still do think: nothing is impossible for God. And I count those reasons of his as having very little value.

But there's one point he raises—and I wish he'd given its source—that quotation from St. Augustine. Hunting for that one line in the entire body of Augustine's writings would be like hunting for a needle in a meadow. But if we could see the passage where the young man found it, I don't doubt we could reply clearly to it.

Yet even as he quotes them, the words don't serve to make his point. For St. Augustine says no more than that the body in which Christ rose must be in one place, and that it remains in heaven and will do so until the last day. But God help me—unless this young man with his young eyes can see more in these words than I can with my old eyes and spectacles, I think it's remarkable for him to cite them as if they served his purpose.

For in saying that the body in which Christ rose has to be in one place, St. Augustine might mean not that Christ's body mightn't be in two different places at once, but, just as well as anything to the contrary, that it must be in one place (in some place or other, that is). Or he might mean that Christ must have one place for his special place, and that place must be heaven, just as we say God and the angels must be in heaven. Augustine says nothing about the sacrament nor does he say the body with which Christ rose must be so utterly in one place that there's no possibility of its being in more than one.

Also, this word 'must'—in Latin, *oportet*—that this young man quotes St. Augustine as using, doesn't always signify necessity of such a kind as to exclude all possibility of the contrary. Our Savior himself said to the two disciples, *Nonne haec oportuit pati Christum, et ita intrare in gloriam suam?*—"Was it not necessary that the Christ should die and so enter into his glory?" [Lk 24:26]. But he also said he might have chosen whether to die or not: for he says it was placed in his power either to give up his soul or retain it. And the prophet Isaiah says of him, "He was offered up because he willed to be" [Cf. Is 53].

Thus this Latin word *oportet*, which St. Augustine uses here, often refers not to absolute, rigid necessity but to what is expedient and convenient. So it's translated in English not only by the word 'must' (which itself doesn't always signify that the contrary is impossible) but often by saying 'it is fitting,' signifying something to be done for our benefit and advantage rather than something that must be so because there's no avoiding it.

And so all that causes this young man to abandon the literal sense is, as he says, the impossibility of Christ's body being in several different places at once. And this he shows to be impossible by quoting words of St. Augustine that say only that the body must be in one place, not that it may not be in more places than one, that don't refer to the kind of necessity that rules out its contrary, and that don't even mention the sacrament. Since, I repeat, St. Augustine says no more than what he says, I consider it really remarkable that this young man should find something in his words to support his citing them as if they proved his point.

But so that you can grasp clearly that St. Augustine isn't speaking here of strict necessity, consider the following. He says not only that the body with which Christ rose must be in one place, but also declares, if this young man quotes him correctly, that this place where it must be is heaven, there to remain until the last day. But I trust our young man doesn't imagine that in holding that Christ's risen body must be in one place, heaven, until the last day, St. Augustine thereby rules out his being here on earth in that very same body if it pleases him a hundred times before the last day. Reliable accounts testify to the fact of his doing that a number of times since his ascension.

Thus our young man should realize that St. Augustine, while saying the body with which Christ rose must be in one place—heaven, didn't mean by those words such utter necessity as to require abandoning the literal sense of Christ's words in favor of allegory. In saying this, Augustine didn't mean that the body must be in one place, heaven, must be there until the last day, and can in the meantime be nowhere else, and that this is required by an immutable necessity that absolutely excludes the contrary. With respect therefore to St. Augustine's words and our present question, I'm genuinely astonished that this young man should even mention them unless he has something further to say.

Now, as for his natural reasons, they aren't worth paying attention to. The first is that Christ's unglorified body could no more be in two places at once than his own can be, and his body is a natural one as was Christ's and Christ's body was as his. I reject any comparisons between the two bodies. But if Christ were to tell me he could cause both their bodies to be in fifteen places at once, I'd believe he could do as he said of both, without so much as inquiring whether or not he'd first would glorify both. For if he says it, I'm sure he can do it, glorified or not.

Our Savior said a camel or a great rope cable could as easily pass through a needle's eye as a rich man enter the kingdom of heaven, and afterward told his apostles that though both things were impossible with men, all things were possible with God. I think that in saying this he meant that neither the particular instance nor the general category of phenomena was impossible with God [Lk 18:24–27; Lk 1:37]. But supposing it isn't impossible for him to draw either camel or cable through the needle's eye, why should I waste time fretting over whether he can do that just as they are or whether, by reason of his sheer ability to do it, he first must glorify the camel or the cable?

That's what this young man does in saying God couldn't make his body be in two places at once in its present state, since it's now somewhat gross and unglorified, and then, making a comparison with his body, arguing similarly of the blessed body of Christ, on the assumption that Christ's body at the Last Supper was no more glorified than his own body is. Of both their bodies I say again: If he said he would do it, I don't doubt that he could.

If it couldn't be done without his glorifying them first, then I'm sure he would glorify them; and if it were true that he couldn't make his own body be in two places at once at the Last Supper without its then being glorified, I'm sure he glorified it for a time. For it was as much in his power to do that as often as he liked before his death as it was after the resurrection. And it was also in his power to keep his glorified state from being perceived, as he did with his two disciples, who, despite his having a glorified body, took him to be only a pilgrim. Therefore I say: If Christ told me he could make both his body and also this young man's be in a thousand places at once, I wouldn't doubt that somehow or other he could do it.

But here perhaps our young man would say: You make a good point if God said that and, saying it, meant just what he said. But you're surely aware that I deny that in saying it he meant to be understood like that. For I say that in speaking thus he was using an allegory, as when he called himself a vine and a door.

Let the young man reflect on the implications of his arguing that Christ didn't mean what he said in speaking this way since even if he'd meant it, God couldn't have done what he meant—that is, caused Christ's body to be in two places at once. Unless he shows it to be impossible for God to do that, he must concede that God not only said it but really meant it.

Even if Christ hadn't said it, though, I don't doubt he could do it, for otherwise there was something he couldn't do. And in that case God wouldn't be all-powerful.

Now supposing this young man were to say that the idea of making one body be in two places involves a contradiction, and it's beyond God's power to do contradictory things. I'd then make so bold as to reply that to him and me many things may seem contradictory which God knows quite well how to make consistent with each other.

Such blind arguments based on contradiction lead many men into great error. Some ascribe everything to fate, with the power of human free will having nothing to do with it, and some attribute everything to human will, assigning no foreknowledge to God's providence. And this is done simply because poor uncomprehending human reason can't see far enough to grasp how God's knowledge and human freedom can coexist but takes them to be in clear contradiction with each other.

If feeble reason's fancy should once succeed in making us think it so hard and contradictory for a man to be in two places at the same time that the impossibility places it beyond even God's power to bring about, then surely it won't be long before the devil makes us so confident in our reason that we'll be led to think it contradictory and impossible for the one God to be three persons.

I'm quite aware that in this matter many good people have used many good, fruitful examples of God's other works—not only miracles of which Scripture speaks but things that happen in the common course of nature here on earth as well as some things made by human artifice. For instance: a single face reflected in several mirrors or in each piece of one mirror broken into twenty pieces; the marvelous way in which the glass itself is manufactured, considering the material from which it's made; the unbroken repetition of the same word for a whole hundred years; the vision of a single small eye looking upon a whole great expanse of land at one time; and a thousand more such wondrous things. Those for whom such things are everyday events therefore don't marvel at them; and they shall never be able to explain them— nor shall this young man himself—except by saying, against the objection that they're contradictions, that their principal and most obvious explanation lies in being caused by almighty God, who can do whatever he wishes [Ps 115:3].

Also, I can't see why it should be more of a contradiction for one body to be in two places at once by God's power than for two bodies to be in the same place at the same time. And I hardly think our young man denies this point. Truly, I think there is no more semblance of difficulty or contradiction for human reason to accept the simultaneous presence of one body, however gross and unglorified, in twenty places at once, than to accept this world in which all bodies, glorified and unglorified, have their own offices and places. Here, though, is an article of our faith that we shall find some people not slow to deny if men reach the point of considering things naturally impossible to be impossible to nature's master and maker, God [cf. Apostle's Creed: "I believe in God the Father Almighty . . . "]. And their imagination will bring them to this—bring them to do as this young man does, fleeing the literal sense of Scripture, seeking some allegory instead, and saying they're unavoidably compelled to do that by the impossibility of the matter. And so, as you can see plainly, in this way no article of our faith can stand.

King Henry VIII by Unknown artist, oil on panel, circa 1535–1540. First praised as an exemplary earthly prince and awarded the title "Defender of the Faith" by Rome, King Henry later divorced Queen Catherine of Aragon, remarried with Anne Boleyn, and assumed the title "Head of the Church in England." He counseled Thomas More to "look first unto God, and after unto the king."
© *National Portrait Gallery, London*

Catherine of Aragon by Unknown artist, oil on panel, early 18th century. Queen Catherine married Henry in 1509, and the marriage ended in 1533. Until her death, she never ceased regarding herself as Henry's lawful wife and rightful Queen.
© *National Portrait Gallery, London*

Anne Boleyn by Unknown artist, oil on panel, late 16th century (circa 1533–1536). After marrying King Henry in 1533, Anne bore him a daughter, Elizabeth. Three years later, Anne was arrested and executed on charges of adultery, incest, and treason. © *National Portrait Gallery, London*

Left: **Thomas Wolsey** by Unknown artist, oil on panel, late 16th century (circa 1520). Cardinal and Lord Chancellor of England, Wolsey was among the most accomplished statesmen of his day. His work on the divorce of Queen Catherine and his own ambition, however, brought about his fall from Henry's graces and an untimely death. © *National Portrait Gallery, London*

Below: **Thomas Cranmer** by Gerlach Flicke, oil on panel, 1545. Appointed Archbishop of Canterbury after the death of William Warham, Thomas Cranmer pronounced the marriage of Catherine and Henry null and void, and then anointed Anne Boleyn the Queen in 1533. © *National Portrait Gallery, London*

EARL OF ESSEX.

Above: **Thomas Cromwell, Earl of Essex** after Hans Holbein the Younger, oil on panel, late 16th century (1533–1534). Arising from modest origins, Thomas Cromwell became King Henry's key minister and instrument before his own fall and execution in 1540.
© *National Portrait Gallery, London*

Right: **Queen Mary I** by Master John, oil on panel, 1544. The only surviving child of Catherine and Henry's marriage, Princess Mary was first proclaimed a bastard after the divorce, but later became Queen of England when England for a time returned to the old faith. © *National Portrait Gallery, London*

Left: **Sir Thomas More** after Hans Holbein the Younger, oil on panel, late 16th century (1527). Holbein's portrait provides the most famous image of Sir Thomas More. Holbein's portrait expresses More, work in hand, and each of the details carries a meaning suggestive of More's character and life. More was Chancellor of the Duchy of Lancaster in 1527, the year of this sitting.
© *National Portrait Gallery, London*

The Visit: Thomas More in Prison. Piloty, Ferdinand the Elder (1786–1844). Photo: Marino Ierman. Location: Museo Civico Revoltella, Trieste, Italy © *Alinari / Art Resource, NY*

Now, the last argument by which he proves it impossible for Christ's one body to be in two places at once is this. You can show no reason, says he, why he should be in many places at once and not all. But since he can't be in all, we must conclude that he can't be in many.

Here's a remarkable bit of reasoning. Surely any child can see easily that his conclusion can't follow from his premises. His conclusion depends on our inability to give a reason for Christ's being many places at once. But even if I grant that we can't, what good does it do him? Is he then free to conclude that Christ can't be in many places at once—as if God couldn't make his body be in two places at the same time unless we could explain how, and why, and whereby it was done and give his reason for doing it?

Now in making this argument, he begins in the major with "should" and then shifts in the minor and the conclusion to "can", moving between start and finish from one logical category to the other. Just for this reason, his argument can never work.

To reach the conclusion he draws here, he would have to argue like this: If the body could be in many places at once, then it could be in all places at once; but it can't be in all places at once, and so it can't be in many places at once. This is how he must argue to prove anything. But as it stands, both his major and his minor are extremely weak. His major is that if our Savior's body can be in many places at once, then it must be able to be in all places at once. I'd grant this causative proposition for the sake of the truth contained in its second part, but I nevertheless deny it to him on account of its form. For though I grant the first part to be true, it doesn't prove the second part but fails to support it, while the second part instead implies the first. For this is good reasoning: he can be in all places, therefore he can be in many.

But argue it the other way round, as this young man does, and the form is very weak. For there's little support for saying "he can be in many places, therefore he can be in all," "many men run, therefore all men run," "men run in many places, therefore men run in all places," unless the fact of the matter itself sustains the argument, either by reason of the first part's possibility or the second part's necessity: "one man is a stone, therefore all men are stones," "one man is a living creature, therefore all men are living creatures."

But let's pass on from this first proposition and consider the second, upon which his whole argument depends: The body of Christ can't be in all places at once. So he says, but how does he prove it? If he tells me to prove the affirmative, I can reply that I don't need to do that, since that isn't the issue. For since the sacrament isn't everywhere at once, we don't say Christ is. As far as this matter is concerned, we're not obliged to go any further, and I prove my point by the fact that the gospel says it's so.

But let this young man who says it can't be so prove that it can't. If it can be so, then he admits that it's clear from Christ's words that it must be so. But because it can't be so, says he, therefore he has to take these words in an allegorical sense. Thus his proof that the body can't be in many places is that it can't be in all; which he needs to prove or else concede the argument.

But although I needn't take on this particular chore, nevertheless I'm prepared to prove that God can make Christ's body be in all places at once. And because this young man links the one proposition with the other, so shall I: God can make his body be in many places at once and in all places at once because he is almighty and therefore can do all things.

Now the young man must either tell us that this is nothing or else deny that God can do everything, allowing God's power to extend only as far as he will allow. But I think every reasonable man will notice and agree that, in going this far, the young man, youth that he is, hasn't been in school long enough to know everything God can do (unless perhaps he can produce a reliable witness to testify to his having learned every last bit of God's wisdom—although the apostle Paul, he who was caught up to the third heaven, judged that to be so far beyond his reach that he exclaimed, "Oh, the height of the riches of the wisdom and knowledge of God" [Rom 11:33]).

And then this young man tries to make his point from Scripture. He says that unless we grant the truth of his claim, we make a liar of the angel who said "he is not here" and also imply that Christ's body didn't pass from earth to heaven in a cloud at his ascension, but that he simply hid himself in the cloud, while remaining here below and playing peekaboo.

Really, I'm sorry to find this young man relying so much on his intelligence before it's mature. This is the kind of amour-propre that causes many wits to rot before they ripen. And truly, if his intelligence goes on shrinking and retrogressing in this manner, it may not last very long. For already he forgets himself so badly in the end that I daresay he'd have been sorely embarrassed had he seen himself acting like this as a young scholar in a public disputation at Oxford.

Now, observe that what he says, and therefore must prove, is that God could in no way make Christ's body be everywhere at once. But the texts he cites to prove his point say no more than that the body wasn't everywhere at once, not that by no power available to his very godhead could God have brought that about. So, as you will note, this young man is proceeding childishly; and truly everyone should shun like the plague all this unreasonable reasoning that argues against God's almighty power by appealing to unnatural nonsense supposedly drawn from nature. We can be sure the good spiritual counsel of St. Paul has such nonsense particularly in mind when he warns us, "Beware lest any man beguile you by vain philosophy" [Col 2:8].

God forbid that anyone should be more disposed and ready to believe this young man in this great matter because he says at the outset that he's going to bring everyone to a meeting of minds and tranquility of conscience. For he offers the worst imaginable tranquility by telling us as he does that in this matter anyone can believe as he likes without any danger to himself. Soon, without further counsel from him, every man will be taking his ease in choosing to believe as he likes in every matter and not troubling himself further about it.

But had that been a safe way of proceeding, St. Paul would never have declared that many were in peril of sickness and death because they failed reverently to discern the presence of our Lord's body in that sacrament when they came to receive him [1 Cor 11:23–30]. Standing against this young brother's teaching is the plain teaching of the old, holy fathers in interpreting Scripture. But what is one to make of someone's saying we can believe our Lord's real body is truly present here if we choose to believe it, and then telling us that the honest-to-goodness truth is that such a belief can't be true because God could never make his body be present there?

I'm very sure the old, holy doctors, who believed in the presence of Christ's body and blood and, as you can see clearly in their books, taught others so to believe, would for nothing in the world have written as they did if they'd thought either that the body couldn't be or wasn't there. Do you think those holy men would have taught that people were obliged to believe the true body and blood of Christ were there if they thought they weren't so obliged? Would they have insisted that men honor and worship as the true body and blood of Christ that which they themselves thought was not? Such trifling is too childish to waste time on.

Still, he does do us one great favor in allowing us to believe without fear of damnation what we believed before—namely, that in the Blessed Sacrament the whole substance of the bread and wine is transmuted and changed into the very body and blood of Christ. And if we can believe that without fear of damnation, as he allows that we may, then he allows us also to believe without fear of damnation that he lies in saying it's impossible that what we believe should be true.

So, with regard to him, I shall conclude as our Sovereign Lord the King's Highness concludes regarding Luther at a point in his well-known book the *Assertio Septem Sacramentorum*. In his *Babylonica* Luther admits that there's no danger in men's believing what they believed before about the sacrament of the altar according to the common faith. "Well then," says His Grace the King, "you yourself concede that there is no danger in our belief. But the whole Church believes that there is certain damnation in your way. Therefore, if you are to take the safest path for yourself, as wisdom dictates you should, you ought to quit your unsafe way of believing, and yourself adopt our belief and counsel all those whom you would wish to have do the right thing to adopt it."

Now, notice that this reasoning by the King's Grace clearly forces this young man back upon what he has conceded. It shows plainly that unless he abandons this belief of his, which all good Christian people regard as damnable, and comes home to his old faith—the common faith of the whole Church—in which, as he himself admits, there is no danger, though (as a matter of courtesy) I won't call him stark raving mad, I'll certainly say that the young man is playing a very childish game with his own soul at stake.

He has yet another way of soothing consciences. Let everyone be bold, he says, and whether the Blessed Sacrament be consecrated or unconsecrated (this is said specifically of the wine, but he means both), there is no need for concern. Receive it unblessed as it is, says he; for neither by changing the words nor leaving them unsaid can the priest cheat us or take from us the benefit of the sacrament's institution by God. Isn't that a wonderful teaching by our young man—making it so clear that the priest can't injure us by his carelessness or malice in the absence of fault on our part? For whatever is lacking on the priest's part we can count on God in his mercy to supply out of his goodness. And so, as holy St. John Chrysostom says, no one can suffer any harm except by his own doing.

Suppose, though, that we ourselves notice the priest to be behaving out of line and thereby thwarting Christ's will in instituting the sacrament; yet we then knowingly receive it unblessed and unconsecrated, not caring whether Christ's manner of instituting the sacrament is kept and respected and observed and reckoning what we receive to be as good without it as with it. In that case, we make ourselves partners in the fault, lose the benefit of the sacrament, and receive it to our damnation—not due to the priest's fault but due to our own.

As for him who believes that what's here is no more than ordinary bread and wine, he hardly cares whether it be consecrated or not: but the more surely consecrated it is, the more harm it does him who receives it with a conscience burdened by this execrable heresy that causes him to make no distinction between our Lord's body in the Blessed Sacrament and the common bread he eats at dinner, but rather to esteem it less. For, lacking a priest, the one sort of man will bless the bread himself before he begins, but the other sort, as he says, doesn't care whether it's blessed or not. May our Lord in his great mercy deliver him from this abominable heresy and all his other errors. May he shut every good man's ears against these wicked spells—I mean his arguments. Far more infectious are they for those simple people whom the wind of every new doctrine tosses about like weathercocks than was the evil doctrine so sharply reproved by St. Paul by which false prophets bewitched the Galatians.

But as for those good, steadfast people who have a bit of grace or a hint of reason in their heads, I feel sure they'll never go so far astray in this matter—to whose truth God himself has testified by as many striking miracles as he has ever worked in testimony to anything—as to believe this one young man and his empty arguments contradicting the faith and reasoning both of all the old holy writers and all good Christian people for these fifteen hundred years. Without any doubt or hesitation, all rejected *his* doctrine on the Blessed Sacrament until Berengarius first began to fall into this error. But having thought better of that, he turned away from it and utterly forsook it; and because he had once held it, that good man determined on his own, without being compelled, voluntarily to do great penance all the rest of his life as you can read in folio 190 of the *Cronica Cronicarum.*

Brother Barnes, too, though in many other matters, as you well know, one of this young man's brothers in the same sect, nevertheless in this instance has a great abhorrence of his heresy (unless he's lying about it). For when he was here last, he wrote me a letter by his own hand saying I'd wrongfully accused him of heresy, and appealing to God and his conscience as his witnesses, thus showing himself deeply offended that any man should believe this of him because of what I wrote. He will, he says, write a book rebutting me and in it will declare and testify to his faith concerning this Blessed Sacrament. The book will make it clear, he says, that I've spoken falsely of him and that he abhors this abominable heresy.

I shall defer replying to his letter until the book appears. Since he forsakes this heresy, we shall see what manner of faith he will profess—the true faith or heresy of some other kind. But if he declares his acceptance of the true Catholic faith, he and I will readily agree on that point, and I shall then respond to him in a way he can be well satisfied with.

In the meantime, though, I find it gratifying that Brother Barnes, an older man of more mature discretion, possessing a doctorate in divinity, and more learned in these matters than our young man, abhors the heresy of the latter on this point while agreeing with him about much else.

I trust, then, that every wise man will resist the spell of childish reasoning like his and will refrain from acting like Christ's listeners, who, reacting to the strangeness of this matter, rejected our Savior as this young man does now and turned away from him.

Let those go who will! The ones who stay with our Savior stay with him who has, not the false, shallow sophistry of this young man's vain and childish rationalizations, but the very words of eternal life.

I beseech our Lord to give this young man the grace to believe those words in preference to his own brazen fantasies, and to bring both him and us to that same life where we shall behold our blessed Savior face to face, without sacramental veil or covering, along with the one godhead of the three Persons, all equally mighty and each almighty. Then we shall clearly grasp and comprehend both the possibility and the fact of Christ's one body being many places at once, as well as how that is brought about which foolish boldness moves many who'll never reach that point to pronounce flatly impossible.

Now, just look at that—instead of a letter, you have nearly a book, which I trust is longer than good Christians will need on the subject of something so clearly an article of faith and so far beyond being doubted by people of solid faith. Still, in returning your copy of his book to you, I thought I should say a bit about what I thought of it. And once begun, though it was no pleasure to me, the abominable character of that pestilential heresy and the danger inherent in his specious treatment nevertheless drew me further and further, till I could hardly make an end. For I was of half a mind to take up the schism of the Bohemians, something else he mentions in his book, saying it deserves to be treated at length, and in that connection also to reply to Brother Barnes, who, as you're well aware, has composed a whole treatise on the subject (and I wonder if even he thinks he's handled it well).

As for the holy prayer that this devout young man—like some new Christ—teaches his congregation to make upon receiving the Blessed Sacrament, even if his prayer were better than it is, I wouldn't give the parings of a pear for a prayer that tears down the true faith. But be that as it may, his prayer is so conceived and composed and decked out by leisure and study that I trust any good Christian woman, by reason of faith-filled feeling and God's silent inspiration, makes a much better prayer when receiving the sacrament. For alongside God's other kindnesses, she thanks him, I think, for the lofty and singular privilege he confers upon her in kindly receiving her and seating her, simple and unworthy as she is, at his own blessed table.

There, in remembrance of the bitter passion he suffered for her sin, he allows her to receive not bread—though it resembles bread—but in the form of bread, his own very precious body, flesh, blood, and bones. This is the very same body with which he died and rose and appeared again to his apostles, ate with his disciples, and ascended into heaven. This is the body with which he shall return to pass judgment and reign in eternal glory with his Father and the Holy Spirit, along with all his truly faithful, believing and loving people, then and forever henceforth merrily nourishing and feeding them as the mystical members of his glorious body, satisfying their insatiable hunger with the sight of his glorious godhead [cf. Ps 145:16; Mt 25; Lk 12:37; 1 Jn 3:2; Rev 22:1–7, 17].

Here, he comforts and feeds their hunger for heaven by hope and by the sure token and sign of salvation—I mean the gift of his own true and blessed body under the sign and likeness of bread, to be eaten and received into our bodies. And so our souls, by faith in this sacrament, and our bodies, by its reception, are spiritually and corporeally joined to and united with his body here on earth. In union with his holy soul and blessed body, joined in his godhead with the Father and their Holy Spirit, they shall live gloriously in heaven forever.

And mark this—good Christian women can make this prayer in deed if not in word (and perhaps some will express it much better, too). For, as the prophet says, God can empower not only women of maturity, faith, and intelligence but also the mouths of infants and suckling babes to proclaim his glory and praise. Thus we have no need for this young man to come teaching us how and what we shall pray, like Christ teaching his disciples the Our Father [Mt 6:9–15].

Frith is hardly the instructor to teach us what to pray when receiving the Blessed Sacrament, considering that he refuses to accept it for what it is but takes Christ's blessed body to be nothing but mere bread while attaching so little significance to the reception of the sacrament that it scarcely matters to him whether it be blessed or not. I pray God by his grace will drive these poisonous errors from his blind heart and make him his faithful servant.

May all go exceedingly well with you.

At Chelsea, the seventh day of December, by the hand of him who is all yours and yet more.

Thomas More, Knight

Letter 56

To Erasmus [191]

A year after his resignation on 16 May 1532, More sent this letter to Erasmus, with a copy of his epitaph, which More had etched in stone at his parish church in Chelsea. More remained for a short while in King Henry's favor after his resignation, but when he wrote against Henry's chief legal propagandist, Christopher St. German, twice in 1533, he fell out of the crown's favor. On May 23 of the same year, newly appointed Archbishop Thomas Cranmer declared Henry's marriage to Queen Catherine annulled, though Catherine would go to her grave claiming the marriage between her and Henry's brother Arthur had never been consummated, one of the key issues in the dispute over the marriage. Days later on May 28, Cranmer pronounced Henry's remarriage to Anne Boleyn valid; Henry and an expecting Anne had secretly married earlier in January 1533 (*ODNB*). When More refused to attend Anne's coronation on 1 June 1533, he incurred the royal wrath further.

The epitaph summarizes his life, education, and professional work—it is More's statement of record about his public career, the resignation of the Lord Chancellorship, and his personal integrity, pronounced upon in public several times by Henry himself. As pointed out earlier, More was the first English writer to use the word "integrity," and Wegemer explains that More understood integrity to be "consistency in thought, word, and action," a demanding but liberating form of life requiring "sure conscience" and "sure delibera-tion" as well (*Young Thomas More,* 17).

In this letter, More places special emphasis on the peace treaty signed at Cambrai in 1529, and again voices his hope that peace will endure and reign in a unified Christendom. More's con-cluding account of having two wives in heaven may have a slight ironic edge given the greater political context of Henry's marital struggles with Catherine of Aragon and Anne Boleyn, as Frank Mitjans has suggested. The strength of More's affection for Lady Alice, whose widowly plainness has been much remarked upon, is noteworthy, as is his tribute to his father, Sir John More. The writing of his epitaph and the construction of his tomb is char-acteristic of More's understanding of the need for preparation, be it for the demands and crosses of life, or death. The epitaph remains on his tombstone, now in Chelsea Old Church, London, where it survived air raid bombing in World War Two when most of the rest of the old church was destroyed.

For a full discussion of the challenges of More's public career and the contemporary debate over it, see John Guy's *Thomas More* (Oxford University Press, 2000); Cathy Curtis' "More's Public Life" in the *Cambridge Companion to Thomas More* (Cambridge University Press, 2011); and Travis Curtright's *The One Thomas More* (Catholic University of America Press, 2012). For a full account of More's statesmanship and the principles informing it, see Wegemer, *Thomas More on Statesmanship*, especially the chapters "The Limits of Reason and the Need for Law," "Reform over Revolution," and "The Limits of Government and the Domain of Conscience" (pp. 153–214).

CHELSEA

<JUNE? 1533>

THOMAS MORE SENDS GREETINGS TO ERASMUS OF ROTTERDAM.

. . . Concerning the remark in your earlier letter that you were hesitant about publishing my letter in spite of motives for wanting to have it published, there is no reason, my dear Erasmus, for hesitation on your part. Some chatterboxes around here began to spread the rumor that I had resigned my office unwillingly and that I had kept that detail a secret. So, after making arrangements for the construction of my tomb, I did not hesitate to make, on my Epitaph, a public declaration of the actual facts, to allow anyone a chance to refute them, if he could. As soon as those fellows noted the Epitaph, since they were unable to deny its truth, they charged it with being boastful. However, I preferred this charge rather than allow the other rumor take hold, not for any selfish reason, since I do not have a high regard for what men may say, provided I have the approval of God; but having written several pamphlets in English in defense of the Faith against some fellow countrymen who had championed rather perverse doctrines, I considered it my duty to protect the integrity of my reputation; and so that you can find out how boastful I was, you will receive a copy of my Epitaph; you will notice, in reading it, that, out of confidence in my own position, I do not bait those fellows at all, so as to prevent them from making whimsical remarks about me.

After resigning my office, I waited until the opening of the new term, and, so far, no one has advanced a complaint against my integrity. Either my life has been so spotless or, at any rate, I have been so circumspect that, if my rivals oppose my boasting of the one, they are forced to let me boast of the other. As a matter of fact, the King himself has pronounced on this situation at various times, frequently in private, and twice in public. It is embarrassing for me to relate—but on the occasion of the installation of my most distinguished successor, the King used as his mouthpiece the most illustrious Duke, I mean the Duke of Norfolk, who is the Lord High Treasurer of England, and he respectfully ordered the Duke to proclaim publicly that he had unwillingly yielded to my request for resignation; the King, however, was not satisfied even with that extraordinary manifestation of good will toward me; at a much later date, he had the same pronouncement repeated, in his presence, at a solemn session of the Lords and Commons, this time using my successor as his mouthpiece, on the formal occasion of his opening address to that assembly which, as you know, we call Parliament. Therefore, if you agree, there is no good reason for holding back the publication of my letter. As to the statement in my epitaph that I was a source of trouble for heretics—I wrote that with deep feeling. I find that breed of men absolutely loathsome, so much so that, unless they regain their senses, I want to be as hateful to them as anyone can possibly be; for my increasing experience with those men frightens me with the thought of what the world will suffer at their hands. I shall follow your advice and make no reply to the person about whom you wrote, although I have held a lengthy letter in readiness for some time now. My reason for holding back is not that I have any regard for what he, or all of his coworkers, may think or write about me, but because I do not want to be burdened with the obligations of writing replies to outsiders, when I feel the more immediate responsibility of answering our own associates. Best wishes, my dear Erasmus, and a long farewell; the best of luck always.

From my rural home at Chelsea.

Thomas More

Epitaph on the Tomb of Thomas More

Thomas More was born in London of respectable, though not distinguished, ancestry; he engaged to some extent in literary matters, and after spending several years of his youth as a pleader in the law courts and after having held the office of judge as an Under-Sheriff in his native city, he was admitted to the Court by the Unconquerable Henry the Eighth, who is the only King to have ever received the unique distinction of meriting the title "Defender of the Faith," a title earned by deeds of sword and pen; he was received at Court, chosen member of the King's Council, knighted, appointed Under-Treasurer and then Chancellor of Lancaster, and finally Chancellor of England by the special favor of his Sovereign. Meanwhile he was elected Speaker of the House of Commons; furthermore, he served as the King's ambassador at various times and in various places, last of all at Cambrai, as an associate and colleague of Cuthbert Tunstall, then Bishop of London and shortly after Bishop of Durham, a man whose equal in learning, wisdom, and virtue is seldom seen in the world today. In that place he witnessed, in the capacity of ambassador, to his great joy, the renewal of a peace treaty between the supreme monarchs of Christendom and the restoration of a long-desired peace to the world.

May heaven confirm this peace and make it a lasting one.

He so conducted himself all through this series of high offices or honors that his Excellent Sovereign found no fault with his service, neither did he make himself odious to the nobles nor unpleasant to the populace, but he was a source of trouble to thieves, murderers, and heretics. His father, John More, was a knight and chosen by the King as member of the group of judges known as the King's Bench; he was an affable man, charming, irreproachable, gentle, sympathetic, honest, and upright; though venerable in age, he was vigorous for a man of his years; after he had lived to see the day when his son was Chancellor of England, he deemed his sojourn upon earth complete and gladly departed for heaven. The son, all through his father's lifetime, had been compared with him, and was commonly known as the young More, and so he considered himself to be; but now he felt the loss of his father, and as he looked upon the four children he had reared and his eleven grandchildren, he began, in his own mind, to grow old. This feeling was increased by a serious chest ailment, that developed soon after, as an indication of approaching old age. Now sated with the passing things of this life, he resigned office and, through the unparalleled graciousness of a most indulgent Sovereign (may God smile favorably upon his enterprises), he at length reached the goal which almost since boyhood had been the object of his longing—to have the last years of his life all to himself, so that he could gradually retire from the affairs of this world and contemplate the eternity of the life to come. Then he arranged for the construction of this tomb for himself, to be a constant reminder of the unrelenting advance of death, and had the remains of his first wife transferred to this place. That he may not have erected this tomb in vain while still alive, and that he may not shudder with fear at the thought of encroaching death, but may go to meet it gladly, with longing for Christ, and that he may find death not completely a death for himself but rather the gateway to a happier life, I beg you, kind reader, attend him with your prayers while he still lives and also when he has done with life.

My beloved wife, Jane, lies here. I, Thomas More, intend that this same tomb shall be Alice's and mine, too. One of these ladies, my wife in the days of my youth, has made me father of a son and three daughters; the other has been as devoted to her stepchildren (a rare attainment in a stepmother) as very few mothers are to their own children. The one lived out her life with me, and the other still lives with me on such terms that I cannot decide whether I did love the one or do love the other more. O, how happily we could have lived all three together if fate and morality permitted. Well, I pray that the grave, that heaven, will bring us together. Thus death will give what life could not.

Letter 57

To Elizabeth Barton [192]

Elizabeth Barton (c. 1506–1534) was the much discussed "Holy Maid of London" and "Nun of Kent," the Benedictine nun who became something of a notorious local visionary after suffering severe illness in 1525 (*ODNB*). Among her other pronouncements and revelations, she prophesied that if King Henry divorced Queen Catherine, he would undo himself—in particular, Barton warned "that if his Highness proceeded to the accomplishment of said divorce and married another, that then his Majesty should not be king of this realm by the space of one month after. And in the reputation of God should not be king one day nor one hour after" (*ODNB* 202). Barton's foretellings, of course, left Henry more piqued than pleased, and the quick spread of these and other prophecies throughout England led to her questioning by the authorities, including Sir Thomas More, who was later himself accused but then acquitted of supporting her (see letters 59–62). Interrogated by Thomas Cranmer and imprisoned in the Tower in 1533, she was forced to make a public confession at St. Paul's Cross and to denounce herself as a heretic and a traitor, a spectacle described by Chapuys, the Spanish ambassador as "a comedy staged 'to blot out from people's minds the impression they have that the Nun is a saint and a prophet'" (*ODNB* 203). After this last performance, she was hanged and beheaded for treason at Tyburn on 20 April 1534.

In this letter, More urges Barton to avoid discussing "princes' affairs" with any person in the realm and counsels the nun to speak only of matters profitable to the soul. As Cranmer himself noted, the problem for Barton was that "many learned men . . . often resorted unto her, to the intent they might by her know the will of God; and chiefly concerning the king's marriage, the great heresies and schisms within the realms, and the taking away the liberties of the church" (*ODNB* 202). On the very day Barton was executed, the Oath of Succession was first required of all London citizens; in the words of a contemporary observer, John Husee, "this day most part of this City are sworn to the King and his legitimate issue by the Queen's Grace [i.e., Anne Boleyn] now had and hereafter to come, and so shall all the realm over be sworn in like manner" (*ODNB* 203). For the text of the Oath of Succession, which More and Fisher would later refuse to take at the peril of their heads, see Appendix II. A "beadsman," the word More often uses to characterize himself in these late letters, is a "man of prayer, one who prays for the soul or spiritual welfare of another" (*OED*).

CHELSEA
TUESDAY <1533?>

GOOD MADAM, AND MY RIGHT DEARLY BELOVED SISTER
IN OUR LORD GOD:

After my most hearty recommendation, I shall beseech you to take my good mind in good worth, and pardon me that I am so homely as of myself unrequired, and also without necessity, to give counsel to you, of whom for the good inspirations, and great revelations that it likes Almighty God of his goodness to give and show, as many wise, well learned, and very virtuous folk testify, I myself have need, for the comfort of my soul, to require and ask advice, for surely, good Madam, since it pleases God sometime to suffer such as are far under and of little estimation, to give yet fruitful advertisement to other as are in the light of the Spirit, so far above them, that there were between them no comparison; as he suffered his high prophet Moses to be in some things advised and counseled by Jethro [see Ex 18], I cannot for the love that in our Lord I bear you refrain to put you in remembrance of one thing, which in my poor mind I think highly necessary to be by your wisdom considered, referring the end and order thereof, to God and his holy Spirit to direct you.

Good Madam, I doubt not, but that you remember that in the beginning of my communication with you, I showed you that I neither was, nor would be, curious of any knowledge of other men's matters, and least of all any matter of princes or of the realm, in case it so were that God had, as to many good folks before time he hath, any things revealed unto you, such things, I said unto your ladyship, that I was not only not desirous to hear of, but also would not hear of. Now, Madam, I consider well that many folk desire to speak with you, which are not all peradventure of my mind in this point, but some hap to be curious and inquisitive of things that little pertain unto their parts; and some might peradventure happen to talk of such things as might peradventure after turn to much harm, as I think you have heard how the late Duke of Buckingham moved with the fame of one that was reported for an holy monk and had such talking with him as after was a great part of his destruction and disinheriting of his blood, and great slander and infamy of religion. It suffices me, good Madam, to put you in remembrance of such thing, as I nothing doubt your wisdom and the spirit of God shall keep you from talking with any persons, specially with lay persons, of any such manner things as pertain to princes' affairs, or the state of the realm, but only to common and talk with any person high and low, of such manner things as may to the soul be profitable for you to show and for them to know.

And thus my good Lady, and dearly beloved sister in our Lord, I make an end of this my needless advertisement unto you, whom the blessed Trinity preserve and increase in grace, and put in your mind to recommend me and mine unto him in your devout prayers.

At Chelsea this Tuesday by the hand of your hearty loving Brother and Beadsman,
Thomas More, Knight

Letter 58

To Thomas Cromwell [194]

Thomas Cromwell, Earl of Essex (c. 1485–1540), rose from a self-styled ruffian youth in Putney to become first a lawyer, then a member of the House of Commons in 1523, and later close advisor to Cardinal Wolsey in 1526; after surviving the fall of Wolsey in 1529, Cromwell eventually made his fortunes again and became Henry's chief secretary in 1534 by working in rigorous support of the marriage to Anne Boleyn and the Royal Supremacy (*ODNB*). He proved the most powerful royal minister in support of Henry's reforms—and marriages—until the fiasco of Henry's fourth marriage to Anne of Cleves left him farther from the king's good pleasure than the homely Anne herself by the middle of 1540. Having fallen from royal grace with the help of some invidious noble enemies, Cromwell was arrested and executed on July 28, 1540, in Hall's account, by the "stroke of the axe, by a ragged butcherly miser which very ungoodly performed the Office." The last letter of the man who has been called the lay head of England under Henry concludes with the passionate imprecation to his King: "Most gracious prince, I cry for mercy, mercy, mercy!" (*ODNB*).

In this "rude long letter," Thomas More denies having written and prepared for publication a book against the "book of certain articles" prepared by the King's council. This book was "Articles Devised by the Whole Consent of the King's Council," published as royal propaganda in 1533 (commentary by Silva in *The Last Letters of Thomas More*, 133). More's last book, he contends, was *Answer to a Poisoned Book*, published in response to the anonymous *Supper of the Lord*, perhaps written by William Tyndale (*CW* 11). More also explains that he does not write unless he has "meetly sure knowledge" of the subject, a remark that casts light on his approach to writing and religious controversy. Most importantly, the letter records More's willingness to discharge his conscience upon the controversial articles "as becomes a poor honest true man, wheresoever I shall be by his Grace commanded." In the meantime, accusations against More were intensifying. First this charge, then one of bribe-taking and corruption, and finally the Nun of Kent saga—all attest to the increasing power and persistence of More's enemies in Henry's court, and one who listens well may hear the sounds of a great gathering storm, with thunder and tempest less and less remote.

William Rastell (1508–1565) was son of John Rastell, husband of More's sister Elizabeth; he became a printer in 1529 and later published More's complete English works in 1557 (*ODNB*). After the death of Queen Mary and the crowning of Elizabeth I, it became illegal to own a copy of More's English or Latin works, though the writer Ben Jonson, rival and friend of Shakespeare, possessed a copy of More's Latin works. Jonson annotated *The History of Richard the Third* and the 1509 *Coronation Ode* in particular. See *www.thomasmorestudies. org* for the texts of these works and study guides to them.

CHELSEA

1 FEBRUARY <1533/4>

RIGHT WORSHIPFUL, IN MY MOST HEARTY WISE I RECOM-
MEND ME UNTO YOU:

Sir, my cousin William Rastell has informed me that your Mastership of your goodness showed him that it has been reported
that I have against the book of certain articles (which was late put
forth in print by the King's honorable Council) made an answer,
and delivered it unto my said cousin to print. And albeit that he
for his part truly denied it, yet because he somewhat remained in
doubt, whether your Mastership gave him therein full credence
or not, he desired me for his farther discharge to declare you the
very truth, sir, as help me God neither my said cousin nor any
man else, never had any book of mine to print, one or other,
since the said book of the King's Council came forth. For of truth
the last book that he printed of mine was that book that I made
against an unknown heretic, which has sent over a work that walks
in over many men's hands, named the *Supper of the Lord*, against
the blessed sacrament of the altar. My answer whereunto, albeit
that the printer (unaware to me) dated it Anno 1534, by which it
seems to be printed since the Feast of the Circumcision, yet was it

of very truth both made and printed and many of them gone before Christmas. And myself never espied the printer's oversight in the date, in more than three weeks after. And this was in good faith the last book that my cousin had of mine. Which being true as of truth it shall be found, suffices for his declaration in this behalf.

As touching mine own self, I shall say thus much farther, that on my faith I never made any such book nor ever thought to do. I read the said book once over and never more. But I am for once reading very far off from many things, whereof I would have meetly sure knowledge, ere ever I would make an answer, though the matter and the book both, concerned the poorest man in a town, and were of the simplest man's making too. For of many things which in that book be touched, in some I know not the law, and in some I know not the fact. And therefore would I never be so childish nor so play the proud arrogant fool, by whomsoever the book had been made, and to whomsoever the matter had belonged, as to presume to make an answer to the book, concerning the matter whereof I never were sufficiently learned in the laws, nor fully instructed in the facts.

And then while the matter pertained unto the King's Highness, and the book professes openly that it was made by his honorable Council, and by them put in print with his Grace's license obtained thereunto I verily trust in good faith that of your good mind toward me, though I never wrote you word thereof, yourself will both think and say so much for me, that it were a thing far unlikely, that an answer should be made thereunto by me. I will by the grace of Almighty God, as long as it shall please him to lend me life in this world, in all such places (as I am of my duty to God and the King's Grace bound) truly say my mind, and discharge my conscience, as becomes a poor honest true man, wheresoever I shall be by his Grace commanded.

Yet surely if it should happen any book to come abroad in the name of his Grace or his honorable Council, if the book to me seemed such as myself would not have given mine own advice to the making, yet I know my bound duty, to bear more honor to my prince, and more reverence to his honorable Council, than that it could become me for many causes, to make an answer unto such a book, or to counsel and advise any man else to do it. And therefore as it is a thing that I never did nor intended, so I heartily beseech you if you shall happen to perceive any man, either of evil will or of lightness, any such thing report by me, be so good master to me, as help to bring us both together. And then never take me for honest after, but if you find his honesty somewhat impaired in the matter.

Thus am I bold upon your goodness to encumber you with my long rude letter, in the contents whereof, I eftsoons [again] heartily beseech you to be in manner aforesaid good master and friend unto me, whereby you shall bind me to be your beadsman while I live, as knows our Lord, whose especial grace both bodily and ghostly long preserve and keep you.

At Chelsea on the Vigil of the Purification of our Blessed Lady [i.e., Candelmas] by the hand of

Assuredly all your own, Thomas More, Knight

Letter 59

To Thomas Cromwell [195]

In this letter, More defends himself against charges associating him with the prophecies of the Nun of Kent, Elizabeth Barton. More's name was eventually dropped from the dangerous act of attainder that brought about the imprisonment, trial, and death of the Nun of Kent and several others associated with her (*ODNB*). As is clear at this point, More was no stranger to potential political peril. Recall that as a "beardless" young man, he had fled England after arousing the displeasure of Henry VII, and that later he had been forced to defend himself when the French humanist Brixius dangerously accused him of disloyalty to Henry the Eighth in the *Antimorus,* published in 1519.

CHELSEA
SATURDAY <FEBRUARY–MARCH 1533/4>

RIGHT WORSHIPFUL:

After right hearty recommendation, so it is that I am informed, that there is a bill put in against me into the higher house before the Lords, concerning my communication with the Nun of Canterbury, and my writing unto her, whereof I not a little marvel, the truth of the matter being such as God and I know it is, and as I have plainly declared unto you by my former letters, wherein I found you then so good, that I am now bold eftsoons [again] upon your goodness to desire you to show me that favor, as that I might the rather by your good means, have a copy of the bill. Which seen, if I find any untrue surmise therein as of likelihood there is, I may make mine humble suit unto the King's good Grace, and declare the truth, either to his Grace or by his Grace's commandment, wheresoever the matter shall require. I am so sure of my truth toward his Grace, that I cannot mistrust his gracious favor toward me, upon the truth known, nor the judgment of any honest man. Nor never shall there loss in this matter grieve me, being myself so innocent as God and I know me, whatsoever should happen me therein, by the grace of Almighty God, who both bodily and ghostly preserve you.

At Chelsea this present Saturday by the hand of
Heartily all your own,
Thomas More, Knight

Letter 60

TO THOMAS CROMWELL [197]

In this letter, More again defends himself against charges associating him with support of the Nun of Kent and the spreading of her prophecies and revelations. He recounts the conversation he had with Father Resby, in which the Friar Observant first praised the Nun's holiness and then shared with More the Nun's revelation about "the three swords," which More would not discuss further with him. Father Resby would later be condemned to death with Barton, along with Father Hugh Rich, whom More also mentions (*ODNB*). More also notes that Barton had shared her prophecies with Henry directly, in what was surely a memorable audience between nun and King. Regarding her other visions and revelations, More regards them as "too marvelous to be true" and indicates his conviction that Barton has been proven to be a fraud upon investigation. In the letter, the "Lord Legate" is likely Cardinal Thomas Wolsey. The "tale of Mary Magdalene" refers to Barton's claim to have received revelations from Mary Magdalene in 1532; the "tale of the host" refers to Barton's claim that she was mystically present during a Mass that Henry VIII attended in Calais, and that she received communion from an angel after the king was denied the host (Silva, 139–40).

<MARCH? 1534>

RIGHT WORSHIPFUL:

After my most hearty recommendation, with like thanks for your goodness in the accepting of my rude long letter, I perceive that of your further goodness and favor toward me, it liked your

Mastership to break with my son Roper of that, that I had had communication, not only with divers that were of acquaintance with the lewd Nun of Canterbury, but also with herself; and had, over that, by my writing, declaring favor toward her, given her advice and counsel; of which my demeanor, that it likes you to be content to take the labor and the pain, to hear, by mine own writing, the truth, I very heartily thank you, and reckon myself therein right deeply beholden to you.

It is, I suppose, about eight or nine years ago since I heard of that huswife first; at which time the Bishop of Canterbury that then was, God assail his soul, sent unto the King's Grace a roll of paper in which were written certain words of hers, that she had, as report was then made, at sundry times spoken in her trances; whereupon it pleased the King's Grace to deliver me the roll, commanding me to look thereon and afterward show him what I thought therein. Whereunto, at another time, when his Highness asked me, I told him, that in good faith I found nothing in these words that I could anything regard or esteem, for saving that some part fell in rhyme, and that, God know, full rude, else for any reason, God know, that I saw therein, a right simple woman might, in my mind, speak it of her own wit well enough; howbeit, I said, that because it was constantly reported for a truth, that God wrought in her, and that a miracle was showed upon her, I dared not nor would not, be bold in judging the matter. And the King's Grace, as methought, esteemed the matter as light as it after proved lewd.

From that time till about Christmas was twelvemonth, albeit that continually, there was much talking of her, and of her holiness, yet never heard I any talk rehearsed, either of revelation of hers, or miracle, saving that I had heard some times in my Lord Cardinal's days, that she had been both with his Lordship and with the King's Grace, but what she said either to the one or to the other, upon my faith, I had never heard any one word.

Now, as I was about to tell you, about Christmas was twelve-month, Father Resby, Friar Observant, then of Canterbury, lodged one night at mine house; where after supper, a little before he went to his chamber, he fell in communication with me of the Nun, giving her high commendation of holiness, and that it was wonderful to see and understand the works that God wrought in her; which thing, I answered, that I was very glad to hear it, and thanked God thereof. Then he told me, that she had been with my Lord Legate in his life and with the King's Grace, too, and that she had told my Lord Legate a revelation of hers, of three swords that God has put in my Lord Legate's hand, which if he ordered not well, God would lay it sore to his charge, the first he said was the ordering of the spiritualty under the Pope, as Legate, the second the rule that he bare in order of the temporalty under the King, as his Chancellor. And the third, she said, was the meddling he was put in trust with by the King, concerning the great matter of his marriage. And therewithal I said unto him that any revelation of the King's matters I would not hear of, I doubt not but the goodness of God should direct his highness with his grace and wisdom, that the thing should take such end, as God should be pleased with, to the King's honor and surety of the realm. When he heard me say these words or the like, he said unto me, that God had specially commanded her to pray for the King; and forthwith he broke again into her revelations, concerning the Cardinal that his soul was saved by her mediation; and without any other communication went into his chamber. And he and I never talked any more of any such manner of matter, nor since his departing on the morrow, I never saw him after to my remembrance, till I saw him at St. Paul's Cross.

After this, about Shrovetide [i.e., the week before Lent], there came unto me, a little before supper, Father Rich, Friar Observant of Richmond. And as we fell in talking, I asked him of Father Resby, how he did? and upon that occasion, he asked me whether Father Resby had anything showed me of the Holy Nun of Kent? and I said yea, and that I was very glad to hear of her virtue. I would not, said he, tell you again that you have heard of him already, but I have heard and known many great graces that God has wrought in her, and in other folk, by her, which I would gladly tell you if I thought you had not heard them already. And therewith he asked me, whether Father Resby had told me anything of her being with my Lord Cardinal? and I said yea. Then he told you, said he, of the three swords; yea verily, said I. Did he tell you, said he, of the revelations that she had concerning the King's Grace? Nay, forsooth, said I, nor if he would have done I would not have given him the hearing; nor verily no more I would in deed, for since she has been with the King's Grace herself, and told him, methought it a thing needless to tell the matter to me, or any man else. And when Father Rich perceived that I would not hear her revelations concerning the King's Grace he talked on a little of her virtue and let her revelations alone; and therewith my supper was set upon the board where I required him to sit with me, but he would in no wise tarry but departed to London.

After that night I talked with him twice, once in mine own house, another time in his own garden at the Friars, at every time a great space, but not of any revelation touching the King's Grace, but only of other mean folk I knew not whom, of which things some were very strange and some were very childish. But albeit that he said that he had seen her lie in her trance in great pains and that he had at other times taken great spiritual comfort in her communication, yet did he never tell me she had told him those tales herself; for if he had I for the tale of Mary Magdalene which he told me, and for the tale of the host, with which, as I heard, she said she was houseled [given the Eucharist], at the King's Mass at Calais; if I had heard it of him as told unto himself by her mouth for a revelation, I would have both liked him and her the worse. But whether ever I heard that same tale of Rich or

of Resby or of neither of them both, but of some other man since
she was in hold, in good faith I cannot tell. But I know well when
or where so ever I heard it, methought it a tale too marvelous to
be true, and very likely that she had told some man her dream,
which told it out for a revelation. And in effect, I little doubted
but that some of these tales that were told of her were untrue;
but yet since I never heard them reported, as spoken by her own
mouth, I thought nevertheless that many of them might be true,
and she a very virtuous woman too; as some lies peradventure
written of some that be saints in heaven, and yet many miracles in
deed done by them for all that.

   After this I being upon a day at Syon [i.e., the abbey house
of the Order of St. Bridget, London] talking with divers of the
Fathers together at the grate, they showed me that she had been
with them, and showed me divers things that some of them mis-
liked in her and in this talking, they wished that I had spoken with
her and said they would fain see how I should like her; whereupon,
afterward, when I heard that she was there again, I came thither
to see her and to speak with her myself. At which communication
had, in a little chapel, there were none present but we two. In the
beginning whereof I showed that my coming to her was not of any
curious mind, anything to know of such things as folk talked, that
it pleased God to reveal and show unto her, but for the great virtue
that I had heard for so many years, every day more and more spoken and reported of her, I therefore had a great mind to see her, and
be acquainted with her, that she might have somewhat the more
occasion to remember me to God in her devotion and prayers;
whereunto she gave me a very good virtuous answer that as God
did of his goodness far better by her than such a poor wretch was
worthy, so she feared that many folk yet beside that spoke of their
own favorable minds many things for her, far above the truth, and
that of me she had many such things heard, that already she prayed
for me and ever would, whereof I heartily thanked her.

I said unto her, "Madam, one Helen, a maiden dwelling about Totnam, of whose trances and revelations there has been much talking, she has been with me late and showed me that she was with you, and that after the rehearsal of such visions as she had seen, you showed her that they were no revelations, but plain illusions of the devil and advised her to cast them out of her mind, and verily she gave therein good credence unto you and thereupon has left to lean any longer unto such visions of her own, whereupon she said, she finds your words true, for ever since she has been the less visited with such things as she was wont to be before." To this she answered me, "Forsooth, Sir, there is in this point no praise unto me, but the goodness of God, as it appears, has wrought much meekness in her soul, which has taken my rude warning so well and not grudged to hear her spirit and her visions reproved." I liked her in good faith better for this answer than for many of those things that I heard reported by her. Afterward she told me, upon that occasion how great need folk have, that are visited with such visions, to take heed and prove well of what spirit they come of, and in the communication she told me that of late the devil, in likeness of a bird, was fleeing and flickering about her in a chamber, and suffered himself to be taken; and being in hands suddenly changed, in their sight that were present, into such a strange ugly fashioned bird, that they were all afraid, and threw him out at a window.

For conclusion, we talked no word of the King's Grace or any great personage else, nor in effect, of any man or woman, but of herself, and myself, but after no long communication had for or ever we met, my time came to go home, I gave her a double ducat and prayed her to pray for me and mine, and so departed from her and never spoke with her after. Howbeit, of truth I had a great good opinion of her, and had her in great estimation, as you shall perceive by the letter that I wrote unto her. For afterward because I had often heard, that many right worshipful folks

as well men as women used to have much communication with
her, and many folk are of nature inquisitive and curious, whereby
they fall sometime into such talking, as better were to forbear, of
which thing I nothing thought while I talked with her of charity,
therefore I wrote her a letter thereof, which since it may be peradventure, that she broke or lost, I shall insert the very copy thereof
in this present letter.

Good Madam and my right dearly beloved Sister in our Lord
God. . . .

[*More here inserts Letter 57 above into this letter*]

At the receipt of this letter she answered my servant that
she heartily thanked me. Soon after this there came to house the
proctor of the Charterhouse at Sheen and one brother William
with him, which nothing talked with me but of her and of the
great joy that they took in her virtue, but of any of her revelations they had no communication. But at another time brother
William came to me, and told me a long tale of her, being at the
house of a Knight in Kent, that was sore troubled with temptation to destroy himself; and none other thing we talked of nor
should have done of likelihood, though we had tarried together
much longer. He took great pleasure, good man, to tell that tale
with all the circumstances at length.

When I came again another time to Syon on a day in which
there was a profession, some of the fathers asked me how I liked
the Nun? And I answered that, in good faith, I liked her very well
in her talking; "Howbeit," said I, "she is never the nearer tried by
that, for I assure you she were likely to be very bad, if she seemed
good, ere I should think her other, till she happed to be proved
naught"; and in good faith that is my manner indeed, except I
were set to search and examine the truth upon likelihood of some
cloaked evil; for in that case, although I nothing suspected the
person myself, yet no less than if I suspected him sore, I would
as far as my wit would serve me search to find out the truth as

yourself has done very prudently in this matter: wherein you have done, in my mind, to your great laud and praise, a very meritorious deed in bringing forth to light such detestable hypocrisy, whereby every other wretch may take warning, and be feared to set forth their own devilish dissimuled falsehood, under the manner and color of the wonderful work of God: for verily, this woman so handled herself, with help of the evil spirit that inspired her, that after her own confession declared at Paul's cross, when I sent word by my servant unto the Proctor of the Charterhouse, that she was undoubtedly proved a false deceiving hypocrite; the good man had had so good opinion of her so long that he could at the first scantly believe me therein. Howbeit it was not he alone that thought her so very good, but many another right good man beside, as little marvel was upon so good report, till she was proved naught.

I remember me further, that in communication between Father Rich and me, I counseled him, that in such strange things as concerned such folk as had come unto her, to whom, as she said, she had told the causes of their coming ere themselves spoke thereof; and such good fruit as they said that many men had received by her prayer he and such other as so reported it, and thought that the knowledge thereof should much pertain to the glory of God, should first cause the things to be well and surely examined by the ordinaries, and such as had authority thereunto; so that it might be surely known whether the things were true or not, and that there were no lies intermingled among them or else the lies might after hap to away the credence of those things that were true. And when he told me the tale of Mary Magdalene, I said unto him, "Father Rich, that she is a good virtuous woman, in good faith, I hear so many good folk so report her, that I verily think it true; and think it well likely that God works some good and great things by her. But yet these strange tales are, you know well, no part of our creed; and therefore before you see them

surely proved, you shall have my poor counsel not to wed yourself so far forth to the credence of them, as to report them very
surely for true, lest that if it should hap that they were afterward
proved false, it might diminish your estimation in your preaching, whereof might grow great loss." To this he thanked me for
my counsel, but how he used it after that, I cannot tell.

Thus have I, good Master Cromwell, fully declared you, as
far as myself can call to remembrance, all that ever I have done or
said in this matter wherein I am sure that never one of them all
shall tell you any farther thing of effect, for if any of them, or any
man else, report of me as I trust verily no man will, and I know
well truly no man can, any word or deed by me spoken or done,
touching any breach of my loyal troth and duty toward my most
redoubted sovereign and natural liege lord, I will come to mine
answer, and make it good in such wise as becomes a poor true
man to do; that whosoever any such thing shall say, shall therein
say untrue; for I neither have in this matter done evil nor said
evil, nor so much as any evil thing thought, but only have been
glad, and rejoiced of them that were reported for good; which
condition I shall nevertheless keep toward all other good folk, for
the false cloaked hypocrisy of any of these, no more than I shall
esteem Judas the true apostle, for Judas the false traitor.

But so purpose I to bear myself in every man's company,
while I live, that neither good man nor bad, neither monk, friar
nor nun, nor other man or woman in this world shall make me
digress from my troth and faith, either toward God, or toward my
natural prince, by the grace of Almighty God; and as you therein
find me true, so I heartily therein pray you to continue toward
me your favor and good will, as you shall be sure of my poor daily
prayer, for other pleasure can I none do you. And thus the blessed
Trinity, both bodily and ghostly, long preserve and prosper you. I
pray you pardon me, that I write not unto you of mine own hand,
for verily I am compelled to forbear writing for a while by reason

of this disease of mine, whereof the chief occasion is grown, as it is thought, by the stooping and leaning on my breast, that I have used in writing. And this, eftsoon [again], I beseech our Lord long to preserve you.

    Thomas More, Knight

Letter 61

To Henry VIII [198]

In this letter, "a most heavy" More appeals to the prudence and wisdom of King Henry VIII for help in dealing with the still dangerous matter of the Nun of Kent and the "grievous bill" of attainder in Parliament accusing More and others of supporting her. As in the earlier letters to Cromwell, More reiterates his *fides* or "duty of faithfulness" to crown and country. According to Cicero, *fides* is "truth and fidelity to promises and agreements," and as such *fides* is the "foundation of justice" (*De Officiis* 1.22–23). *Fides*—and the consequences of its absence in political life—is a crucial concern in More's earlier humanist writings such as his remarkable *History of Richard the Third*, a work widely admired and praised after More's death and the crucial literary and philosophical source informing the young Shakespeare's first great tragedy, *Richard the Third*. The story of Regulus, the Roman general who went freely to his death rather than prove false to his word and promises, provides a classical example of the firm *fides* much admired by Cicero and other Romans, such as the poet Horace (see book three of *De Officiis*, and *Odes* 3.5).

CHELSEA
5 MARCH <1534>

It may like your Highness to call to your gracious remembrance, that at such time as of that great weighty room and office of your Chancellor (with which so far above my merits or qualities able and meet therefore, your Highness had of your incomparable goodness honored and exalted me), you were so good and gracious unto me, as at my poor humble suit to discharge and disburden me, giving me license with your gracious favor to bestow the residue of my life in mine age now to come, about the provision for my soul in the service of God, and to be your Grace's beadsman and pray for you. It pleased your Highness further to say unto me, that for the service which I before had done you (which it then liked your goodness far above my deserving to commend) that in any suit that I should after have unto your Highness, which either should concern mine honor (that word it liked your Highness to use unto me) or that should pertain unto my profit, I should find your Highness good and gracious lord unto me. So is it now, gracious Sovereign, that worldly honor is the thing, whereof I have resigned both the possession and the desire, in the resignation of your most honorable office; and worldly profit, I trust experience proves, and daily more and more shall prove, that I never was very greedy thereon.

But now is my most humble suit unto your excellent Highness, partly to beseech the same, somewhat to tender my poor honesty, but principally that of your accustomed goodness, no sinister information move your noble Grace to have any more distrust of my truth and devotion toward you than I have, or shall during my life give the cause. For in this matter of the wicked woman of Canterbury I have unto your trusty Counselor Master Thomas Cromwell, by my writing, as plainly declared the truth as I possibly can, which my declaration of his duty toward your

Grace and his goodness toward me he has, I understand, declared unto your Grace. In any part of all which my dealing, whether any other man may peradventure put any doubt, or move any scruple of suspicion, that can I neither tell, nor lies in mine hand to let, but unto myself is it not possible any part of my said demeanor to seem evil, the very clearness of mine own conscience knows in all the matter my mind and intent so good.

Wherefore most gracious Sovereign, I neither will nor well it can become me with your Highness to reason and argue the matter, but in my most humble manner prostrate at your gracious feet, I only beseech your Majesty with your own high prudence and your accustomed goodness consider and weigh the matter. And then if in your so doing, your own virtuous mind shall give you, that notwithstanding the manifold excellent goodness that your gracious Highness has by so many manner ways used unto me, I be a wretch of such monstrous ingratitude as could with any of them all, or with any other person living, digress from my bound duty of allegiance toward your good Grace, then desire I no further favor at your gracious hand, than the loss of all that ever I may lose in this world, goods, lands, and liberty and finally my life withal, whereof the keeping of any part unto my self could never do me pennyworth of pleasure, but only should then my recomfort be, that after my short life and your long, which with continual prosperity to God's pleasure our Lord for his mercy send you I should once meet with your Grace again in heaven, and there be merry with you, where among mine other pleasures this should yet be one, that your Grace should surely see there then, that (howsoever you take me) I am your true beadsman now and ever have been, and will be till I die, howsoever your pleasure be to do by me.

Howbeit, if in the considering of my cause your high wisdom and gracious goodness perceive (as I verily trust in God you shall) that I none otherwise have demeaned myself, than well may stand with my bound duty of faithfulness toward your royal Majesty, then in my most humble wise I beseech your most noble Grace that the knowledge of your true gracious persuasion in that behalf may relieve the torment of my present heaviness, conceived of the dread and fear (by that I hear such a grievous bill put by your learned Council into your high Court of Parliament against me) lest your Grace might by some sinister information be moved anything to think the contrary, which if your Highness do not (as I trust in God and your great goodness the matter by your own high prudence examined and considered, you will not) then in my most humble manner I beseech your Highness further (albeit that in respect of my former request this other thing is very slight) yet since your Highness has here before of your mere abundant goodness heaped and accumulated upon me (though I was thereto very far unworthy) from time to time both worship and great honor, too, and since I now have left off all such things and nothing seek or desire but the life to come and in the meanwhile pray for your Grace, it may like your Highness of your accustomed benignity somewhat to tender my poor honesty and never suffer by the mean of such a bill put forth against me any man to take occasion hereafter against the truth to slander me; which thing should yet by the peril of their own souls do themselves more hurt than me, which shall, I trust, settle mine heart, with your gracious favor, to depend upon the comfort of the truth and hope of heaven, and not upon the fallible opinion or soon spoken words of light and soon changeable people.

And thus, most dread and most dear sovereign Lord, I beseech the blessed Trinity preserve your most noble Grace, both in body and soul, and all that are your well willers, and amend all the contrary, among whom if ever I be or ever have been one, then pray I God that he may with mine open shame and destruction declare it. At my poor house in Chelsea, the fifth day of March, by the known rude hand of

Your most humble and most heavy faithful subject
and beadsman,
Thomas More, Knight

Letter 62

To Thomas Cromwell [199]

After again requesting Cromwell's help in the matter of the Nun of Kent, More describes in detail his earlier conversations with Henry about the "great matter" of his contested marriage with Queen Catherine. Most importantly, he recalls to mind "the first lesson" King Henry taught him upon entering the royal service—namely, "that I should first look unto God and after God unto [the King]." More will invoke these directions from Henry several times in later letters (see letters 71 and 79) as he defends himself and his silence. Moreover, he will summon this princely lesson to remembrance again in the last words he utters before his death: "I die the King's good servant, and God's first." See Appendix III for the Paris Newsletter account of More's trial and execution, and see *A Thomas More Sourcebook* for a more detailed discussion of More's last words (357–58).

The scriptural texts at the heart of Henry's appeal are Exodus 25:5 and Leviticus 18:16, as well as Leviticus 20:21. According to the common canonical interpretation and law, however, the prohibition in Leviticus was not seen as an immutable decree of divine law (*ODCC* 757), and the Exodus text in fact provided Henry the right to marry his sister-in-law in the first place, since Catherine was a widow from an heir-less marriage (*ODNB* 525–26). It seems clear from More's account in the letter that he did disclose his mind privately to King Henry on the "great matter" (see letter 71), though More's particular judgment remains discretely undisclosed in this letter. The "master

Fox" in the letter is Edward Fox (1496–1538), bishop of Hereford and author of several works, such as *Glasse of Truth* (1532), composed in support of Henry's "scruple" that the marriage to Queen Catherine was not lawful (*ODNB*). "Master Abell" is Thomas Abell, chaplain to Queen Catherine, who published *A Treatise against the Royal Divorce with the Title Invicta Veritas* in 1532. Abell was imprisoned several times and eventually executed in 1540; he was beatified in 1886 (*ODNB*).

For his part, More records his resolve to turn his mind to other business and not to meddle in the matter of the divorce and the questions over papal primacy; he also indicates his perhaps surprising willingness to accept the recently anointed Queen Anne, though he refused to attend her coronation in 1533. In his *Life of Sir Thomas More*, son-in-law William Roper relates that More merrily counseled certain bishops as follows in regards to attending the coronation: "And so though your lordships have in the matter of the matrimony hitherto kept yourselves pure virgins, yet take good heed, my lords, that you keep your virginity still. For some there be that by procuring your lordships first at the coronation to be present, and next to preach for the setting forth of it, and finally to write books to all the world in defense thereof, are desirous to deflower you; and when they have deflowered you, then will they not fail soon after to devour you" (see *A Thomas More Sourcebook*, 44).

More could perhaps have accepted the Act of Succession making Anne's children heirs to the throne because such an act was within Parliament's legal power and competency, though even here there was real trouble, because the Act pronounced Queen Anne Henry's "lawful" wife as well, as Henry Kelly points out in *Thomas More's Trial by Jury*. In any event, it was the Oath of the Act of Succession, which added words requiring acknowledgment of Henry's title "Supreme Head of the Church in England" and repudiating allegiance to any foreign power (e.g., Rome), that would prove impossible to swear for More, Fisher, and others. As Peter Marshall explains,

"More would not swear because the preamble to the oath upheld the spiritual validity of the king's second marriage and implicitly rejected the authority of the pope. For him to swear such an oath against his belief to the contrary would have been perjury, not just a legal transgression but a cause of eternal damnation. Everyone understood that this was the position. [Archbishop Thomas] Cranmer hoped to broker a fudge: More and Fisher should be allowed to swear to the succession without affirming the act's preamble, and the exact form of the oath they swore could be kept secret. But Henry was having none of it" (*Cambridge Companion*, 122–23). More's rejection of the oath, however, was not simply because the words were against his "belief" and faith; the record of More's trial suggests that, in his judgment, Parliament was exceeding its legal powers in these matters, especially in the 1534 Act of Supremacy. See Appendix II for texts of the relevant laws, acts, and oaths in question here.

In this letter, More also reminds Cromwell of King Henry's own part, through his book *Defense of the Seven Sacraments* (1523), in persuading More of the primacy of Peter, something More's long study of Scripture, Church Fathers, and general councils later confirmed and strengthened, though it is important to note More's aversion to exaggerating that primacy and papal power, especially its temporal jurisdiction. His appeal to the "common corps" of Christendom with a "common head" and "lawful councils" anticipates part of the defense he will make of himself at his trial in July 1535; the other side of his defense involves an appeal to English law and the Magna Carta, specifically to the words, "the English Church shall be free." See *Thomas More's Trial by Jury* for the best current account of More's trial and the many legal issues at stake. The book also contains a remarkable reconstruction of More's trial.

CHELSEA

5 MARCH <1534>

RIGHT WORSHIPFUL:

After my most hearty recommendation, it may please you to
understand that I have perceived by the relation of my son Roper
(for which I beseech almighty God reward you) your most charitable labor taken for me toward the King's gracious Highness, in
the procuring at his most gracious hand, the relief and comfort of
this woeful heaviness in which mine heart stands, neither for the
loss of goods, lands, or liberty, nor for any respect either, of this
kind of honesty that stands in the opinion of people and worldly
reputation, all which manner things (I thank our Lord), I so little
esteem for any affection therein toward myself that I can well be
content to jeopard, lose, and forgo them all and my life herewith,
without any further respite than even this same present day, either
for the pleasure of God or of my prince.

But surely good Master Cromwell, as I by mouth declared
unto you, some part (for all could I neither then say nor now
write) it thoroughly pierces my poor heart, that the King's Highness (whose gracious favor toward me far above all the things
of this world I have evermore desired, and whereof both for the
conscience of mine own true faithful heart and devotion toward
him, and for the manifold benefits of his high goodness continually bestowed upon me, I thought myself always sure), should
conceive any such mind or opinion of me, as to think that in my
communication either with the nun or the friars, or in my letter
written unto the nun, I had any other manner mind, than might
well stand with the duty of a tender loving subject toward his
natural prince, or that his Grace should reckon in me any manner
of obstinate heart against his pleasure in any thing that ever I said
or did concerning his great matter of his marriage or concerning
the primacy of the Pope. Never would I wish other thing in this

world more lief, than that his Highness in these things all three, as perfectly knew my dealing, and as thoroughly saw my mind, as I do myself, or as God himself, whose sight pierces deeper into my heart, than mine own.

For, Sir, as for the first matter, that is to wit my letter or communication with the nun (the whole discourse whereof in my former letter I have as plainly declared unto you as I possibly can), so pray I God to withdraw that scruple and doubt of my good mind, out of the King's noble breast and none other wise, but as I not only thought none harm, but also purposed good, and in that thing most, in which (as I perceive) his Grace conceives most grief and suspicion, that is to wit in my letter which I wrote unto her. And therefore Sir, since I have by my writing declared the truth of my deed, and am ready by mine oath to declare the truth of mine intent, I can devise no further thing by me to be done in that matter, but only beseech almighty God to put into the King's gracious mind, that as God knows the thing is indeed, so his noble Grace may take it. Now touching the second point concerning his Grace's great matter of his marriage, to the intent that you may see cause with the better conscience to make suit unto his highness for me, I shall as plainly declare you my demeanor in that matter as I have already declared you in the other, for more plainly can I not.

Sir, upon a time at my coming from beyond the sea, where I had been in the King's business, I repaired as my duty was unto the King's Grace being at that time at Hampton Court. At which time suddenly his Highness walking in the gallery, broke with me of his great matter, and showed me that it was now perceived, that his marriage was not only against the positive laws of the Church and the written law of God, but also in such wise against the law of nature, that it could in no wise by the Church be dispensable. Now so was it that before my going over the sea, I had heard certain things moved against the bull of the dispensation concerning the words of the Law Levitical and the Law Deuteronomical to prove the prohibition to be *de iure diuino* [i.e., by divine law; see Deut 25:5 and Lev 18:16 and 20:21], but yet perceived I not at that time but that the greater hope of the matter stood in certain faults that were found in the bull, whereby the bull should by the law not be sufficient. And such comfort was there in that point as far as I perceived a good season, that the Council on the other part were fain to bring forth a brief, by which they pretended those defaults to be supplied, the truth of which brief was by the King's Council suspected, and much diligence was thereafter done for the trial of that point, wherein what was finally found either I never knew or else I not remember.

But I rehearse you this to the intent you shall know that the first time that ever I heard that point moved, that it should be in such high degree against the law of nature, was the time in which as I began to tell you the King's Grace showed it me himself, and laid the Bible open before me, and there read me the words that moved his Highness and divers other erudite persons so to think, and asked me further what myself thought thereon. At which time not presuming to look that his Highness should anything take that point for the more proved or unproved for my poor mind in so great a matter, I showed nevertheless as my duty was at his commandment what thing I thought upon the words which I there read. Whereupon his Highness accepting benignly my sudden unadvised answer commanded me to commune further with Master Fox, now his Grace's Almoner, and to read a book with him that then was in making for that matter. After which book read, and my poor opinion eftsoons [again] declared unto his Highness thereupon, his Highness like a prudent and a virtuous prince assembled at another time at Hampton Court a good number of very well learned men, at which time as far as ever I heard there were (as was in so great a matter most likely to be) diverse opinions among them. Howbeit I never heard but that they agreed at that time upon a certain form in which the book should be made, which book was afterward at York Place in my Lord Cardinal's chamber read in the presence of divers bishops and many learned men. And they all thought that there appeared in the book good and reasonable causes that might well move the King's Highness, being so virtuous a prince, to conceive in his mind a scruple against his marriage, which, while he could not otherwise avoid, he did well and virtuously for the acquitting of his conscience to sue and procure to have his doubt decided by judgment of the Church.

After this the suit began, and the Legates sat upon the matter, during all which time I never meddled therein, nor was a man meet to do, for the matter was in hand by an ordinary process of the spiritual law, whereof I could little skill. And yet while the Legates were sitting upon the matter, it pleased the King's Highness to send me in the company of my Lord of London now of Durham in embassy about the peace that at our being there was concluded at Cambrai, between his Highness and the Emperor and the French King.

And after my coming home his Highness of his only goodness (as far unworthy as I was thereto) made me, as you well know, his Chancellor of this realm, soon after which time his Grace moved me again yet eftsoons [a second time], to look and consider his great matter, and well and indifferently to ponder such things as I should find therein. And if it so were that thereupon it should hap me to see such things as should persuade me to that part, he would gladly use me among other of his councilors in that matter, and nevertheless he graciously declared unto me that he would in no wise that I should other thing do or say therein, than upon that that I should perceive mine own conscience should serve me, and that I should first look unto God and after God unto him, which most gracious words was the first lesson also that ever his Grace gave me at my first coming into his noble service.

This motion was to me very comfortable and much I longed beside anything that myself either had seen, or by further search should hap to find for the one part or the other, yet specially to have some conference in the matter with some such of his Grace's learned Council as most for his part had labored and most have found in the matter.

Whereupon his Highness assigned unto me the now most reverend fathers Archbishops of Canterbury and York with Master Doctor Fox, now his Grace's Almoner and Master Doctor Nicholas the Italian friar, whereupon I not only sought and read, and as far forth as my poor wit and learning served me, well weighed and considered every such thing as I could find myself, or read in any other man's labor that I could get, which anything had written therein, but had also diligent conference with his Grace's councilors aforesaid, whose honors and worships I nothing mistrust in this point, but that they both have and will report unto his Highness that they never found obstinate manner or fashion in me, but a mind as toward and as conformable as reason could in a matter disputable require.

Whereupon the King's Highness being further advertised both by them and myself of my poor opinion in the matter (wherein to have been able and meet to do him service I would as I then showed his Highness have been more glad than of all such worldly commodities as I either then had or ever should come to) his Highness graciously taking in good part my good mind in that behalf used of his blessed disposition in the prosecuting of his great matter only those (of whom his Grace had good number) whose conscience his Grace perceived well and fully persuaded upon that part, and as well myself as any other to whom his Highness thought the thing to seem otherwise, he used in his other business, abiding (of his abundant goodness) nevertheless gracious lord unto any man, nor never was willing to put any man in ruffle or trouble of his conscience.

After this did I never nothing more therein, nor never any word wrote I therein to the impairing of his Grace's part neither before nor after, nor any man else by my procurement, but settling my mind in quiet to serve his Grace in other things, I would not so much as look nor wittingly let lie by me any book of the other part, albeit that I gladly read afterward divers books that were made on his part yet, nor never would I read the book that Master Abell made on the other side, nor other book which were as I heard say made in Latin beyond the sea, nor never give ear to the Pope's proceedings in the matter.

Moreover, whereas I had found in my study a book that I had before borrowed of my Lord of Bath, which book he had made of the matter at such time as the Legates sat here thereupon, which book had been by me merely gently cast aside, and that I showed him I would send him home his book again, he told me that in good faith he had long time before discharged his mind of that matter, and having forgotten that copy to remain in my hands, had burned his own copy that he had thereof at home, and because he no more minded to meddle anything in the matter, he desired me to burn the same book too. And upon my faith so did I.

Besides this, divers other ways have I so used myself that if I rehearsed them all, it should well appear that I never have had against his Grace's marriage any manner demeanor whereby his Highness might have any manner cause or occasion of displeasure toward me, for likewise as I am not he which either can, or whom it could become, to take upon him the determination or decision of such a weighty matter, nor boldly to affirm this thing or that therein, whereof divers points a great way pass my learning, so am I he that among other his Grace's faithful subjects, his Highness being in possession of his marriage and this noble woman really anointed Queen, neither murmur at it nor dispute upon it, nor never did nor will, but without any other manner meddling of the matter among his other faithful subjects faithfully pray to God for his Grace and hers both, long to live and well and their noble issue too, in such wise as may be to the pleasure of God, honor and surety to themselves, rest, peace, wealth, and profit unto this noble realm.

As touching the third point, the primacy of the Pope, I nothing meddle in the matter. Truth it is, that as I told you, when you desired me to show you what I thought therein, I was myself sometime not of the mind that the primacy of that See should be begun by the institution of God, until that I read in that matter those things that the King's Highness had written in his most famous book against the heresies of Martin Luther [i.e., Henry's *Defense of the Seven Sacraments*], at the first reading whereof I moved the King's Highness either to leave out that point, or else to touch it more slenderly for doubt of such things as after might hap to fall in question between his Highness and some pope as between princes and popes divers times have done. Whereunto his Highness answered me that he would in no wise anything diminish of that matter, of which thing his Highness showed me a secret cause whereof I never had anything heard before. But surely after that I had read his Grace's book therein, and so many other things as I have seen in that point by this continuance of these ten year since and more have found in effect the substance of all the holy doctors from St. Ignatius, disciple to St. John the Evangelist, unto our own days both Latins and Greeks so consonant and agreeing in that point, and the thing by such general councils so confirmed also, that in good faith I never neither read nor heard anything of such effect on the other side, that ever could lead me to think that my conscience were well discharged, but rather in right great peril if I should follow the other side and deny the primacy to be provided by God, which if we did, yet can I nothing (as I showed you) perceive any commodity that ever could come by that denial, for that primacy is at the leastwise instituted by the corps of Christendom and for a great urgent cause in avoiding of schisms and corroborate by continual succession more than the space of a thousand year at the least, for there are passed almost a thousand year since the time of holy St. Gregory.

And therefore since all Christendom is one corps, I cannot perceive how any member thereof may without the common assent of the body depart from the common head. And then if we may not lawfully leave it by ourselves, I cannot perceive (but if the thing were a treating in a general council) what the question could avail whether the primacy were instituted by God or ordained by the Church. As for the general councils assembled lawfully, I never could perceive but that in the declaration of the truths to be believed and to be stood to, the authority thereof ought to be taken for undoubtable, or else were there in nothing no certainty, but through Christendom upon every man's affectionate reason, all thing might be brought from day to day to continual ruffle and confusion, from which by the general councils, the spirit of God assisting, every such council well assembled keeps and ever shall keep the corps of his Catholic Church.

And verily since the King's Highness has (as by the book of his honorable council appears) appealed to the general council from the Pope, in which council I beseech our Lord send his Grace comfortable speed, methinks in my poor mind it could be no furtherance there unto his Grace's cause if his Highness should in his own realm before, either by laws making or books putting forth, seem to derogate and deny not only the primacy of the see apostolic, but also the authority of the general councils too, which I verily trust his Highness intends not, for in the next general council it may well happen that this Pope may be deposed and another substituted in his room with whom the King's Highness may be very well content; for albeit that I have for mine own part such opinion of the pope's primacy as I have showed you, yet never thought I the Pope above the general council nor never have in any book of mine put forth among the King's subjects in our vulgar tongue, advanced greatly the Pope's authority. For albeit that a man may peradventure somewhat find therein that after the common manner of all Christian realms I speak of him as primate, yet never do I stick thereon with reasoning and proving of that point. And in my book against the Masker [i.e., More's *Answer to a Poisoned Book*, 1532], I wrote not I know well five lines, and yet of no more but only St. Peter himself, from whose person many take not the primacy, even of those that grant it none of his successors, and yet was that book made, printed, and put forth of very truth before that any of the books of the council was either printed or spoken of. But where as I had written thereof at length in my *Confutation* [i.e., More's *Confutation of Tyndale,* 1533] before, and for the proof thereof had compiled together all that I could find therefore, at such time as I little looked that there should fall between the King's Highness and the Pope such a breach as is fallen since, when I after that saw the thing likely to draw toward such displeasure between them, I suppressed it utterly and never put word thereof into my book, but put out the remnant without it, which thing well declares that I never intended anything to meddle in that matter against the King's gracious pleasure, whatsoever mine own opinion were therein.

And thus have I, good Master Cromwell, long troubled your Mastership with a long process of these matters, with which I neither dared nor it could become me to encumber the King's noble Grace, but I beseech you for our Lord's love, that you be not so weary of my most cumbrous suit but that it may like you at such opportune time or times as your wisdom may find to help that his Highness may by your goodness be fully informed of my true faithful mind, and that in the matter of that wicked woman there never was on my part any other mind than good, nor yet in any other thing else never was there nor never shall there be any further fault found in me, than that I cannot in everything think the same way that some other men of more wisdom and deeper learning do, nor can find in mine heart otherwise to say than as mine own conscience gives me, which condition has never grown in anything that ever might touch his gracious pleasure of any obstinate mind or misaffectionate appetite, but of a timorous conscience rising happily for lack of better perceiving, and yet not without tender respect unto my most bound duty toward his noble Grace, whose only favor I so much esteem that I nothing have of mine own in all this world, except only my soul, but that I will with better will forgo it than abide of his Highness, one heavy displeasant look. And thus I make an end of my long, troublous process, beseeching the blessed Trinity for the great goodness you show me, and the great comfort you do me, both bodily and ghostly to prosper you, and in heaven to reward you. At Chelsea the fifth day of March by

Yours deeply bounden,
Thomas More, Knight

Letter 63

To Margaret Roper [200]

More's Account of his First Interrogation, Lambeth Palace

More was sent to the Tower of London on April 17, 1534 for refusing to take the Oath of the Act of Succession because he judged that the oath was against his conscience, though he remained silent as to why during the interrogations. The only lay man summoned to take the oath, More describes his refusal of the oath and the subsequent "pageant" he was allowed to behold of troubled men entering Lambeth to take the oath and then emerging relieved and incredibly happy, even "waxen wonten."

This letter is the first of three accounts More writes of the interrogations he underwent while imprisoned (see letters 77 and 79). The setting is Lambeth Palace, the London residence of the Archbishop of Canterbury. The principal figures in the interrogation scenes are Thomas More himself; Thomas Audley, Lord Chancellor; Thomas Cromwell, Master Secretary; Thomas Cranmer, Archbishop of Canterbury; the Dukes of Norfolk and Suffolk; and William Benson, abbot and Lord of Westminster. Other figures mentioned are Rowland Philipps, Vicar of Croyden, who according to long-standing tradition is the anonymous preacher who pined, in happier days, to be appointed first bishop of the Utopians, something More alludes to in jest in *Utopia* (*ODNB*); Hugh Latimer, bishop of Worcester; Bishop John Fisher of Rochester; and Doctor Nicholas Wilson, formerly chaplain of Henry, who fell out of favor and was imprisoned with More but later released after he took the Oath (see letters 70–71). During More's fifteen month imprisonment in the hospitable Tower of London, he also wrote two of his masterpieces, *A Dialogue of Comfort against Tribulation,* and the striking scriptural commentary on the Garden of Gethsemane, *On the Sadness of Christ,* as well as the remaining letters in this volume and various spiritual counsels and prayers. *The Sadness of Christ* offers a striking variation on More's famous advice from his earlier *Utopia.* In those happier days of his youth More had counseled Raphael Hythloday, "Don't give up the ship in a storm because you cannot hold back the winds" (35); now, from his cell in the Tower, he again urges the reader not to be "like a cowardly ship's captain who is so disheartened by the furious din of a storm that he deserts the helm, hides away cowering in some cranny, and abandons the ship to the waves" (47).

Daughter:

When I was before the Lords at Lambeth, I was the first that was called in, albeit Master Doctor the Vicar of Croydon [i.e., Rowland Philipps] was come before me, and divers others. After the cause of my sending for was declared unto me (whereof I somewhat marveled in my mind, considering that they sent for no more temporal men but me), I desired the sight of the oath, which they showed me under the great seal. Then desired I the sight of the Act of the Succession, which was delivered me in a printed roll. After which read secretly by myself, and the oath considered with the act, I showed unto them that my purpose was not to put any fault either in the act or any man that made it, or in the oath or any man that swore it, nor to condemn the conscience of any other man. But as for myself in good faith my conscience so moved me in the matter that though I would not deny to swear to the succession, yet unto the oath that there was offered me I could not swear, without the jeoparding of my soul to perpetual damnation. And that if they doubted whether I did refuse the oath only for the grudge of my conscience, or for any other fantasy, I was ready therein to satisfy them by mine oath. Which if they trusted not, what should they be the better to give me any oath? And if they trusted that I would therein swear true, then trusted I that of their goodness they would not move me to swear the oath that they offered me, perceiving that for to swear it was against my conscience.

Unto this my Lord Chancellor [i.e., Thomas Audley] said that they all were sorry to hear me say thus, and see me thus refuse the oath. And they said all that on their faith I was the very first that ever refused it; which would cause the King's Highness to conceive great suspicion of me and great indignation toward me.

And therewith they showed me the roll, and let me see the names of the lords and the commons which had sworn, and subscribed their names already. Which notwithstanding when they saw that I refused to swear the same myself, not blaming any other man that had sworn, I was in conclusion commanded to go down into the garden, and thereupon I tarried in the old burned chamber, that looks into the garden and would not go down because of the heat. In that time saw I Master Doctor Latimer come into the garden, and there walked he with divers other doctors and chaplains of my Lord of Canterbury [i.e., Thomas Cranmer], and very merry I saw him, for he laughed, and took one or twain about the neck so handsomely, that if they had been women, I would have went he had been waxen wanton. After that came Master Doctor Wilson forth from the lords and was with two gentlemen brought by me, and gentlemanly sent straight unto the Tower. What time my Lord of Rochester [i.e., John Fisher] was called in before them, that cannot I tell. But at night I heard that he had been before them, but where he remained that night, and so forth till he was sent hither, I never heard. I heard also that Master Vicar of Croydon, and all the remnant of the priests of London that were sent for, were sworn, and that they had such favor at the Council's hand that they were not lingered nor made to dance any long attendance to their travail and cost, as suitors were sometimes wont to be, but were sped apace to their great comfort so far forth that Master Vicar of Croydon, either for gladness or for dryness, or else that it might be seen (*quod ille notus erat pontifici* [i.e., he that was known to the high priest; see John 18:15–16, RSV]) went to my Lord's buttery bar and called for drink, and drank (*valde familiariter* [i.e., on familiar terms]).

When they had played their pageant and were gone out of the place, then was I called in again. And then was it declared unto me what a number had sworn, even since I went inside, gladly, without any sticking. Wherein I laid no blame in no man, but for my own self answered as before. Now as well before as then, they somewhat laid unto me for obstinacy, that where as before, since I refused to swear, I would not declare any special part of that oath that grudged my conscience, and open the cause wherefore. For thereunto I had said to them, that I feared lest the King's Highness would as they said take displeasure enough toward me for the only refusal of the oath. And that if I should open and disclose the causes why, I should therewith but further exasperate his Highness, which I would in no wise do, but rather would I abide all the danger and harm that might come toward me, than give his Highness any occasion of further displeasure than the offering of the oath unto me of pure necessity constrained me. Howbeit when they divers times imputed this to me for stubbornness and obstinacy that I would neither swear the oath nor yet declare the causes why, I declined thus far toward them that rather than I would be accounted for obstinate, I would upon the King's gracious license or rather his such commandment had as might be my sufficient warrant that my declaration should not offend his Highness, nor put me in the danger of any of his statutes, I would be content to declare the causes in writing; and over that to give an oath in the beginning, that if I might find those causes by any man in such wise answered as I might think mine own conscience satisfied, I would after that with all mine heart swear the principal oath, too.

To this I was answered that though the King would give me license under his letters patent, yet would it not serve against the statute. Whereto I said that yet if I had them, I would stand unto the trust of his honor at my peril for the remnant. But yet it thinks me, lo, that if I may not declare the causes without peril, then to leave them undeclared is no obstinacy.

My Lord of Canterbury taking hold upon that that I said, that I condemned not the conscience of them that swore, said unto me that it appeared well that I did not take it for a very sure thing and a certain that I might not lawfully swear it, but rather as a thing uncertain and doubtful. But then (said my Lord) you know for a certainty and a thing without doubt that you be bound to obey your sovereign lord your King. And therefore are you bound to leave off the doubt of your unsure conscience in refusing the oath, and take the sure way in obeying of your prince, and swear it. Now all was it so that in mine own mind methought myself not concluded, yet this argument seemed me suddenly so subtle and namely with such authority coming out of so noble a prelate's mouth, that I could again answer nothing thereto but only that I thought myself I might not well do so, because that in my conscience this was one of the cases in which I was bound that I should not obey my prince, since that whatsoever other folk thought in the matter (whose conscience and learning I would not condemn nor take upon me to judge), yet in my conscience the truth seemed on the other side. Wherein I had not informed my conscience neither suddenly nor slightly but by long leisure and diligent search for the matter. And of truth if that reason may conclude, than have we a ready way to avoid all perplexities. For in whatsoever matters the doctors stand in great doubt, the King's commandment given upon whither side he list soils all the doubts.

Then said my Lord of Westminster [i.e., William Benson] to me that howsoever the matter seemed unto mine own mind, I had cause to fear that mine own mind was erroneous when I see the great council of the realm determine of my mind the contrary, and that therefore I ought to change my conscience. To that I answered that if there were no more but myself upon my side and the whole Parliament upon the other, I would be sore afraid to lean to mine own mind only against so many. But on the other side, if it so be that in some things for which I refuse the oath, I have (as I think I have) upon my part as great a council and a greater too, I am not then bound to change my conscience, and confirm it to the council of one realm, against the general council of Christendom. Upon this Master Secretary [i.e., Thomas Cromwell], as he that tenderly favors me, said and swore a great oath that he had lever that his own only son (which is of truth a goodly young gentleman, and shall I trust come to much worship) had lost his head than that I should thus have refused the oath. For surely the King's Highness would now conceive a great suspicion against me, and think that the matter of the nun of Canterbury was all contrived by my drift. To which I said that the contrary was true and well known, and whatsoever should mishap me, it lay not in my power to help it without peril of my soul.

Then did my Lord Chancellor repeat before me my refusal unto Master Secretary, as to him that was going unto the King's Grace. And in the rehearsing, his Lordship repeated again that I denied not but was content to swear to the succession. Whereunto I said that as for that point, I would be content, so that I might see my oath in that point so framed in such a manner as might stand with my conscience. Then said my Lord: "Marry, Master Secretary mark that too, that he will not swear that neither but under some certain manner." "Verily no, my Lord," said I, "but that I will see it made in such wise first, as I shall myself see, that I shall neither be forsworn nor swear against my conscience. Surely as to swear to the succession I see no peril, but I thought and think it reason that to mine own oath I look well myself, and be of counsel also in the fashion, and never intended to swear for a piece, and set my hand to the whole oath. Howbeit (as help me God), as touching the whole oath, I never withdrew any man from it, nor never advised any to refuse it, nor never put, nor will, any scruple in any man's head, but leave every man to his own conscience. And methinks in good faith that so were it good reason that every man should leave me to mine.

Thomas More, Knight

Letter 64

To Margaret Roper [201]

As the 1557 edition of More's *English Works* attests, this letter was written "with a coal" by Sir Thomas More to his daughter Mistress Margaret Roper. A "fillip" is a smart blow or stroke (*OED*).

Tower of London
<April–May? 1534>

Mine Own Good Daughter:

Our Lord be thanked, I am in good health of body, and in good quiet of mind; and of worldly things I no more desire than I have. I beseech him make you all merry in the hope of heaven. And such things as I somewhat longed to talk with you all, concerning the world to come, our Lord put them into your minds, as I trust he doth, and better, too, by his Holy Spirit, who bless you and preserve you all. Written with a coal by your tender loving father, who in his poor prayers forgets none of you all, nor your babes, nor your nurses, nor your good husbands, nor your good husbands' shrewd wives, nor your father's shrewd wife neither, nor our other friends. And thus fare you heartily well for lack of paper.

Thomas More, Knight

Our Lord keep me continually true, faithful and plain, to the contrary whereof I beseech him heartily never to suffer me to live. For as for long life (as I have often told thee, Meg), I neither look for, nor long for, but am well content to go, if God call me hence tomorrow. And I thank our Lord I know no person living that I would had one fillip for my sake, of which mind I am more glad than of all the world beside.

Recommend me to your shrewd Will and mine other sons, and to John Harris my friend, and yourself knows to whom else, and to my shrewd wife above all, and God preserve you all, and make and keep you his servants all.

Letter 65

To Margaret Roper [202]

Sometime in the month after More's imprisonment, Meg Roper had written her father a letter in which, as the 1557 editor relates, "she seemed somewhat to labor to persuade More to take the oath (though she nothing so thought) to win thereby credence with Master Thomas Cromwell, that she might the rather get liberty to have free resort unto her father. . . ." More's brief reply anticipates the longer, later pair of letters known as the *Dialogue on Conscience* (letters 68 and 69), which may have been co-authored by father and daughter.

The sole Latin scriptural quotation, repeated often by More in these late letters, is from Proverbs: "The king's heart is a stream of water in the hand of the LORD; he turns it wherever he will" (21.1). The proverb continues: "Every way of a man is right in his own eyes, but the LORD weighs the heart" (21:2).

<Tower of London
May? 1534>

Our Lord Bless You All:

If I had not been, my dearly beloved daughter, at a firm and fast point (I trust in God's great mercy), this good great while before, your lamentable letter had not a little abashed me, surely far above all other things, of which I hear divers times not a few terrible toward me. But surely they all touched me never so near, nor were so grievous unto me, as to see you, my well-beloved child, in such vehement piteous manner labor to persuade unto me that thing wherein I have of pure necessity for respect unto mine own soul so often given you so precise answer before. Wherein as touching the points of your letter, I can make none answer, for I doubt not but you well remember that the matters which move my conscience (without declaration whereof I can nothing touch the points) I have sundry times showed you that I will disclose them to no man. And therefore daughter Margaret, I can in this thing no further, but like as you labor me again to follow your mind, to desire and pray you both again to leave off such labor, and with my former answers to hold yourself content.

A deadly grief unto me, and much more deadly than to hear of mine own death (for the fear thereof, I thank our Lord, the fear of hell, the hope of heaven and the passion of Christ daily more and more assuage) is that I perceive my good son your husband, and you my good daughter, and my good wife, and mine other good children and innocent friends, in great displeasure and danger of great harm thereby. The let whereof [i.e. the hindrance], while it lies not in my hand, I can no further but commit all unto God. *Nam in manu Dei*, said the scripture, *cor regis est, et sicut diuisiones aquarum quocunque voluerit, impellit illud* [Prov 21:1, "Like flowing water is the heart of the king in the hand of God who turns it where he pleases"], whose high goodness I most humbly beseech to incline the noble heart of the King's Highness to the tender favor of you all, and to favor me no better than God and myself know that my faithful heart toward him and my daily prayer for him, do deserve. For surely if his Highness might inwardly see my true mind such as God knows it is, I would (I trust) soon assuage his high displeasure. Which while I can in this world never in such wise show but that his Grace may be persuaded to believe the contrary of me, I can no further go, but put all in the hands of him, for fear of whose displeasure for the safeguard of my soul stirred by mine own conscience, without insectation [i.e., railing and calumniation] or reproach laying to any other man's, I suffer and endure this trouble. Out of which I beseech him to bring me, when his will shall be, into his endless bliss of heaven, and in the meanwhile, give me grace and you both in all our agonies and troubles, devoutly to resort prostrate unto the remembrance of that bitter agony, which our Savior suffered before his passion at the Mount. And if we diligently so do, I verily trust we shall find therein great comfort and consolation. And thus my dear daughter the blessed spirit of Christ for his tender mercy govern and guide you all, to his pleasure and your weal and comforts both body and soul.

Your tender loving father,
Thomas More, Knight

Letter 66

From Margaret Roper [203]

In this letter to her father, Meg Roper invokes the old Latin phrase, *ut sit mens sana in corpore sano*, originally found in Juvenal's tenth satire. The full text is *Orandum est ut sit mens sana in corpore sano*—that

is, that one should pray for a healthy mind in a sound body. See the
Loeb edition of Juvenal for the complete text of this satire.

<MAY? 1534>

Mine own good father, it is to me no little comfort, since I cannot
talk with you by such means as I would, at the least way to delight
myself among in this bitter time of your absence, by such means
as I may, by as often writing to you, as shall be expedient, and by
reading again and again your most fruitful and delectable letter, a
faithful messenger of your very virtuous and ghostly mind, rid from
all corrupt love of worldly things, and fast knit only in the love of
God, and desire of heaven, as becomes a very true worshipper and
a faithful servant of God, which I doubt not good father holds
his holy hand over you, and shall (as he has) preserve you both
body and soul, *ut sit mens sana in corpore sano,* and namely, now
when you have abjected [i.e., cast off] all earthly consolations, and
resigned yourself willingly gladly and fully, for his love, to his holy
protection. Father, what think you has been our comfort since your
departing from us? Surely the experience we have had of your life
past, and godly conversation, and wholesome counsel, and virtuous example, and a surety not only of the continuance of that same,
but also of great increase by the goodness of our Lord to the great
rest and gladness of your heart devoid of all earthly dregs, and gar-
nished with the noble vesture of heavenly virtue, a pleasant palace
for the holy spirit of God to rest in, who defend you (as I doubt not
good father but of his goodness he will) from all trouble of mind
and of body, and give me your most loving obedient daughter and
handmaid, and all us your children and friends, to follow that that
we praise in you, and to our only comfort remember and coming
together of you, that we may in conclusion meet with you mine
own dear father in the bliss of heaven to which our most merciful
Lord has bought us with his precious blood.

Your own most loving obedient daughter and beadswoman Margaret Roper, which desires above all worldly things to be in John Wood's stead, to do you some service. But we live in hope that we shall shortly receive you again, I pray God heartily we may, if it be his holy will.

Letter 67

To All His Friends [204]

After Meg Roper obtained license from the King to visit her imprisoned father, she did so. While she was there, More wrote this letter, again with a coal, to his family and friends worried and awaiting, they hoped, his release from the Tower of London.

TOWER OF LONDON
<1534>

To All My Loving Friends:

For as much as being in prison I cannot tell what need I may have, or what necessity I may hap to stand in, I heartily beseech you all, that if my well beloved daughter Margaret Roper (which only of all my friends has by the King's gracious favor license to resort to me) do anything desire of any of you, of such things as I shall hap to need, that it may like you no less to regard and tender it, than if I moved it unto you and required it of you personally present myself. And I beseech you all to pray for me, and I shall pray for you.

Your faithful lover and poor beadsman,

Thomas More, Knight, prisoner

Letter 68

FROM ALICE ALINGTON TO MARGARET ROPER [205]

PART ONE OF *A DIALOGUE ON CONSCIENCE*

This letter and the following comprise what has come to be called *A Dialogue on Conscience*. The second part is the longest letter from More addressing the controversies and his conscience, and the *Dialogue* has been compared to Plato's *Crito*, the dialogue wherein Socrates' friends visit him in prison before his death. The background of the *Dialogue of Conscience* is this: On 16 and 17 August 1534, Lord Chancellor Thomas Audley visited the home of More's step-daughter, Alice Aldington. While the pretense of his visit was hunting, Audley really wished to communicate a message to Thomas More through Alice Alington, whom Audley summoned for a meeting the day after "he killed his deer." Audley and More were friends, despite the present controversies of state and church. In fact, Audley had helped protect More from the King's anger on several occasions, especially in the matter of the Nun of Kent.

Still, as these two letters indicate, Audley was growing increasingly concerned about the effect of More's conscience and noticeable silence. He marvels that out of all lords and clergy, only More and Fisher maintain "obstinate" or willful silence on the Oath, despite all arguments and persuasions to the contrary. Thus in part one (letter 68), Audley urges More to overcome his scruples and take the Oath, while part two (letter 69) represents Margaret Roper's account of her father's long response to the first letter—and to Meg herself, who begins the *Dialogue* agreeing with Audley and presenting the Chancellor's positions to her father like another "Mistress Eve." These two letters contain several pointed "fables," such as the tale of the fools in the rain and the tale of the lion, the ass, and the wolf, told first by Audley, then wittily retold and reinterpreted by More.

More also adds a merry tale of his own, the tale of Good Company, a poor fellow who finds himself alone and in the middle of a drama of conscience in the second letter.

Letters 68 and 69 have been modernized by Mary Gottschalk. The original text may be found in *The Correspondence of Sir Thomas More*, ed. Elizabeth Rogers (Princeton University Press, 1947).

17 AUGUST <1534>

SISTER ROPER, WITH ALL MY HEART I GIVE YOU MY
REGARDS, THANKING YOU FOR ALL YOUR KINDNESS.

The reason I am writing at this time is to let you know that when I got home, within two hours after, my Lord Chancellor [i.e., Thomas Audley] came over to hunt a buck in our park—which was to my husband a source of great encouragement, that it would please him to do this. Then, when he had enjoyed himself and killed his deer, he went to spend the night at the home of Sir Thomas Barmeston. The next day, I went to see him there at his request, which I could not say no to, since I thought he asked me with genuine sincerity, and most especially since I wanted to speak to him on behalf of my father.

And when I saw my chance, I did ask him, as humbly as I could, that he would still be, as I have heard it said that he has been, a good lord to my father. And he said that when it came to his being charged with the matter of the Nun of Kent, things did look very good. But as for this other matter, he marveled that my father is so obstinate in his thinking, when everybody else went ahead with the rest, except only the obstinate Bishop of Rochester [John Fisher] and himself. "And in all honesty," said my Lord, "I am very glad that I have no learning outside of a few of Aesop's fables, of which I shall tell you one. There was a country full of almost nothing but fools. There were only a few who were wise.

And they, by their wisdom, knew that there was going to fall a heavy rain which would turn into a fool everyone who got dirtied or wet with it. They, seeing that, made for themselves caves under the ground and stayed there till the rain was all over. Then they came out, thinking to make the fools do what they wanted them to, and rule them as they would. But the fools would have none of that. Despite all this crafty planning, the fools would have the rule themselves. And when the wise men saw that they could not achieve their goal, they wished that they had been in the rain, and dirtied their clothes, with them."

When this tale was told, my Lord laughed very delightedly. Then I said to him that for all the delightfulness of his fable I had no doubt that he would be a good lord to my father when he saw his chance. He said, "I would not have your father so scrupulous of conscience." And then he told me another fable, one about a lion, an ass, and a wolf, all going to confession. First the lion confessed that he had devoured all the beasts that he could come by. His confessor absolved him, on the grounds that he was a king and also that it was his nature so to do. Then came the poor ass. He said that he took but one straw out of his master's shoe, for hunger, and that because of this he thought his master had caught a cold. His confessor could not absolve this great trespass, but immediately sent him to the bishop. Then the wolf came and made his confession, and he was strictly commanded not to eat more than a sixpence's worth of food at any one meal. But when the wolf had been on this diet a little while, he grew very hungry. So much so that one day, when he saw come by him a cow with her calf, he said to himself, "I am very hungry and would gladly eat, except that I am bound by my spiritual father. Well, notwithstanding that, my conscience must be my judge. So, then, if that be so, my conscience will be thus: that the cow does now seem to me to be worth but fourpence, and then, if the cow is worth but fourpence, then the calf is worth but twopence." And so the wolf ate both the cow and the calf.

Now, good sister, has not my Lord told me two clever fables? Actually I liked them not at all, nor did I know what to say, because I was embarrassed by this answer. Anyway, I see no better recourse than to Almighty God, for he is the comforter of all sorrows and will not fail to send his comfort to his servants when they are most in need of it. And so, farewell, my own good sister. Written the Monday after Saint Lawrence, in haste, by

> Your sister Dame,
> Alice Alington

Letter 69

From Margaret Roper to Alice Alington [206]

PART TWO OF *A DIALOGUE ON CONSCIENCE*

In this letter, More responds to Audley's attempts at persuasion in the previous letter and engages Margaret, or "Mistress Eve," in a conversation about the workings and demands of conscience. More assures his daughter that his conscience is "clear" and "sure" in regard to the great matter of the Oath. The formation of conscience was a lifelong concern of More's, as the much earlier letter to William Gonell, his children's tutor, makes clear: "the whole fruit of their endeavors," More wrote then, "should consist in the testimony of God and a good conscience." This present letter to Meg is More's most extended reflection on conscience in his collected letters, and his "tale of Good Company" one of his most pointed and powerful stories.

More's understanding of conscience is the traditional one; conscience is "the capacity for judging the rightness of actions, either considered generally, or actually proposed or already performed"

(*ODCC* 405). In Thomas Aquinas' concise sentence, "Conscience is nothing else than the application of knowledge to some action," a work and application performed by the practical reason, but presuming formation in the natural law, Scripture, and doctrine, at least in the best case (*Summa Theologica IaIIae.19.5;* see also *Summa Theologica Ia.79.13*). Because conscience intimately involves judgment of what the person sees and judges to be right, conscience must be obeyed and followed, even in the case of an erroneous conscience, though following an erroneous conscience does not make the decision or the deed right.

Faulty forms of conscience include the scrupulous conscience, which fears it sees sin where there is no sin, and the lax, erroneous, or "cheveril" conscience, which sees objective sins not as sins at all, or sees them as less serious than they are. In Aquinas' view, conscience errs because of ignorance, either vincible ignorance, which we are responsible for, or invincible ignorance, which we are not responsible for. In any event, More understood the proper education and formation of the conscience—the "law of the mind" and the "aboriginal Vicar" of God in man, in John Henry Newman's later words—to be one of the ends of learning.

<AUGUST 1534>

The next time I went to see my father after your letter arrived, I thought it both desirable and necessary to show it to him. Desirable, in that he might see thereby the labor of love you undertook for him. And necessary, in that he might perceive thereby that if he stands firm in this scruple of his conscience (as it is at least called by many who are his friends and wise), all his friends that seem most able to do him good either will end up forsaking him or perhaps not actually be able to do him any good at all.

And so, the next time I was with him after receiving your letter, first I talked with him a while about his physical ailments, both his chronic chest pains and his recent problems with kidney stones, and also about the cramps that grip him in his legs some nights, and I found by what he said that they were not much worse, but were about the same as before, sometimes very bad and sometimes giving him little trouble. At that time I found him not in pain and (as much as one in his situation could be) fairly well disposed, once we had said our seven psalms and the litany, to sit and talk and have a good time. So I began first with other things, about how well my mother is holding up and the good attitudes of my brother and all my sisters, how they are disposing themselves every day more and more to set little by the world and to draw more and more to God, and I told him that his household, his neighbors, and other good friends out there are diligently remembering him in their prayers. And then I added this: "Good Father, I pray to God that their prayers and ours, and your own with them, may procure from God the grace that in this great matter (because of which you are in this trouble, on account of which so also are all of us who love you), you may take, soon, a way that while being pleasing to God will also content and please the King—whom you have always found so singularly gracious to you that if you should stubbornly refuse to do what would please him when you could do it without displeasing God (which many great, wise, and very learned men say you could in this thing), it would both be a great blot on your honor, in every wise man's opinion, and, as I myself have heard some say (some that you yourself have always taken for very learned and good), put your soul in danger too. But that point, Father, I will not be so bold as to dispute upon, since I trust in God and your good disposition that you will surely look at that. And your learning I know to be such that I know well you can.

"But there is one thing which I and your other loved ones find and perceive out there which needs to be brought to your attention, because otherwise you may, to your great peril, mistakenly hope for less harm (for as for good, I well know that with regard to this matter you are not expecting any in this world) than I am terribly afraid is likely to happen to you. For I assure you, Father, I have recently received a letter from my sister Alington by which I can well see that if you do not change your mind, you are likely to lose all those friends that are able to do you any good. Or that if you do not lose their good wills, you will at least lose the effect of them, for any good that they will be able to do you."

With this my father smiled at me and said, "What, mistress Eve (as I called you the first time you came), has my daughter Alington played the serpent with you, and with a letter set you at work to come tempt your father again, and for the love that you bear him, labor to make him swear against his conscience, and so send him to the devil?" And after that he looked sad again, and said to me earnestly, "Daughter Margaret, the two of us have talked of this thing more than two or three times, and the same story, in effect, that you're telling me now, and the same fear too, you have told me twice before. And I have twice answered you, too, that if in this matter it were possible for me to do the thing that might content the King's Grace without God thereby being offended, there is no man who has taken this oath already who has done so more gladly than I would—as he that considers himself more deeply bound to the King's Highness for his most singular bounty, many ways shown and expressed, than all the rest of them. But since, my conscience remaining unchanged, I can in no way do it, and since for the instruction of my conscience I have not looked into this matter lightly, but have for many years given it serious study and consideration, and never yet have been able to see or hear anything, nor think I ever will, that could induce my own mind to think otherwise than I do, I have no way out of the bind that God has me in: that I must either mortally displease him or else endure whatever worldly harm he will for my other sins, under name of this thing, let happen to me. Of which (as I have also told you before now) I have, before I came here, not failed to think of and ponder the very worst and absolute most that can possibly happen. And although I know full well my own frailty and the natural faintness of my own heart, if I had not yet trusted that God would give me strength rather to endure all things than to offend him by blasphemously swearing against my own conscience, you can be very sure I would not have come here. And since in this matter I look only to God, it matters little to me if men call it as it pleases them and say it is not a matter of conscience but just a foolish scruple."

At this last word I took advantage of a good opportunity and said to him this: "Really and truly, Father, for my part, neither do I nor could it become me to question either your good disposition or your learning. But since you speak of what some call only a scruple, I must tell you that, as you will see by my sister's letter, one of the greatest dignitaries in this realm, and a learned man too, and (as I dare say you yourself will think when you find out who he is, and as you have already very effectively proved him) your tender friend and very specially good lord, accounts your problem of conscience in this matter for nothing but a scruple, and you can be sure he says it in good faith and gives no little reason. For he says that whereas you say your conscience moves you to this, all the nobles of this realm, and almost all other men too, are boldly going forth with the contrary, with no hesitation, excepting only yourself and one other man [i.e., Bishop John Fisher]—who is very good, and very learned too, yet I believe few who love you would advise you to rely on his mind alone, against all other men."

And with this I gave him your letter, that he might see that what I said was not something I made up, but was said by this person whom he much loves and highly esteems. Then he read over your letter, and when he came to the end, he began it afresh and read it over again. And he did this in no kind of hurry, but took his time and emphasized every word.

After that he paused, and then he said this: "Indeed, daughter Margaret, I find my daughter Alington just as I have always found her and, I trust, always will—as naturally watching out for me as you who are my own. Of course, I truly take her for my own too, since I married her mother and have brought her up from childhood as I brought you up, both in other things and in learning, in which, I thank God, she is now finding some fruit. She is bringing up very virtuously and well her own children, of whom God, I thank him, has sent her a good supply. May our Lord safeguard them and send her much joy of them and of my good son, her gentle husband, too, and have mercy on the soul of my other good son, her first husband. I pray daily (please write her so) for them all.

"In this matter she has been very much herself, acting wisely and like a true daughter toward me. And at the end of her letter she gives as good counsel as any man with any sense would wish for. God give me the grace to follow it, and God reward her for it.

"Now, daughter Margaret, as for my Lord, I not only think but also have found that he is undoubtedly my exceptionally good lord. And in my other business, concerning the poor nun, as my case was good and blameless, so in it was he my good lord, and Master Secretary [i.e., Thomas Cromwell] my good master too. For which I shall never cease to pray faithfully for them both. Upon my honor, I pray for them daily as I do for myself. And if at any time it should happen (which I trust in God it never will) that I be found other than a man true to my king, let them never favor me, neither of them. Nor, in truth, could it become them to do so any more than they do.

"But in this matter, Meg, to tell the truth between you and me, my Lord's Aesop fables do not greatly move me. But as his Wisdom for his pastime cheerfully told them to my own daughter, so I for my pastime will answer them to you, Meg, another daughter of mine.

"The first fable, the one about the rain that washed away the wits of all who stayed outside when it fell, I have often heard before. It was a tale told so often among the King's Council by my Lord Cardinal [Thomas Wolsey], when his Grace was chancellor, that I could not easily forget it. For in truth, in times past, when dissension began to come up between the Emperor and the French king in such a way that they were likely to, and did indeed, go to war, there were in the Council here sometimes different opinions. Some were of the mind that they thought it would be wise for us to sit still and leave them alone. But ever against that way of thinking, my Lord used this fable of those wise men who, because they did not want to be washed with the rain that would make all the people fools, went themselves into caves and hid themselves under the ground. But once the rain had made all the rest fools, and these men came out of their caves wanting to utter their wisdom, the fools agreed together against them and there and then soundly beat them. And so, said his Grace, if we were to be so wise as to sit in peace while the fools fought, they would not fail afterwards to make peace and agree among themselves and eventually all fall upon us.

"I will not dispute his Grace's counsel, and I trust we never made war but as reason would dictate. But yet his telling of this fable did in his day help the King and the realm to spend many a fair penny. But that business is over and his Grace is gone, God rest his soul.

"And therefore I shall come now to this Aesop's fable as my Lord so cheerily laid it out for me. If those wise men, Meg, when the rain was gone and they came outside, where they found all men fools, wished that they too were fools just because they could not rule them, then it would seem that the fools' rain was so severe a shower that even through the ground it sank into their caves and poured down upon their heads and wet them to the skin, and made them more noodle-headed than those that stayed outside. For if they'd had any sense, they might well have seen that if they had been fools too, that would not have sufficed to make them rulers over the other fools, no more than the other fools over them, and that of so many fools, not all could be rulers. Now, when they longed so badly to bear a rule among fools that, so that they could, they would have been glad to lose their good sense and be fools too, the fools' rain had washed them fairly well. Although, to tell the truth, if before the rain came they thought that all the rest would turn into fools, and they were then either so foolish that they wanted to, or so crazy as to think that they would, being so few, rule so many fools, and did not have sense enough to realize that there are none so unruly as they that lack sense and are fools, then these wise men were stark fools before the rain came.

"Anyway, daughter Roper, whom my Lord takes here for the wise men, and whom he means by the fools, I cannot very well guess; I cannot well read such riddles. For to adapt what Davus says in Terence, '*Non sum Oedipus*'—you're quite familiar with this, I may say—I'll make this, '*Non sum Oedipus, sed Morus*' [i.e., I am not Oedipus, but More], which name of mine, what it means in Greek, I need not tell you. But I trust my Lord reckons me among the fools, and so I reckon myself, as my name is in Greek. And I find, I thank God, not a few reasons why I should indeed.

"But among those that long to be rulers—that is something that certainly God and my own conscience clearly know no man can rightly number and reckon me. And I suppose every other man's conscience can tell him the same, since it is so well known that, of the King's great goodness, I was one of the greatest rulers in this noble realm, and that, at my own great effort, I was by his great goodness discharged. But whomever my Lord means the wise men to stand for, and whomever he means by the fools, and whoever longs for the rule, and whoever longs for none, I beg our Lord to make us all so wise as that we may, every one of us here, so wisely rule ourselves in this time of tears, this vale of misery, this plain wretched world—in which, as Boethius says [*Consolation of Philosophy* 2.Pro.6], for one man to be proud that he bears rule over other men is much as if one mouse were to be proud to bear a rule over other mice in a barn—may God, I say, give us the grace to rule ourselves so wisely here that when we shall depart posthaste to meet the great Spouse, we shall not be taken asleep and for lack of light in our lanterns shut out of heaven with the five foolish virgins [Matt 25:1–13].

"The second fable, Margaret, seems not to be Aesop's. Since it has to do with confession, it would seem to have been invented after Christendom began. For in Greece before Christ's days they did not make use of confession, no more the people then than the beasts now. And Aesop was a Greek, and died long before Christ was born.

"But so what? Who made up the fable makes little difference. Nor do I envy Aesop for his getting the credit. But surely it is somewhat too subtle for me. For whom his Lordship means by the lion and the wolf, the both of which confessed to destroying and devouring all that they could get their hands on, and one of which enlarged his conscience as he pleased in the interpretation of his penance, or whom he supposes to be the good, discerning confessor that imposed on the one a small penance and the other none at all—none of these things can I tell. But as for the foolish, scrupulous ass, that had so sore a conscience on account of taking a straw for hunger out of his master's shoe, my Lord's other words about my scruple make clear that his Lordship teasingly meant by that me—signifying (as it seems by that similitude) that on account of over-conscientiousness and foolishness, my scrupulous conscience is taking for a huge danger to my soul something that my Lordship thinks would in reality be but a trifle: namely, if I were to take this oath. And I well suppose, Margaret, as you told me just now, that so think many more besides—clergy as

well as lay people—including even some whom, for their learning and their virtue, I myself hold in not a little esteem. And yet,
although I suppose this to be true, I do not believe very surely
even that everyone who says so actually thinks so. But even if they
did, daughter, that would not make much difference to me—not
even if I should see my Lord of Rochester [Bishop Fisher] say the
same and take the oath himself, right in front of me.

"For since you told me just now that those who love me do
not think it advisable that, against all other men, I should rely
on his mind alone, let me assure you, daughter, that no more
do I. For although it is very true that I have him in that reverent an estimation that I reckon not one man in this realm fit to
be matched and compared with him in wisdom, learning, and
long-proved virtue put together, yet the fact that in this matter
I was not led by him appears very well and plainly both in that I
refused the oath before it was presented to him and also in that
he might have been content to take that oath (as I gathered later
by you, when you suggested that I do the same) either to a somewhat further extent or in some other manner than I ever thought
of doing.

"Truly, daughter, I never intend—God being my good
lord—to pin my soul to another man's back, not even if he's the
best man I know who is alive today; for I do not know where he
might happen to carry it. There is no man living of whom, while
he is still living, I can make myself sure. Some might do something
for favor, and some might do it for fear, and so they might carry
my soul a wrong way. And some might happen to frame themselves a conscience and think that as long as they did it for fear,
God would forgive it. And some may perhaps think that they will
repent and be absolved of it, and so God will remit it. And some
may perhaps be thinking that if they say one thing while thinking the contrary, God more regards their heart than their tongue,
and that therefore their oath goes by what they think and not by

what they say, as a woman reasoned once. I believe, daughter, you were nearby. But honestly, Margaret, I can use no such ploys [i.e., mental reservation] in so great a matter. Just as, if my own conscience permitted me to, I would not refrain from doing it even if other men refused to, so also even if others do not refuse to do it, I dare not, my own conscience being against it. If I had, as I told you, looked but lightly into the matter, I would have reason to fear. But by now I have looked into it so much and so long that I intend at the least to have no less regard for my soul than once did a poor honest countryman, named Company, for his."

And with this he told me a story—I think I can hardly tell it again to you, because it involves some legal terms and proceedings. But as far as I can recall, my father's story was this. There is a court that as a matter of course is set up at every fair, to do justice in such things as happen within that fair. This court has a pretty funny name—I can't think of it, but it begins with "pie," and the rest goes, I think, much like the name of a knight that I have met (and you too, I believe, for he has been at my father's often before this, at times when you were there), a fairly tall, dark-complexioned man, his name was Sir William Pounder. But never mind, let the name of the court go for now, or call it, if you want, a court of "pie Sir William Pounder" [i.e., the Court of Piepowder, held at fairs and markets]. But look, here was what happened. Once upon a time, at such a court held at Bartholomew Fair, there was an escheator from London [i.e., a government official in charge of confiscating forfeited property]. This escheator arrested an outlaw and seized the goods that he had brought into the fair, getting him out of the fair by a trick. The man who was arrested and had his goods seized was a Northerner. By way of friends of his, he caused the escheator at the fair to be arrested upon some charge, I don't know what, and so he was brought before the judge of the court of pie Sir William Pounder, and in the end had to go through a certain proceeding in which he was tried by an inquest of twelve men—a jury, as I remember they call it, or else a perjury.

Now the clothier, through his friendship with the officials, had found the means to have the inquest almost all made up of Northerners who had had their booths standing there at the fair. Now it came to the last day of the trial, in the afternoon. Having heard both parties, and their lawyers, tell their sides of the story at the bar, the twelve men were taken from the courtroom to a place where they could talk and discuss and agree upon the sentence. No, let me get my terms a little more accurate: I believe the judge gives the sentence and the jury's statement is called a verdict. Well, scarcely had they come in together when the Northerners were agreed, and practically all the others too, to convict our London escheator. They thought they needed no more proof that he had done wrong than just the mere name of his occupation. But then there was, as the devil would have it, this honest man from another region, the man called Company. And because the fellow seemed but a fool and sat still and said nothing, they took no account of him, but said, "We are agreed now. Come, let's go give our verdict."

Then, when the poor fellow saw that they were in such a hurry, and that his mind was going not at all the way theirs were (if their minds were going the way they said), he begged them to wait and discuss the matter and give him a reason whereby he might think as they did. When he should do so, he would be glad to go along with them; but otherwise, he said, they must pardon him, for since he had a soul of his own to keep, as did they, he must say as he thought for his, as they must for theirs.

When they heard this, they were half angry with him. "What, good fellow," said one of the Northerners, "what's the matter with you? Are there not eleven of us here and you just one, all alone, all the rest of us in agreement? What's holding you back? What is your name, good fellow?" "Sirs," he said, "my name is Company."

"Company," they said, "now by your word, good fellow, play then the good companion. Come along with us on that basis; go ahead, just as good company."

"I wish to God, good sirs," the man replied, "that there was no more to it than that. But, now, when we depart and come before God, and he sends you to heaven for doing according to your conscience, and me to the devil for doing against mine by going along, at your request here, for the sake of companionship, now, by God, Master Dickenson"—that was the name of one of the Northerners—"if I then say to all of you, 'Sirs, I went once for companionship's sake with you, for which reason I am going now to hell; now it's your turn to play good fellows with me; as I went with you then to keep you good company, so some of you go with me now, to keep me good company,' would you go, Master Dickenson? No, no, by our Lady, nor never a one of you all. And therefore you must excuse me from going along with you unless I can think in the matter as you do. I dare not in such a matter go along for good company. For the passage of my poor soul passes all good company."

And when my father had told me this story, he then said: "I ask you now, good Margaret, to tell me this. Would you wish your poor father, who is at least somewhat learned, to have less regard for the peril of his soul than that honorable unlearned man did for his? I do not meddle, as well you know, with the conscience of any man who has taken the oath, nor do I take it upon myself to be their judge. But now, if they do well and their consciences do not trouble them, if I with my conscience to the contrary should for companionship's sake go along with them and swear as they do, then when our souls later on shall pass out of this world and stand in judgment at the bar before the high Judge, if he sends them to heaven and me to the devil, because I did as they did, not thinking as they thought, if I should then say (as the good man Company said), 'My old good lords and friends,' naming such-and-such a lord—yes, and perhaps some of the bishops I love best—'I swore because you swore, and went the way that you went; now do the same for me; don't let me go alone; if there be any good fellowship among us, some of you come with me,' upon my honor, Margaret, I may say to you, in confidence, here between the two of us (but let it go no further, I beg you with all my heart), that I find the friendship of this wretched world so fickle that no matter how much entreating and begging I might do, among them all I think I would find not one who would for good fellowship go to the devil with me. And so, by God, Margaret, if you think so too, I suppose it is best that for all the consideration I might have for them, even were they twice as many as they are, I have myself a consideration for my own soul."

"Surely, Father," I said, "without any scruple at all you could be bold enough, I dare say, to swear to that. But, Father, those who think you should not refuse to swear this thing that you see so many—such good men, and so learned—swear before you, do not mean that you should swear in order to bear them fellowship, or go along with them for companionship's sake. They mean, rather, that the credence that you may reasonably give to their persons on account of those aforesaid qualities should well move you to think the oath such of itself that everyone may well swear it without endangering their soul, if there is not the obstacle of their own private conscience being to the contrary, and that you well ought and have good reason to change your own conscience, conforming your own conscience to the conscience of so many others, precisely because they are such as you know they are. And since it is also commanded by a law made by Parliament, they think that you are, under pain of losing your soul, bound to change and reform your conscience, and conform your own, as I said, to other men's."

"Indeed, Margaret," replied my father, "for the part you are playing, you are not doing a bad job. But Margaret, first, as for the law of the land, though everyone born in and inhabiting it is bound to keep it in every case under pain of some temporal punishment, and in many cases also under pain of God's displeasure, still no one is bound to swear that every law is well made, or bound under pain of God's displeasure to perform any point of the law that is actually unlawful. That a law of this kind can happen to be made in any part of Christendom, I suppose no one doubts—the one exception on that point always being a General Council of the whole body of Christendom. Though it may lay down some things better than others, and some things may develop in such a way that by another law they may need to be reformed, yet to institute anything in such a way, to God's displeasure, that it could not lawfully be performed at the time that the law was made, that is something that the Spirit of God that governs his Church has never allowed, nor ever hereafter shall allow, to happen to his whole Catholic Church lawfully gathered together in a General Council. Christ has clearly promised this in Scripture.

"Now, should it so happen that in some particular part of Christendom a law is made that is such that because of some part of it, some think that the law of God cannot bear it, and some others think yes—the thing being in such a way in question that through different regions of Christendom some good and intelligent men, both of our own time and before our time, think one way, and some others of like learning and goodness think the contrary—in such a case, those who think against the law neither may swear that the law was lawfully made, their own consciences telling them the contrary, nor are bound under pain of God's displeasure to change their own consciences on that matter. This applies to any particular law made anywhere, other than by a General Council of the Church or by a general faith grown by a universal working of God throughout all Christian nations—no authority other than one of these two (barring special revelation or an express commandment from God). Where the contrary opinions of good and very learned men (as I put to you the case) have cast doubt on what is the correct understanding of Scripture, I cannot see that any other authority may lawfully command and compel anyone to change their own opinion and transfer their own conscience from the one side to the other.

"For an example of that kind of thing, I have, I believe, before now mentioned to you that whether our Blessed Lady was or was not conceived with original sin was at one time in great question among the great learned men of Christendom. And whether that has yet been determined and defined by any General Council, I do not remember. But this I remember well, that notwithstanding the fact that the feast of her conception was then celebrated in the Church (at least in some places), yet Saint Bernard—who, as his many books written in honor and praise of our Lady make clear, was of as devout an affection toward all things tending to her commendation, that he thought could well be verified or allowed, as any man then living—yet, I say, that holy, devout man was against that part of her praise. This shows up very clearly in a letter of his in which he very vehemently and with great reasoning argues against it, and does not approve of the institution of that feast either. Nor was he alone in this way of thinking. There were many other very learned men with him, and very holy men too. Now, there was on the other side the blessed, holy bishop Saint Anselm, and he not alone either, but many very learned and very virtuous men also with him. And the both of them are now holy saints in heaven, and so are many more that were on either side. And neither side there was bound to change their opinion for the other, not for any provincial council either.

"But just as after a determination by a well-assembled General Council, everyone is bound to give credence that way and conform their own conscience to the determination of the General

Council, and all those that held the contrary before cannot be blamed for that, so too, if before that determination was made, someone had against his own conscience sworn to maintain and defend the other side, that person did not fail to offend God very grievously. But, indeed, if, on the other hand, a person were on some issue to take a way all by himself, going by his mind alone, or with some few, or with however many, against an evident truth appearing by the common faith of Christendom, this conscience is very damnable, yes. Or even if it is not so fully plain and evident, yet if he sees but himself with the far smaller side thinking the one way, against the far larger side—of people as learned and as good as those who affirm the thing that he thinks—thinking and affirming the contrary, and these latter folk are such that he has no good reason not to suppose that in this matter, those who say they think against his mind are saying this for no reason other than that they think so indeed, then in all truth this is a very good reason why he should be moved, and yet not compelled, to conform his mind and conscience to theirs.

"But Margaret, for what reasons I refuse the oath, that—as I have often said to you—is something I will never tell you, neither you nor anybody else, except if the King's Highness should choose to command me. Which if his Grace did, I have before now told you how obediently I would respond at such time. But let me assure you, daughter, I have refused it, and do, for more than one reason. And whatever my reasons for refusing it, of this much I am sure—it is a well-known fact—that of those who have taken it, some of the most learned, before the oath was presented to them, clearly said and affirmed the contrary of some things that they have now sworn to in the oath, and did so then upon their honor and their learning, and not in haste or suddenly, but often and after very diligently exerting themselves to seek and find out the truth."

"That might be, Father," I said.

"And yet," he said, "since they may see more than they did before, I will not, daughter Margaret, dispute that, nor presume to judge any other person's conscience, which lies in their own heart, far out of my sight. But this I will say: that I myself never heard the reason for their change being any new, further thing found in the words of some authority than, as far as I can tell, they had looked at and, I would suppose, very seriously considered before. Now, of the very same things that they saw before, if some seem otherwise to them now than they did before, I am for their sake a great deal the gladder. But anything that I ever saw before, it still to this day seems to me just as it did. And therefore, even if they may now do otherwise than they might before, still, daughter, I may not.

"Now, as for things that some would perhaps say—such as, that I might with good reason take into less account those people's change, and be less inclined to change my conscience on account of any example of theirs, because their desire to keep the King happy and avoid his indignation, their fear of losing their worldly possessions, in consideration of the discomfort this would cause their relatives and friends, might have made them swear otherwise than they think or else frame their conscience afresh to think otherwise than they thought—any such opinion as this, I will not conceive of them. I have better hope of their goodness than to think that of them. For if such things should have turned them, the same things would likely have made me do the same; for in all honesty, I know few so fainthearted as myself. Therefore I will, Margaret, by my will, think no worse of other folk, in this thing that I do not know, than I find in myself. Rather, as I know well that it is my own conscience that causes me to refuse the oath, so I will trust in God that it was in accord with their conscience that they took the oath and swore.

"But whereas you think, Margaret, that there are so many more on that side than there are on the side that think in this thing as I think, let me assure you, for your own comfort, that this is a thought you should never have: that your father is throwing himself away so like a fool that he would risk the loss of his possessions, and perhaps his body, for no reason having to do with a danger to his soul, but, rather, is thereby putting his soul at risk too. To this I will say to you, Margaret, that with respect to some of my reasons, I have no doubt at all that, even if not in this realm, yet in the rest of Christendom, of all those very learned and virtuous men who are still living, they are not the smaller part that are of my mind. And besides that, it is, you know, quite possible that some men in this realm, too, think not so clearly the contrary as, by the oath they have taken, they have sworn that they think.

"Now, that much I say about those who are still living. But now we go to those who have died, and who are, I trust, in heaven. I am sure that it is not the smaller part of them that, all the time that they lived, thought in some of these things the way that I think now. I am also, Margaret, plenty sure of this: that of all those holy doctors and saints, who no Christian doubts are long since with God in heaven, whose books we still to this day can get our hands on, many thought in some of these things as I think now. I do not say that they all thought so, but certainly so many and of such a caliber, as well appears in their writings, that I pray that God may give me the grace that my soul may follow theirs. And still I am not telling you everything, Margaret, that I have for myself in the sure discharge of my conscience. But in conclusion, daughter Margaret, in this whole thing, as I have often told you, I do not take it upon myself either to define or to dispute in these matters, nor do I rebuke or impugn any other man's deed, nor have I ever written, nor so much as spoken to anyone, any word of criticism about anything that Parliament has passed, nor have I meddled with the conscience of any man who either thinks or says he thinks contrary to mine. But as concerns my own self, for your comfort I will say, daughter, to you, that my own conscience on this matter (I condemn no one else's) is such as may well stand with my own salvation—of that I am as sure, Meg, as that God is in heaven. And therefore, as for all the rest—goods, lands, and life too (if it should come to that)—since this conscience is sure for me, I truly trust in God that he shall strengthen me to bear the loss rather than against this conscience to take the oath and put my soul in peril, since all the reasons I see moving other men to the contrary do not seem to me such that could make any change in my conscience."

When he saw me sitting there looking very sad at this—since, I promise you, sister, my heart was very heavy for the peril of his person, though in all honesty I have no fear for his soul—he smiled at me and said, "What now, daughter Margaret? What now, mother Eve? Where is your mind now? Is it not musing with some serpent in your breast upon some new line of persuasion by which to offer father Adam the apple yet once again?"

"Truly, Father," I said, "I can go no further. I am, as I believe Cressida says in Chaucer, 'come to Dulcarnon, even at my wit's end' [*Troilus and Criseyde* 3.929–31]. For since in this matter the example of so many wise men cannot move you, I can't see what more I could say, unless I should try to persuade you with the argument that Master Harry Patenson [i.e., the More family fool] came up with. For one day he came across one of our men, and when he asked where you were, and heard that you were still in the Tower, he actually got angry with you, and said, 'Why? What's wrong with him, that he will not take that oath? Why should he hesitate to take it? I myself have taken it.' And so, in all truthfulness, I can now go no further either, after your taking so many wise men for no example, unless I should say like Master Harry, 'Why should you refuse to take the oath, Father? For I myself have taken it.'"

At this he laughed and said, "That was like Eve too, for she offered Adam no worse fruit than she had eaten herself."

"But yet, Father," I said, "really and truly, I am terribly afraid that this matter will bring you into dreadfully deep trouble. You well know, since I mentioned it to you, that Master Secretary sent you word, as your true friend, to remember that Parliament is still in session."

"Margaret," said my father, "I thank him with all my heart. But as I explained to you then, I have not failed to think about that. And although I know well that if they were to make a law designed to do me any harm, that law could never be lawful, and I trust that God will so keep me in grace that concerning my duty to my king, no man will be able to hurt me without doing me wrong (and then, as I told you, this is like a riddle, a case in which a man may lose his head and not be harmed), and notwithstanding also that I have good hope that God will never allow so good and wise a king to requite in such a way the long service of his true, faithful servant, yet, since there is nothing that couldn't possibly happen, I do not forget in this matter the counsel of Christ in the Gospel, that before beginning to build this castle for the safeguarding of my own soul, I should sit and calculate what the cost could be. I counted, Margaret, you can be very sure, during many a restless night, while my wife slept and thought I did too, all the perils that could possibly come upon me. I went so far that I am sure there can come nothing more than what I thought of. And in thinking this through, daughter, I did have a very heavy heart. But yet, I thank our Lord, for all that, I never thought of changing my mind, even should the very worst happen to me that my fear ran upon."

"No, Father," I said, "to think about something that could happen is not the same as to see a thing that will happen, as you would—our Lord save you—if it should go that way. And then you perhaps would think what you do not think now, but by then it might be too late."

"Too late, daughter Margaret?" said my father. "I beg our Lord that if ever I make such a change, it will indeed be too late. For well I know the change could not be good for my soul—that change, I say, that would be caused only by fear. And therefore I pray to God that in this world I never benefit from such a change. For, however much pain I may have to take here, I at least will on that account have the less to take when I am gone. And even if I now knew for sure that I would afterwards faint and fall and out of fear take the oath, I would still wish to take the pain that comes of refusing at first, for so I would have the better hope of being given the grace to rise again.

"And even though, Margaret, I know well that my wickedness has been such that I know I well deserve for God to let me slip, yet I cannot but trust in his merciful goodness, that as his grace has strengthened me up till now, and has made me content in my heart to lose goods, land, and life too rather than swear against my conscience, and has also put in the King that good and gracious a mind toward me that as yet he has taken from me nothing but my liberty (by which, so help me God, his Grace has done me such great good, by the spiritual profit that I trust I am taking from it, that among all the great benefits he has heaped so thickly upon me, I reckon upon my faith my imprisonment the very greatest)—I therefore cannot, I say, doubt that by the grace of God, either he shall conserve and keep the King in that gracious intention still to do me no harm, or else, if it be his pleasure that for my other sins I shall suffer things that I seemingly shall not deserve, his grace shall give me the strength to take it docilely, and maybe somewhat gladly too, whereby his high goodness shall—by the merits of his bitter passion joined to, and far surmounting in merit for me, all that I can suffer myself—make it serve for release of my pain in purgatory, and over that for increase of some reward in heaven.

"Mistrust him, Meg, I will not, even if I feel myself faint. Yes, and even if I should feel my fear rise to the point of overthrowing me, I shall yet remember how Saint Peter, with a blast of wind, began to sink for his faint faith, and I shall do as he did—call upon Christ and beg him to help. And then I trust he shall set his holy hand on me, and in the stormy seas, hold me up from drowning. Yes, and if he suffers me to play Saint Peter further, and fall flat on my face and swear and forswear too—which our Lord, for his tender passion, keep me from, and if it does happen, let me lose and never win anything by—yet afterwards I shall trust that in his goodness he will look upon me tenderly and compassionately, as he did upon Saint Peter, and make me stand up again and confess the truth of my conscience afresh and endure here the shame and the harm of my own failing.

"And finally, Margaret, this I know well: that except by my own fault he will not let me be lost. I shall therefore with good hope commit myself wholly to him. And if he allows me to perish eternally for my failings, then I still shall serve for a praise of his justice. But in all honesty, Meg, I trust that his tender pity shall keep my poor soul safe and make me praise his mercy.

"And therefore, my own good daughter, never let your mind be troubled over anything that ever shall happen to me in this world. Nothing can come but what God wills. And I make myself very sure that whatever that may be, no matter how bad it seems, it will indeed be the best. And with this, my good child, I beg you with all my heart—you and all your sisters and my sons too—to be of comfort and service to your good mother, my wife. And of your good husband's dispositions, I have no doubt whatsoever. Give my regards to them all, and to my good daughter Alington, and to all my other relatives—sisters, nieces, nephews, in-laws—and all our servants, man, woman, and child, and all my good neighbors and our acquaintances out there. And with all my heart I beg both you and them to serve God and be merry and rejoice in him. And if anything happens to me that you would hate to happen, pray to God for me, but do not let yourself be troubled, as I shall wholeheartedly pray for us all that we may one day meet together in heaven, where we shall make merry forever and never have trouble again."

Letter 70

To Rev. Dr. Nicholas Wilson [207]

More sent letters 70 and 71 to Doctor Nicholas Wilson (d. 1548), when both men were imprisoned in the Tower of London. A friend of More and Fisher, Wilson had been chaplain and confessor to King Henry. In 1533, however, he spoke out against the divorce and argued that the pope had been right in the first place to grant Henry a dispensation to marry Catherine in 1509; Wilson then refused to take the Oath in 1534 and was imprisoned along with More and Fisher, though he would in time take the oath and eventually receive a royal pardon in 1537 (*ODNB*).

In this letter, More discerns that his friend intends to take the Oath, but More nevertheless reiterates his duty to follow the clear prompting and regulation of his own conscience. He hopes he will finally have "the grace to do according to mine own conscience" in the matter of the Oath.

TOWER OF LONDON

1534

Our Lord be your comfort and whereas I perceive by sundry means that you have promised to swear the Oath, I beseech our Lord give you thereof good luck. I never gave any man counsel to the contrary in my days nor never used any ways to put any scruple in other folks' conscience concerning the matter. And whereas I perceive that you would gladly know what I intend to do, you know well that I told you when we were both abroad that I would therein neither know your mind nor no man's else, nor you nor no man else should therein know mine, for I would be no part taker with no man nor of truth never I will, but leaving every other man to their own conscience myself will with good grace follow mine. For against mine own to swear were peril of my damnation and what mine own shall be tomorrow myself cannot be sure and whether I shall have finally the grace to do according to mine own conscience or not hangs in God's goodness and not in mine, to whom I beseech you heartily remember me in your devout prayers and I shall and daily do remember you in mine, such as they be, and as long as my poor short life shall last, any thing that I have, your part shall be therein.

Letter 71

To Rev. Dr. Nicholas Wilson [208]

The still-imprisoned Wilson seeks comfort from More on account of his troubled conscience and "great heaviness of heart" as he struggles with the question of whether or not to take the oath. More invokes their past conversations and shared searching of scripture and tradition in regard to the "great matter" and subsequent controversies of King Henry. More reminds Wilson of their deep communing on these questions, and of Wilson's well-known care for Henry's body, soul, and honor in the past. More again invokes the "commandment" and "gracious lesson" Henry taught him when More first entered the king's service—specifically, that More should "look first unto God and after God unto him." He then reiterates his desire to remain silent, and thus safe under the law, in the great matter of the Oath. For a full elaboration of the many scriptural and patristic texts More touches on in this letter, see Silva's excellent commentary, 177–81.

TOWER OF LONDON
1534

MASTER WILSON IN MY RIGHT HEARTY WISE I
RECOMMEND ME TO YOU:

And very sorry am I to see you, beside the trouble that you be in by this imprisonment with loss of liberty, goods, revenues of your livelihood and comfort of your friends' company, fallen also into such agony and vexation of mind through doubts falling in your mind that diversely to and fro toss and trouble your conscience to your great heaviness of heart as I (to no little grief of mine own mind for your sake) perceive. And so much am I for you, good Master Doctor, the more sorry for that it lies not in me to give you such kind of comfort as meseems you somewhat desire and look for at mine hand.

For whereas you would somewhat hear of my mind in your doubts, I am a man at this day very little meet therefore. For this you know well, good Master Doctor, that at such time as the matter came in such manner in question as mine opinion was asked therein amongst other and yet you made privy thereunto before me, you remember well that at that time you and I many things talked together thereof. And by all the time after by which I did at the King's gracious commandment both seek out and read and comment with all such as I knew made privy to the matter to perceive what I might therein upon both sides and by indifferent weighing of everything as near as my poor wit and learning would serve to see to which side my conscience could incline, and as my own mind should give me so to make his Highness report which way myself should hap to think therein. For other commandment had I never of his Grace in good faith, saving that this knot his Highness added thereto that I should therein look first unto God and after God unto him, which word was also the first lesson that his Grace gave me what time I came first into his noble service and neither a more indifferent commandment nor a more gracious lesson could there in my mind never King give his counselor or any his other servant.

But as I began to tell you by all this long time, I cannot now tell how many years, of all those that I talked with of the matter and with whom I most conferred those places of Scripture and of the old holy Doctors that touched either the one side or the other, with the councils and laws on either side, that speak thereof also, the most, as I trust you know well, was yourself. For with no man communed I so much and so often thereof as with you, both for your substantial learning and for your mature judgment, and for that I well perceived ever in you that no man had or lightly could have a more faithful respect unto the King's honor and surety both of body and soul than I ever saw that you had.

And yet among many other things which I well liked in you, one specially was that I well perceived in the thing that the King's Grace did put you in trust with, your substantial secret manner. For where I had heard (I know not now of whom) that you had written his Highness a book of that matter from Paris before, yet in all those years of our long acquaintance and often talking and reasoning upon the thing, I never heard you so much as make once any mention of that book. But else (except there were any other things in that book that you peradventure thought not on) I suppose that all that ever came to your mind, that might in the matter make for the one side or the other comprised either in the Scripture or in the old ancient Doctors, I verily think in my mind that you did communicate with me and I likewise with you and at the least wise I remember well that of those points which you call now newly to your remembrance there was none at that time forgotten.

I remember well also by your often conference in the matter that by all the time in which I studied about it, you and I were in every point both twain of one opinion and remember well that the laws and councils and the words of Saint Augustine's *De Civitate Dei* and the epistle of Saint Ambrose, *Ad Paternum*, and the epistle of Saint Basil translated out of Greek and the writing of Saint Gregory you and I read together and over that the places of the Scripture self both in Leviticus and in the Deuteronomy and in the Gospel and in Saint Paul's epistles and over this in that other place of Saint Augustine that you remember now and beside that other places of his, wherein he properly touches the matter expressly with the words of Saint Jerome and of Saint Chrysostom too, and I cannot now remember of how many more. But I verily think that on your part, and I am very sure that on my part, albeit that it had been peradventure over long to show and read with you every man's book that I read by myself, whereto the parties peradventure that trusted me therewith gave me no leave to show their books further as you peradventure used the like manner with me; yet in good faith as it was of reason my part in that case to do, you and I having both one commandment indifferently to consider the matter, everything of Scripture and of the Doctors I faithfully communed with you and as I suppose verily so did you with me too, so that of me, good Master Doctor, though I had all the points as ripe in mind now as I had then and had still all the books about me that I then had, and were as willing to meddle in the matter as any man could be, yet could you now no new thing hear of me, more than you have, I think, heard often before, nor I think I of you neither.

But now stands it with me in far other case. For afterward when I had signified unto the King's Highness mine own poor opinion in the matter which his Highness very graciously took in good part and that I saw further progress in the matter wherein to do his Grace service to his pleasure I could not, and anything meddle against his pleasure I would not, I determined utterly with myself to discharge my mind of any farther studying or musing of the matter and thereupon I sent home again such books as I had saving that some I burned by the consent of the owner that was minded as myself was no more to meddle of the matter, and therefore now good Master Doctor I could not be sufficient and able to reason those points again though I were minded thereto since many things are out of my mind which I never purpose to look for again nor though I would were never like to find again while I live. Besides this, all that ever I looked for was, you know well, concerning two or three questions to be pondered and weighed by the study of scripture and the interpreters of the same, save for somewhat that has been touched in the same by the canon laws of the Church.

But then were there at that time in the matter other things more, divers faults found in the bull of the dispensation, by which the King's Council learned in the spiritual law reckoned the bull vicious, partly for untrue suggestion, partly by reason of insufficient suggestion. Now concerning those points I never meddled. For I neither understand the doctors of the law nor well can turn their books. And many things have there since in this great matter grown in question wherein I neither am sufficiently learned in the law nor full informed of the fact and therefore I am not he that either murmur or grudge, make assertions, hold opinions or keep disputations in the matter, but like the King's true, poor, humble subject daily pray for the preservation of his Grace, and the Queen's Grace and their noble issue and of all the realm, without harm doing or intending, I thank our Lord, unto any man living.

Finally as touching the oath, the causes for which I refused it, no man know what they be for they be secret in mine own conscience, some other peradventure, than those that other men would think, and such as I never disclosed unto any man yet nor never intend to do while I live. Finally as I said unto you, before the oath offered unto us when we met in London at adventure I would be no part taker in the matter but for mine own self follow mine own conscience, for which myself must make answer unto God, and shall leave every other man to his own, so say to you still and I dare say further that no more never intended you neither. Many things every man learned know well there are, in which every man is at liberty without peril of damnation to think which way him list till the one part be determined for necessary to be believed by a general council, and I am not he that take upon me to define or determine of what kind or nature everything is that the oath contains, nor am so bold or presumptuous to blame or dispraise the conscience of other men, their truth nor their learning neither, nor I meddle with no man but of myself, nor of no man's conscience else will I meddle but of mine own. And in mine own conscience I cry God mercy, I find of mine own life, matters enough to think on.

I have lived, methinks, a long life and now neither I look nor I long to live much longer. I have since I came in the Tower looked once or twice to have given up my ghost ere this and in good faith mine heart waxed the lighter with hope thereof. Yet forget I not that I have a long reckoning and a great to give account of, but I put my trust in God and in the merits of his bitter passion, and I beseech him give me and keep me the mind to long to be out of this world and to be with him. For I can never but trust that who so long to be with him shall be welcome to him and on the other side my mind gives me verily that any that ever shall come to him shall full heartily wish to be with him or ever he shall come at him. And I beseech him heartily to set your heart at such rest and quiet as may be to his pleasure and eternal weal of your soul and so I verily trust that he shortly shall and shall also if it be his pleasure incline the King's noble heart to be gracious and favorable to you and me both, since we be both twain of true faithful mind unto him, whether we be in this matter of one mind both, or of diverse. *Sicut diuisiones aquarum, ita cor regis in manu Domini, quocunque voluerit, inclinabit illud* [i.e., "The king's heart is a stream of water in the hand of the Lord; he turns it wherever he will" (Prov 21:1)]. And if the pleasure of God be on any of us both otherwise to dispose, I need to give you no counsel nor advice.

But for myself I most humbly beseech him to give me the grace in such wise patiently to conform my mind unto his high pleasure therein, that after the troublous storm of this my tempestuous time his great mercy may conduct me into the sure haven of the joyful bliss of heaven, and after at his further pleasure (if I have any) all mine enemies too, for there shall we love together well enough and I thank our Lord for my part so do I here too. Be not angry now though I pray not like for you; you be sure enough I would my friends fare no worse than they, nor yet they, so help me God, no worse than myself.

For our Lord's sake, good Master Wilson, pray for me for I pray for you daily and sometime when I would be sorry but if I thought you were asleep. Comfort yourself, good Master Doctor, with remembering God's great mercy and the King's accustomed goodness, and by my troth I think that all his Grace's Council favors you in their hearts. I cannot judge in my mind any one of them so evil as to be of the mind that you should do otherwise than well. And for conclusion in God is all. *Spes non confundit* [i.e., "hope does not disappoint" (Rom 5:5)]. I pray you pardon my scribbling for I cannot always so well endure to write as I might sometime. And I pray you when ye see time convenient at your pleasure, send me this rude bill again. *Quia quanquam nihil inest mali, tamen propter ministrum nolim rescire* [i.e "though there is nothing evil in it, still, on account of the minister, I would not want to bring it to light"].

Letter 72

From Margaret Roper [209]

Meg Roper wrote this letter of thanks to her father for his recent coal-quilled letter, "written in letters of gold" in Meg's judgment. Meg also recalls that More had prepared his family for the worst that might befall him beforehand. As William Roper relates in his *Life of Sir Thomas More*, "[More] showed unto them afore what trouble might after fall unto him, wherewith and the like virtuous talk he had so long before his trouble encouraged them, that when he after fell into trouble indeed, his trouble to them was a great deal the less. *Quia spicula previsa minus laedunt* [i.e., because spears foreseen hurt less]." More's response follows in Letter 73.

1534

Mine own most entirely beloved father, I think myself never able to give you sufficient thanks, for the inestimable comfort my poor heart received in the reading of your most loving and godly letter, representing to me the clear shining brightness of your soul, the pure temple of the holy spirit of God, which I doubt not shall perpetually rest in you and you in him. Father, if all the world had been given to me, as I be saved, it had been a small pleasure, in comparison with the pleasure I conceived of the treasure of your letter, which though it were written with a coal is worthy in mine opinion to be written in letters of gold.

Father, what moved them to shut you up again? We can nothing hear. But surely I conjecture that when they considered that you were of so temperate mind, that you were contented to abide there all your life with such liberty, they thought it were never possible to incline you to their will, except it were by restraining you from the church, and the company of my good mother, your dear wife, and us your children and beadsfolk. But, father, this chance was not strange to you. For I shall not forget how you told us when we were with you in the garden, that these things were like enough to chance you shortly after. Father, I have many times rehearsed to mine own comfort, and divers others, your fashion and words you had to us when we were last with you: for which I trust, by the grace of God, to be the better while I live, and when I am departed out of this frail life, which I pray God I may pass and end in his true obedient service, after the wholesome counsel and fruitful example of living I have had (good father) of you, whom I pray God give me grace to follow: which I shall the better through the assistance of your devout prayers, the special stay of my frailty. Father I am sorry I have no longer leisure at this time to talk with you, the chief comfort of my life, I trust to have occasion to write again shortly. I trust I have your daily prayer and blessing.

Your most loving obedient daughter and beadswoman Margaret Roper, which daily and hourly is bound to pray for you, for whom she prays in this wise, that our Lord of his infinite mercy give you of his heavenly comfort, and so assist you with his special grace, that you never in anything decline from his blessed will, but live and die his true obedient servant. Amen.

Letter 73

TO MARGARET ROPER [210]

In this letter, More explains to Margaret that his silence on the Oath is not obstinate and stubborn: "And now you see well, Margaret, that it is no obstinacy to leave the causes undeclared, while I could not declare them without peril." He also likens his present predicament to a strange riddle, as he did in *A Dialogue of Conscience*, that "a man may lose his head and have no harm."

Tower of London

1534

The Holy Spirit of God Be With You:

If I would with my writing (mine own good daughter) declare how much pleasure and comfort your daughterly loving letters were unto me, a peck of coals would not suffice to make me the pens. And other pens have I (good Margaret) none here: and therefore can I write you no long process, nor dare adventure good daughter, to write often.

The cause of my close keeping again did of likelihood grow of my negligent and very plain true word, which you remember. And verily where as my mind gave me (as I told you in the garden) that some such thing were likely to happen, so does my mind always give me that some folk yet think that I was not so poor as it appeared in the search, and that it may therefore happen that yet eftsoon [i.e., again] more often than once, some new sudden searches may hap to be made in every house of ours as narrowly as is possible. Which thing if ever it so should hap can make but game to us that know the truth of my poverty but if they find out my wife's gay girdle and her golden beads. Howbeit I verily believe in good faith that the King's Grace of his benign pity will take nothing from her.

I thought and yet think that it may be that I was shut up again upon some new causeless suspicion, grown peradventure upon some secret sinister information, whereby some folk haply thought that there should be found out against me some other greater things. But I thank our Lord whensoever this conjecture has fallen in my mind, the clearness of my conscience has made my heart hop for joy. For one thing am I very sure of hitherto, and trust in God's mercy to be while I live, that as often I have said unto you, I shall for anything toward my prince never take great harm, but if I take great wrong, in the sight of God, I say, howsoever it shall seem in the sight of men. For to the world, wrong may seem right sometime by false conjecturing, sometimes by false witnesses, as that good Lord said unto you, which is I dare say my very good lord in his mind, and said it of very good will.

Before the world also, my refusing of this oath is accounted an heinous offense, and my religious fear toward God is called obstinacy toward my Prince. But my Lords of the Council before whom I refused it might well perceive by the heaviness of my heart appearing well more ways than one unto them that all sturdy stubbornness whereof obstinacy grows was very far from my mind. For the clearer proof whereof, since they seemed to take for one argument of obstinacy in me that refusing of the oath, I would not declare the causes why, I offered with a full heart, that albeit I rather would endure all the pain and peril of the statute than by declaring of the causes, give any occasion of exasperation unto my most dread Sovereign Lord and Prince, yet rather than his Highness should for not disclosing the causes account me for stubborn and obstinate, I would upon such his gracious license and commandment as should discharge me of his displeasure and peril of any statute declare those points that letted [i.e., hindered] my poor conscience to receive that oath; and would over that be sworn before, that if I should after the causes disclosed and declared find them so answered as my conscience should think itself satisfied, I would thereupon swear the oath that I there refused. To this, Master Secretary answered me that though the King's Grace gave me such a license, yet it could not discharge me against the statutes in saying anything that were by them upon heinous pains prohibited. In this good warning he showed himself my special tender friend.

And now you see well, Margaret, that it is no obstinacy to leave the causes undeclared, while I could not declare them without peril. But now is it accounted great obstinacy that I refuse the oath, whatsoever my causes be, considering that of so many wiser and better men none sticked thereat [i.e., resisted it]. And Master Secretary of a great zeal that he bore unto me swore there before them a great oath that for the displeasure that he thought the King's Highness would bear me, and the suspicion that his Grace would conceive of me, which would now think in his mind that all the Nun's business was wrought and devised by me, he had liefer [i.e., rather] than I should have refused the oath that his own only son (which is a goodly young gentleman of whom our Lord send him much joy) had had his head stricken off. This word Margaret, as it was a marvelous declaration of Master Secretary's great good mind and favor toward me, so was it an heavy hearing to me that the King's Grace, my most dread Sovereign Lord, were likely to conceive such high suspicion of me and bear such grievous indignation toward me, for the thing which without the danger and peril of my poor soul lay not in my hand to help, nor does.

Now have I heard since that some say that this obstinate manner of mine in still refusing the oath shall peradventure force and drive the King's Grace to make a further law for me. I cannot let [i.e., prevent] such a law to be made. But I am very sure that if I died by such a law, I should die for that point innocent afore God. And albeit (good daughter) that I think our Lord that has the hearts of Kings in his hand would never suffer of his high goodness, so gracious a Prince, and so many honorable men, and so many good men as be in the Parliament to make such an unlawful law, as that should be if it so mishapped, yet lest I note that point unthought upon, but many times more than one revolved and cast in my mind before my coming here, both that peril and all other that might put my body in peril of death by the refusing of this oath. In devising whereupon, albeit (mine own good daughter) that I found myself (I cry God mercy) very sensual and my flesh much more shrinking from pain and from death than methought it the part of a faithful Christian man, in such a case as my conscience gave me, that in the saving of my body should stand the loss of my soul, yet I thank our Lord, that in that conflict the Spirit had in conclusion the mastery, and reason with help of faith finally concluded that for to be put to death wrongfully for doing well (as I am very sure I do, in refusing to swear against mine own conscience, being such as I am not upon peril of my soul bound to change whether my death should come without law, or by color of a law) it is a case in which a man may lose his head and yet have none harm, but instead of harm inestimable good at the hand of God.

And I thank our Lord, Meg, since I am come here I set by death every day less than other. For though a man lose of his years in this world, it is more than manifold recompensed by coming the sooner to heaven. And though it be a pain to die while a man is in health, yet see I very few that in sickness die with ease. And finally, very sure am I that whensoever the time shall come that may hap to come, God know how soon, in which I should lie sick in my death bed by nature, I shall then think that God had done much for me, if he had suffered me to die before by the color [i.e., under the specious cover] of such a law. And therefore my reason shows me, Margaret, that it were great folly for me to be sorry to come to that death, which I would after wish that I had died. Beside that, that a man may hap with less thank of God and more adventure of his soul to die as violently and as painfully by many other chances as by enemies or thieves. And therefore mine own good daughter I assure you—thanks be to God—the thinking of any such thing, albeit it has grieved me ere this, yet at this day grieves me nothing. And yet I know well for all this mine own frailty, and that Saint Peter which feared it much less than I, fell in such fear soon after that at the word of a simple girl he forsook and forswore our Savior. And therefore am I not, Meg, so mad as to warrant myself to stand. But I shall pray, and I pray thee mine own good daughter to pray with me, that it may please God that has given me this mind, to give me the grace to keep it.

And thus have I, mine own good daughter, disclosed unto you the very secret bottom of my mind, referring the order thereof only to the goodness of God, and that so fully that I assure you, Margaret, on my faith I never have prayed God to bring me hence nor deliver me from death, but referring all thing whole unto his only pleasure, as to him that sees better what is best for me than myself does [cf. 1 Sam 16:7]. Nor never longed I since I came here to set my foot in mine own house, for any desire of or pleasure of my house, but gladly would I sometime somewhat talk with my friends, and specially my wife and you that pertain to my charge. But since that God otherwise disposes, I commit all wholly to his goodness and take daily great comfort in that I perceive that you live together so charitably and so quietly; I beseech our Lord continue it. And thus, mine own good daughter, putting you finally in remembrance that albeit if the necessity so should require, I thank our Lord in this quiet and comfort is mine heart at this day, and I trust in God's goodness so shall have grace to continue, yet (as I said before) I verily trust that God shall so inspire and govern the King's heart that he shall not suffer his noble heart and courage to requite my true faithful heart and service with such extreme unlawful and uncharitable dealing, only for the displeasure that I cannot think so as other do. But his true subject will I live and die, and truly pray for him will I, both here and in the other world too.

And thus mine own good daughter have me recommended to my good bedfellow [Lady Alice] and all my children, men, women and all, with all your babes and your nurses and all the maids and all the servants, and all our kin, and all our other friends abroad. And I beseech our Lord to save them all and keep them. And I pray you all pray for me, and I shall pray for you all. And take no thought for me whatsoever you shall hap to hear, but be merry in God.

Thomas More

Letter 74

To Margaret Roper [211]

Tower of London
1534

THE HOLY SPIRIT OF GOD BE WITH YOU:

Your daughterly loving letter, my dearly beloved child, was and is, I faithfully assure you, much more inward comfort unto me than my pen can well express you, for divers things that I marked therein but of all things most especially, for that God of his high goodness gives you the grace to consider the incomparable difference between the wretched estate of this present life and the wealthy state of the life to come, for them that die in God, and to pray God in such a good Christian fashion that it may please him (it does me good here to rehearse your own words) "of his tender pity so firmly to rest our love in him, with little regard of this world, and so to flee sin and embrace virtue, that we may say with Saint Paul, *Mihi viuere Christus est et mori luchrum* [i.e., "for to me to live is Christ, and to die is gain" (Phil 1.21)]. And this, *Cupio dissolui et esse cum Christo* [i.e., "my desire is to depart and be with Christ" (Phil 1:23)]. I beseech our Lord, my dearly beloved daughter, that wholesome prayer that he has put

in your mind, it may like him to give your father the grace daily
to remember and pray, and yourself as you have written it even so
daily devoutly to kneel and pray it. For surely if God give us that,
he gives us and will give us therewith all that ever we can well
wish. And therefore good Margaret, when you pray it, pray it for
us both, and I shall on my part the like, in such manner as it shall
like our Lord to give me, poor wretch, the grace, that likewise as
in this wretched world I have been very glad of your company
and you of mine, and yet would if it might be (as natural charity binds the father and the child) so we may rejoice and enjoy
each other's company, with our other kinsfolk, allies, and friends
everlastingly in the glorious bliss of heaven, and in the meantime
with good counsel and prayer each help other thitherward [i.e.,
heavenward, Godward].

And where you write these words of yourself, "But good
father, I wretch am far, far, farthest of all other from such point
of perfection, our Lord send me the grace to amend my life,
and continually to have an eye to mine end, without grudge of
death, which to them that die in God, is the gate of a wealthy
life to which God of his infinite mercy bring us all. Amen. Good
Father strengthen my frailty with your devout prayers." The
father of heaven must strengthen your frailty, my good daughter
and the frailty of your frail father too. And let us not doubt but
he so will, if we will not be slack in calling upon him therefore.
Of my poor prayers, such as they be, you may be bold to reckon.
For Christian charity and natural love and your very daughterly
dealing—*funiculo triplici*, as says the Scripture, *dificile rumpitur*
[i.e., "A threefold cord is not quickly broken" (Eccl 4:12)]—
both bind me and strain me thereto. And of yours I put as little
doubt.

That you fear your own frailty Marget, nothing mislikes me.
God give us both twain the grace to despair of our own self, and
whole to depend and hang upon the hope and strength of God.

The blessed apostle Saint Paul found such lack of strength in himself that in his own temptation he was fain thrice to call and cry out unto God, to take that temptation from him. And yet sped he not of his prayer, in the manner that he required. For God of his high wisdom, seeing that it was (as himself said) necessary for him to keep him from pride that else he might peradventure have fallen in, would not at his thrice praying, by and by take it from him, but suffered him to be panged in the pain and fear thereof, giving him yet at the last this comfort against his fear of falling— *Suficit tibi gratia mea* [i.e., "my grace is sufficient for you" (2 Cor 12:9)]. By which words it well seems that the temptation was so strong (whatsoever kind of temptation it was) that he was very afraid of falling, through the feebleness of resisting that he began to feel in himself. Wherefore for his comfort God answered, "*Suficit tibi gratia mea*," putting him in surety, that were he of himself never so feeble and faint, nor never so likely to fall, yet the grace of God was sufficient to keep him up and make him stand. And our Lord said further, "*Virtus in infirmitate proficitur*" [i.e., "My power is made perfect in weakness" (2 Cor 12:9)]. The more weak that man is, the more is the strength of God in his safeguard declared. And so Saint Paul said, "*Omnia possum in eo qui me confortat*" [i.e., "I can do all things in him who strengthens me" (Phil 4:13)].

Surely Meg a fainter heart than your frail father has, canst you not have. And yet I verily trust in the great mercy of God, that he shall of his goodness so stay me with his holy hand that he shall not finally suffer me to fall wretchedly from his favor. And the like trust, dear daughter, in his high goodness I verily conceive of you. And so much the more, in that there is neither of us both, but that if we call his benefits to mind and give him oft thanks for them, we may find tokens many, to give us good hope for all our manifold offenses toward him, that his great mercy, when we will heartily call therefore, shall not be withdrawn from us. And verily, my dear daughter, in this is my great comfort, that albeit I am of nature so shrinking from pain that I am almost afraid of a fillip, yet in all the agonies that I have had, whereof before my coming here (as I have showed you ere this) I have had neither small nor few, with heavy fearful heart, forecasting all such perils and painful deaths, as by any manner of possibility might after fall unto me, and in such thought lain long restless and waking, while my wife had thought I had slept, yet in any such fear and heavy pensiveness (I thank the mighty mercy of God) I never in my mind intended to consent that I would for the enduring of the uttermost do any such thing as I should in mine own conscience (for with other men's I am not a man meet to take upon me to meddle) think to be to myself, such as should damnably cast me in the displeasure of God. And this is the least point that any man may with his salvation come to, as far as I can see, and is bound if he see peril to examine his conscience surely by learning and by good counsel and be sure that his conscience be such as it may stand with his salvation, or else reform it. And if the matter be such as both the parties may stand with salvation, then on whither side his conscience falls, he is safe enough before God. But that mine own may stand with my own salvation, thereof I thank our Lord I am very sure. I beseech our Lord bring all parts to his bliss.

It is now, my good daughter, late. And therefore thus I commend you to the holy Trinity, to guide you, comfort you and direct you with his Holy Spirit, and all yours and my wife with all my children and all our other friends.

Thomas More, Knight

Letter 75

From Lady Alice More to King Henry VIII [212]

In this letter, Lady Alice implores King Henry to help More and the family. Lady Alice argues that More's silence is neither obstinate nor malicious, but of a "long continued and deep rooted scruple." Like Meg Roper, Lady Alice struggled to understand how More could endure imprisonment, the destruction of his name, the imperiling of his family, the confiscation of his goods, and finally the losing of his own life, for what appeared to be a scruple of conscience. The source of this letter is *Bruce,* Archaeologia, *XXVII* (London, 1838).

<c. Christmas 1534>

In lamentable wise, beseech your most noble Grace your most humble subjects and continual beadsfolk, the poor miserable wife and children of your true, poor, heavy subject and beadsman Sir Thomas More Knight, that whereas the same Sir Thomas being your Grace's prisoner in your Tower of London by the space of eight months and above, in great continual sickness of body and heaviness of heart, during all which space notwithstanding that the same Sir Thomas More had by refusing of the oath forfeited unto your most noble Grace all his goods and chattels and the profit of all his lands, annuities and fees that as well himself as your said beadswoman his wife should live by, yet your most gracious Highness of your most blessed disposition suffered your said beadswoman, his poor wife, to retain and keep still his moveable goods and the revenues of his lands to keep her aide husband and her poor household with.

So it is now, most gracious Sovereign, that now late by reason of a new act or twain made in this last passed prorogation of your

Parliament, not only the said former forfeiture is confirmed, but also the inheritance of all such lands and tenements as the same Sir Thomas had of your most bountiful gift, amounting to the yearly value of 60 pounds, is forfeited also. And thus—except your merciful favor be shown—your said poor beadswoman his wife, which brought fair substance to him, which is all spent in your Grace's service, is likely to be utterly undone and his poor son, one of your said humble suppliants, standing charged and bound for the payment of great sums of money due by the said Sir Thomas unto your Grace, stands in danger to be cast away and undone in this world also. But over all this, the said Sir Thomas himself, after his long, true service to his power diligently done to your Grace, is likely to be in his age hard continual sickness, for lack of comfort and good keeping, to be shortly destroyed, to the woeful heaviness and deadly discomfort of all your said sorrowful suppliants.

In consideration of the premises, for that his offence is grown not of any malice or obstinate mind, but of such a long continued and deep rooted scruple, as asset he his power to avoid and put away, it may like your most noble Majesty of your most abundant grace to remit and pardon your most grievous displeasure to the said Sir Thomas and to have tender pity and compassion upon his long distress and great heaviness, and for the tender mercy of God to deliver him out of prison and suffer him quietly to live the remnant of his life with your said poor beadswoman his wife and other of your poor suppliants his children, with only such entertainment of living as it shall like your most noble Majesty of your gracious alms and pity to appoint him. And this in the way of mercy and pity, and all your said poor beadsfolk shall daily during their lives pray to God for the preservation of your most Royal estate.

Letter 76

To Rev. Master Leder [213]

More writes to Master Leder, identified simply as "a virtuous priest" in the 1557 edition of Thomas More's *English Works*.

TOWER OF LONDON
SATURDAY 16 JANUARY 1534/5

The tale that is reported, albeit I cannot but thank you though you would it were true, yet I thank God it is a very vanity. I trust in the great goodness of God, that he shall never suffer it to be true. If my mind had been obstinate indeed I would not let for any rebuke or worldly shame plainly to confess the truth. For I purpose not to depend upon the fame of the world. But I thank our Lord that the thing that I do is not for obstinacy but for the salvation of my soul, because I cannot induce mine own mind otherwise to think than I do concerning the oath.

As for other men's consciences, I will be no judge of, nor I never advised any man neither to swear nor to refuse, but as for mine own self if ever I should mishap to receive the oath (which I trust our Lord shall never suffer me), you may reckon sure that it were expressed and extorted by duress and hard handling. For as for all the goods of this world, I thank our Lord I set not much more by than I do by dust. And I trust both that they will use no violent forcible ways, and also that if they would, God would of his grace and the rather a great deal through good folks' prayers give me strength to stand. *Fidelis Deus,* said Saint Paul, *qui non patitur vos tentari supra id quod potestis ferre, sed dat cum tentatione prouentum vt possitis sustinere* [i.e., "God is faithful, and he will not let you be tempted beyond your strength, but with the temptation will also provide the way of escape, that you may be able to endure it" (1 Cor 10:13)]. For this I am very sure, that if ever I should swear it, I should swear deadly against mine own conscience. For I am very sure in my mind that I shall never be able to change mine own conscience to the contrary; as for other men's, I will not meddle of.

It has been showed me that I am reckoned willful and obstinate because that since my coming here I have not written unto the King's Highness and by mine own writing made some suit unto his Grace. But in good faith I do not forbear it of any obstinacy, but rather of a lowly mind and a reverent, because that I see nothing that I could write but that I fear me sore that his Grace were likely rather to take displeasure with me for it than otherwise, while his Grace believes me not that my conscience is the cause but rather obstinate willfulness. But surely that my let [i.e., hindrance] is but my conscience, that knows God to whose order I commit the whole matter. *In cuius manu corda regum sunt* [i.e., "in whose hands are the heart of the king" (1 Prov 21:1)]. I beseech our Lord that all may prove as true faithful subjects to the King that have sworn as I am in my mind very sure that they be, which have refused to swear.

In haste, the Saturday the sixteenth day of January by the hand of your beadsman,

Thomas More, Knight and prisoner

Letter 77

To Margaret Roper [214]

AN ACCOUNT OF MORE'S SECOND INTERROGATION, 2–3 MAY 1535

More's account of his second interrogation is noteworthy for the emergence of Sir Richard Rich (1496–1567), whom More had known since Rich was a youth in Chelsea parish. Friends with Lord Chancellor Thomas Audley, Rich was appointed attorney general for Wales in 1532 and solicitor general in 1533; he prosecuted the opponents of the royal supremacy, and his sworn testimony doomed to death both Fisher and More (*ODNB*). According to Roper's *Life of Sir Thomas More* and the surviving accounts of More's trial, More judged Rich guilty of perjuring himself during the trial by maliciously misreporting the "hypothetical" legal conversation on 12 June 1535 between More and himself on the question of whether Parliament had the right to make a law establishing the King as the head of the Church. Despite More's critique of Rich's character and motives at the trial, Rich's testimony was accepted and More condemned. Rich was rewarded with the post of chirographer of the Court of Common Pleas after More's death, and he later became Lord Chancellor of England from 1547–1558, after which, in Robert Bolt's words, he "died in his bed," unlike most of the other players in this great drama (*ODNB*). For an account of Rich's role in More's trial and condemnation, see *Thomas More's Trial by Jury* (Boydell & Brewer, 2011).

Among the participants in this second interrogation, "Master Secretary" is Thomas Cromwell, and "Master Solicitor" is Richard Rich. "Master Reynolds" is St. Richard Reynolds (d. 1535), a Bridgetine monk who was executed with other monks for treason on 4 May 1535 (*ODNB*). "Master Lieutenant" is Sir Edmund Walsingham (c. 1480–1550), who guarded More at the Tower and led him to his execution (*ODNB*). "Master Attorney" is Sir Christopher

Hales (d. 1541), judge and lawyer who played a part in the indictment of Wolsey, the submission of the clergy, the fall of the Nun of Kent, and the prosecutions of Fisher, More, and later Anne Boleyn (*ODNB*). "Master Bedill" is Thomas Bedill (d. 1537), who according to Silva worked for Henry VIII by obtaining the oaths of supremacy from religious and assessing their positions (*Last Letters*, 188). "Master Doctor Tregonwell" is Sir John Tregonwell (c.1498–1565), lawyer and administrator known for his later role as "monastic visitor" in the process that brought about the wholesale dissolution of the English monasteries, those soon to be "bare ruined choirs, where late the sweet birds sang," in Shakespeare's words (*ODNB*; Sonnet 73.5).

Tower of London
2 or 3 May 1535

Our Lord bless you, my dearly beloved daughter:

I doubt not but by the reason of the Councilors resorting hither, in this time (in which our Lord be their comfort) these fathers of the Charterhouse and Master Reynolds of Sion that be now judged to death for treason, whose matters and causes I know not, may hap to put you in trouble and fear of mind concerning me, being here prisoner, specially because it is not unlikely but that you have heard that I was brought also before the Council here myself. I have thought it necessary to advertise you of the very truth, to the end that you neither conceive more hope than the matter gives, lest upon other turn it might grieve your heaviness, nor more grief and fear than the matter gives of, on the other side. Wherefore shortly you shall understand that on Friday the last day of April in the afternoon, Master Lieutenant came in here unto me, and showed me that Master Secretary would speak with me. Whereupon I shifted my gown and went out with Master Lieutenant into the gallery to him. Where I met many, some known and some unknown in the way. And in conclusion coming into the chamber where his Mastership sat with Master Attorney, Master Solicitor, Master Bedill and Master Doctor Tregonwell, I was offered to sit with them, which in no wise I would.

Whereupon Master Secretary [i.e., Thomas Cromwell] showed unto me, that he doubted not, but that I had by such friends as hither had resorted to me seen the new statutes made at the last sitting of the Parliament. Whereunto I answered: "Yes, verily. Howbeit for as much as being there, I have no conversation with any people, I thought it little need for me to bestow much time upon them, and therefore I redelivered the book shortly and the effect of the statutes I never marked nor studied to put in remembrance." Then he asked me whether I had not read the first statute of them, of the King being Head of the Church. Whereunto I answered, "Yes." Then his Mastership declared unto me, that since it was now by act of Parliament ordained that his Highness and his heirs be, and ever right have been, and perpetually should be Supreme Head in the earth of the Church of England under Christ, the King's pleasure was that those of his Council there assembled should demand mine opinion, and what my mind was therein. Whereunto I answered that in good faith I had well trusted that the King's Highness would never have commanded any such question to be demanded of me, considering that I ever from the beginning well and truly from time to time declared my mind unto his Highness, and since that time I had, I said, unto your Mastership Master Secretary also, both by mouth and by writing. And now I have in good faith discharged my mind of all such matters, and neither will dispute King's titles nor Pope's, but the King's true faithful subject I am and will be, and daily I pray for him and for all his, and for you all that are of his honorable Council, and for all the realm, and otherwise than thus I never intend to meddle.

Whereunto Master Secretary answered that he thought this manner of answer should not satisfy nor content the King's Highness, but that his Grace would exact a more full answer. And his Mastership added thereunto, that the King's Highness was a prince not of rigor but of mercy and pity, and though that he had found obstinacy at some time in any of his subjects, yet when he should find them at another time conformable and submit themselves, his Grace would show mercy. And that concerning myself, his Highness would be glad to see me take such conformable ways, as I might be abroad in the world again among other men as I have been before.

Whereunto I shortly (after the inward affection of my mind) answered for a very truth, that I would never meddle in the world again, to have the world given me. And to the remnant of the matter, I answered in effect as before, showing that I had fully determined with myself neither to study nor meddle with any matter of this world, but that my whole study should be upon the passion of Christ and mine own passage out of this world.

Upon this I was commanded to go forth for a while, and after called in again. At which time Master Secretary said unto me that though I was prisoner and condemned to perpetual prison, yet I was not thereby discharged of mine obedience and allegiance unto the King's Highness. And thereupon demanded me whether I thought that the King's Grace might exact of me such things as are contained in the statutes and upon like pains as he might of other men. Whereto I answered that I would not say the contrary. Whereto he said that likewise as the King's Highness would be gracious to them that he found conformable, so his Grace would follow the course of his laws toward such as he shall find obstinate. And his Mastership said further that my demeanor in that matter was of a thing that of likelihood made now other men so stifle therein as they be.

Whereto I answered, that I give no man occasion to hold any one point or the other, nor never gave any man advise or counsel therein one way or other. And for conclusion I could no further go, whatsoever pain should come thereof. I am, said I, the King's true faithful subject and daily beadsman and pray for his Highness and all his and all the realm. I do nobody harm, I say none harm, I think none harm, but wish everybody good. And if this be not enough to keep a man alive, in good faith, I long not to live. And I am dying already, and have since I came here been divers times in the case that I thought to die within one hour, and I thank our Lord I was never sorry for it, but rather sorry when I saw the pang past. And therefore my poor body is at the King's pleasure; would God my death might do him good.

After this Master Secretary said: "Well, you find no fault in that statute, find you any in any of the other statutes after?" Whereto I answered, "Sir, whatsoever thing should seem to me other than good, in any of the statutes or in that statute either, I would not declare what fault I found, nor speak thereof." Whereunto finally his Mastership said full gently that of anything that I had spoken, there should none advantage be taken, and whether he said further that there be none to be taken, I am not well remembered. But he said that report should be made unto the King's Highness, and his gracious pleasure known.

Whereupon I was delivered again to Master Lieutenant, which was then called in, and so was I by Master Lieutenant brought again into my chamber, and here am I yet in such case as I was, neither better nor worse. That which shall follow lies in the hand of God, whom I beseech to put in King's Grace's mind that thing that may be to His high pleasure, and in mine, to mind only the weal of my soul, with little regard of my body.

And you with all yours, and my wife and all my children and all our friends both bodily and ghostly heartily well to fare. And I pray you and all them, pray for me, and take no thought whatsoever shall

happen me. For I verily trust in the goodness of God, seem it never
so evil to this world, it shall indeed in another world be for the best.
Your loving father,
Thomas More, Knight.

Letter 78

FROM LADY ALICE MORE TO MASTER SECRETARY THOMAS CROMWELL [215]

The source of this letter, in which Lady Alice implores Thomas
Cromwell for financial assistance, is Cresacre More's *The Life of Sir
Thomas More: With a Biographical Preface, Notes, and Other Illustra-
tions*, ed. Hunter (London, 1828). An "oratrix" is a female petitioner
or plaintiff (*OED*).

MAY 1535

RIGHT HONORABLE, AND MY ESPECIAL GOOD
MASTER SECRETARY:

In my most humble wise I recommend me unto your good Mastership, acknowledging myself to be most deeply bound to your
good Mastership, for your manifold goodness, and loving favor,
both before this time, and yet daily, now also shown towards my
poor husband and me. I pray Almighty God continue your goodness so still, for thereupon hangs the greatest part of my poor
husband's comfort and mine.

The cause of my writing, at this time, is to certify your especial good Mastership of my great and extreme necessity; which,
on and besides the charge of mine own house, do pay weekly

15 shillings for the board-wages of my poor husband, and his servant; for the maintaining whereof, I have been compelled, of very necessity, to sell part of mine apparel, for lack of other substance to make money of. Wherefore my most humble petition and suit to your Mastership, at this time, is to desire your Mastership's favorable advice and counsel, whether I may be so bold to attend upon the King's most gracious Highness. I trust there is no doubt in the cause of my impediment; for the young man, being a ploughman, had been diseased with the ague [i.e., the plague] by the space of 3 years before that he departed. And besides this, it is now five weeks since he departed, and no other person diseased in the house since that time; wherefore I most humbly beseech your especial good Mastership (as my only trust is, and else know not what to do, but utterly in this world to be undone) for the love of God to consider the premises; and thereupon, of your most abundant goodness, to show your most favorable help to the comforting of my poor husband and me, in this our great heaviness, extreme age, and necessity. And thus we, and all ours, shall daily, during our lives, pray to God for the prosperous success of your right honorable dignity.

By your poor continual Oratrix,
Dame Alice More.

Letter 79

To Margaret Roper [216]

An Account of More's Third Interrogation, Star Chamber

During this third interrogation, More was questioned by the highest-ranking members of King Henry's council: Lord Chancellor Thomas

Audley, Archbishop Thomas Cranmer, Master Secretary Thomas Cromwell, Lord Wiltshire (Thomas Boleyn, Anne Boleyn's father), and Lord Suffolk (Henry's brother-in-law). The council reports to More that his example and obstinate silence is the "occasion of much grudge and harm in the realm." More responds to the council that his conscience is clear and sure and that he will not—and cannot— change his position on the Oath. This interrogation took place at the Star Chamber, Westminster.

The sole Latin quotation in the letter, *Suo domino stat et cadit*, is an allusion to Romans 14:4, the full text of which reads: "Who are you to pass judgment on the servant of another? It is before his own master that he stands or falls. And he will be upheld, for the Master is able to make him stand." Around this time, More also composed a short poem, "Lewis the Lost Lover," which reads like a last letter and farewell to fortune and its power: "Eye-flattering fortune, look thou never so fair, / Nor never so pleasantly begin to smile, / As though thou would my ruin all repair, / During my life thou shalt me not beguile. / Trust shall I God, to enter in a while, / His haven of heaven ever sure and uniform: / Ever after thy calm, look I for a storm." The other poem he wrote in 1535, the lighter "Davy the Dicer," also addresses "lady luck," or fortune, and reveals More's good cheer during his imprisonment: "But in faith I bless you again a thousand times, / For lending me now some leisure to make rhymes" (6–7). These modernized texts of the poems are taken from Campbell and Reed, *The English Works of Thomas More*, volume one (London: Eyre and Spottiswoode Limited, 1931), a wonderful but incomplete edition of More's writings, the progress of which was destroyed, along with the plates, during World War Two bombings.

<Tower of London
3 June 1535>

Our Lord bless you and all yours.

For as much, dearly beloved daughter, as it is likely that you either have heard or shortly shall hear that the Council was here this day, and that I was before them, I have thought it necessary to send you word how the matter stands. And verily to be short I perceive little difference between this time and the last, for as far as I can see the whole purpose is either to drive me to say precisely the one way or else precisely the other.

Here sat my Lord of Canterbury, my Lord Chancellor, my Lord of Suffolk, my Lord of Wilshire and Master Secretary. And after my coming, Master Secretary made rehearsal in what wise he had reported unto the King's Highness, what had been said by his Grace's Council to me, and what had been answered by me to them at mine other being before them last. Which thing his Mastership rehearsed in good faith very well, as I acknowledged and confessed and heartily thanked him therefore. Whereupon he added that the King's Highness was nothing content nor satisfied with mine answer, but thought that by my demeanor I had been occasion of much grudge and harm in the realm, and that I had an obstinate mind and an evil toward him and that my duty was being his subject; and so he had sent them now in his name upon my allegiance to command me to make a plain and terminate answer whether I thought the statute lawful or not and that I should either acknowledge and confess it lawful that his Highness should be Supreme Head of the Church of England or else to utter plainly my malignity.

Whereto I answered that I had no malignity and therefore I could none utter. And as to the matter, I could none other answer make than I had before made, which answer his Mastership had there rehearsed. Very heavy I was that the King's Highness should have any such opinion of me. Howbeit if there were one that had informed his Highness many evil things of me that were untrue, to which his Highness for the time gave credence, I would be very sorry that he should have that opinion of me the space of one day. Howbeit if I were sure that other should come on the morrow by whom his Grace should know the truth of my innocence, I should in the meanwhile comfort myself with the consideration of that. And in like wise now though it be great heaviness to me that his Highness have such opinion of me for the while, yet have I no remedy to help it, but only to comfort myself with this consideration that I know very well that the time shall come, when God shall declare my truth toward his Grace before him and all the world. And whereas it might haply seem to be but a small cause of comfort because I might take harm here first in the meanwhile, I thanked God that my case was such in this matter through the clearness of mine own conscience that though I might have pain I could have no harm for a man may in such case lose his head and have no harm. For I was very sure that I had no corrupt affection, but that I had always from the beginning truly used myself to looking first upon God and next upon the King, according to the lesson that his Highness taught me at my first coming to his noble service, the most virtuous lesson that ever prince taught his servant; whose Highness to have of me such opinion is my great heaviness, but I have no means, as I said, to help it but only comfort myself in the meantime with the hope of that joyful day in which my truth towards him shall well be known. And in this matter further I could not go nor other answer thereto I could not make.

To this it was said by my Lord Chancellor and Master Secretary both that the King might by his laws compel me to make a plain answer thereto, either the one way or the other.

Whereunto I answered I would not dispute the King's authority, what his Highness might do in such case, but I said that verily under correction it seemed to me somewhat hard. For if it so were that my conscience gave me against the statutes (wherein how my mind gives me I make no declaration), then I nothing doing nor nothing saying against the statute, it were a very hard thing to compel me to say either precisely with it against my conscience to the loss of my soul, or precisely against it to the destruction of my body.

To this Master Secretary said that I had before this when I was Chancellor examined heretics and thieves and other malefactors and gave me a great praise above my deserving in that behalf. And he said that I then, as he thought and at the leastwise Bishops did use to examine heretics, whether they believed the Pope to be the head of the Church and used to compel them to make a precise answer thereto. And why should not then the King, since it is a law made here that his Grace is Head of the Church, here compel men to answer precisely to the law here as they did then concerning the Pope.

I answered and said that I protested that I intended not to defend any part or stand in contention; but I said there was a difference between those two cases because at that time, as well here as elsewhere through the corps of Christendom, the Pope's power was recognized for an undoubted thing which seems not like a thing agreed in this realm and the contrary taken for truth in other realms. Whereunto Master Secretary answered that they were as well burned for the denying of that as they be beheaded for denying of this, and therefore as good reason to compel them to make precise answer to the one as to the other.

Whereto I answered that since in this case a man is not by a law of one realm so bound in his conscience, where there is a law of the whole corps of Christendom to the contrary in matter touching belief, as he is by a law of the whole corps though there hap to be made in some place a local law to the contrary, the reasonableness or the unreasonableness in binding a man to precise answer, stands not in the respect or difference between beheading and burning, but because of the difference in charge of conscience, the difference stands between beheading and hell.

Much was there answered unto this both by Master Secretary and my Lord Chancellor over long to rehearse. And in conclusion they offered me an oath by which I should be sworn to make true answer to such things as should be asked me on the King's behalf, concerning the King's own person.

Whereto I answered that verily I never purposed to swear any book oath more while I lived. Then they said that I was very obstinate if I would refuse that, for every man does it in the Star Chamber and everywhere. I said that was true, but I had not so little foresight that I might well conjecture what should be part of my interrogatory, and as good it was to refuse it at first as afterward.

Whereto my Lord Chancellor answered that he thought I guessed truth, for I should see them and so they were showed me and they were but two. The first whether I had seen the statute. The other whether I believed that it were a lawful made statute or not. Whereupon I refused the oath and said further by mouth, that the first I had before confessed, and to the second I would make none answer.

Which was the end of the communication and I was thereupon sent away. In the communication before, it was said that it was marveled that I stuck so much in my conscience while at the uttermost I was not sure therein. Whereto I said that I was very sure that my own conscience, so informed as it is by such diligence as I have so long taken therein, may stand with mine own salvation. I meddle not with the conscience of them that think otherwise, every man *suo domino stat et cadit* [i.e "it is before his own master that he stands or falls" (Rom 14:4)]. I am no man's judge. It was also said unto me that if I had rather be out of the world as in it, as I had there said, why did I not speak even out plain against the statute. It appeared well I was not content to die though I had said so. Whereto I answered as the truth is, that I have not been a man of such holy living as I might be bold to offer myself to death, lest God for my presumption might suffer me to fall, and therefore I put not myself forward, but draw back. Howbeit if God draw me to it himself, then trust I in his great mercy, that he shall not fail to give me grace and strength.

In conclusion Master Secretary said that he liked me this day much worse than he did the last time, for then he said he pitied me much and now he thought that I meant not well; but God and I know both that I mean well and so I pray God do by me.

I pray you be, you and my other friends, of good cheer whatsoever fall of me, and take no thought for me but pray for me as I do and shall do for you and all them.

Your tender loving father,
Thomas More, Knight

Letter 80

To Antonio Bonvisi [217]

Shortly before his death, More writes to thank Antonio Bonvisi, the Italian merchant, banker, and resident of London, for the gift of life-long friendship, and especially for supporting More during his imprisonment in the Tower, when most former friends abandoned him or proved distant and silent as fading stars. Bonvisi provided More with food, wine, and a warm camlet gown, something More undoubtedly appreciated in his riverside Tower cell. After More's death, Bonvisi would suffer the displeasure of the crown despite his power and influence in London. He fled England in 1544, but opened his home in Louvain to English exiles, including Nicholas Harpsfield, one of

More's first biographers. This letter has been translated into English by Dr. Elizabeth McCutcheon, and originally appeared in *Moreana* 71–72 (Nov. 1981).

TOWER OF LONDON
1535

TO THE MOST FRIENDLY OF FRIENDS, AND DESERVEDLY
DEAREST TO ME, GREETINGS:

Since my mind has a presentiment (perhaps a false one, but still a presentiment) that before very long I will be unable to write to you, I have decided, while I may, to show by this little letter, at least, how much I am refreshed by the pleasantness of your friendship now that fortune has abandoned me.

To be sure, most excellent sir, in the past I have always been wonderfully delighted by this love for me, but when I remembered that for almost forty years now I have been, not a guest, but a continual habitué of the Bonvisi household, and that in all this time I have not proven to be a friend in repaying my debt to you, but only a barren lover, my sense of shame truly made that genuine sweetness, which I otherwise enjoyed in thinking about the friendship of the Bonvisis, turn a little bit sour because I felt somehow awkward and ashamed, as if I had neglected to do my part. But certainly I now console myself with the thought that there never arose any opportunity for me to pay you back, since your fortune was so large that there was no way left for me to do anything for you. And so I am aware that I did not fail to pay you back through any neglect of my duty towards you, but because there was no opportunity. But now that even the hope of recompense is taken away, when I see you persist in loving and obliging me, nay rather, when I see you push on in your friendship and run the race unwearied, so that few men court their fortunate friends as much as you favor, love, cherish, and regard your More—overthrown as he is, cast aside, struck down, and sentenced to prison—then I not only absolve myself from whatever bitter shame I felt before but also find peace in the sweetness of this wonderful friendship of yours. And my good fortune in having such a faithful friend as you seems somehow—I don't know how—almost to counterbalance this unfortunate shipwreck of my fleet. Certainly, apart from the indignation of the Prince, whom I love no less than I ought to fear him, for the rest, your friendship almost outweighs my losses, since they, after all, are to be counted among the evils of fortune.

But if I were to count the possession of such a constant friendship—which such an unfavorable fall of fortune has not snatched away, but rather cemented more strongly—among the fleeting goods of fortune, truly I should be out of my mind. For the happiness of a friendship so faithful, and so constant against the contrary blast of fortune, is a rare favor, and without a doubt is a higher good, and a more exalted one, arising from a certain special loving-kindness of God. Certainly I do not otherwise accept or understand it than as something arranged by the unparalleled mercy of God, that among my poor little friends, a person such as you, so great a friend, was prepared so long beforehand, who might assuage and lighten by your consolation a great part of that distress which the weight of fortune rushing headlong against me has brought upon me. Therefore, my dear Antonio, dearest of all mortals to me, with all my strength I pray (the only thing I can do) to Almighty God, who provided you for me, that, since he gave you such a debtor, who will never be able to discharge his debt, he himself for his loving-kindness vouchsafe to requite you for those deeds of kindness of yours which you daily expend so profusely upon me; then that he bring us, for his great mercy, from this wretched and stormy world to his peace, where there will be no need for letters, where no wall will separate us, where no porter will prevent us from talking together, but with God the Father unbegotten, and his only-begotten Son, our Lord and Redeemer Jesus Christ, and the Holy Spirit of them both, the Comforter proceeding from them both, we shall fully enjoy eternal joy. Meanwhile may Almighty God bring it about that you, my dear Antonio, and I, and would that all mortals, and everyone everywhere, may hold cheap all the riches of this world, all the glory of the whole universe, and even the sweetness of life itself, for the ardent desire of that joy. Most trusty of all friends, and most beloved by me, and (as I am now long accustomed to call you) the apple of my eye: goodbye. May Christ keep unharmed your whole household, so very like the head of the family in their affection for me.

T. More: If I put down "yours," I'll have done so in vain. For you cannot now not know this, when you have bought it by so many deeds of kindness. Nor am I now such, that it matters whose I am.

Letter 81

TO MARGARET ROPER [218]

On Monday, 5 July 1535, Thomas More wrote his last letter to his daughter, Meg. He was executed the next morning, July the sixth, at 9 o'clock, after receiving the last sacraments. In the letter, he indicates his wish that his execution occur no later than "tomorrow," within the "Utas" or octave of St. Peter, and on the eve of the popular feast of St. Thomas Becket, the archbishop killed at Canterbury Cathedral by the knights of Henry II on 29 December 1190.

As the 1557 editor points out simply, this letter to Meg "was the last thing that ever he wrote."

Tower of London
5 July 1535

Our Lord bless you good daughter and your good husband and your little boy and all yours and all my children and all my god-children and all our friends. Recommend me when you may to my good daughter Cecilye, whom I beseech our Lord to comfort, and I send her my blessing and to all her children and pray her to pray for me. I send her an handkerchief and God comfort my good son her husband. My good daughter Daunce has the picture in parchment that you delivered me from my Lady Coniers; her name is on the back side. Show her that I heartily pray her that you may send it in my name again for a token from me to pray for me.

I like specialwell Dorothy Coly, I pray you be good unto her. I would wit whether this be she that you wrote me of. If not I pray you be good to the other as you may in her affliction and to my good daughter Joan Aleyn to give her I pray you some kind answer, for she sued hither to me this day to pray you be good to her.

I cumber you good Margaret much, but I would be sorry, if it should be any longer than tomorrow, for it is Saint Thomas even, and the Utas [i.e., the Octave] of Saint Peter and therefore tomorrow long I to go to God, it were a day very meet and convenient for me. I never liked your manner toward me better than when you kissed me last for I love when daughterly love and dear charity has no leisure to look to worldly courtesy.

Appendix I

King Henry's "Great Matter": Texts on the Royal Divorce

1. Letter of Anne Boleyn to Henry VIII, 1527

The source of this letter and the next is *The Love Letters of Henry VIII to Anne Boleyn* (Boston: John W. Luce and Company, 1906). The second letter, Henry's reply, would prove most momentous for England; it has been called a letter that changed English history. The original, handwritten in French, survives in the Vatican Library, and was recently displayed in England to mark the 500th anniversary of Henry's coronation in 1509. After these letters there follows the account by Raphael Holinshed (1529–1580) of the King's doubts about his marriage to Catherine and the ensuing papal trial arranged by Cardinal Wolsey in 1529. Unable to gain Rome's approval for his desire to annul the marriage, Henry would have to wait until 1533 to put away Queen Catherine at last and marry Anne Boleyn. Holinshed's text has been lightly modernized in spelling and punctuation.

Sire, it belongs only to the august mind of a great king, to whom Nature has given a heart full of generosity towards the sex, to repay by favors so extraordinary an artless and short conversation with a girl. Inexhaustible as is the treasury of your majesty's bounties, I pray you to consider that it cannot be sufficient to your generosity; for, if you recompense so slight a conversation by gifts so great, what will you be able to do for those who are ready to consecrate their entire obedience to your desires? How great soever may be the bounties I have received, the joy that I feel in being loved by a king whom I adore, and to whom I would with pleasure make a sacrifice of my heart, if fortune had rendered it worthy of being offered to him, will ever be infinitely greater. The warrant of maid of honor to the queen induces me to think that your majesty has some regard for me, since it gives me means of seeing you oftener, and of assuring you by my own lips (which I shall do on the first opportunity) that I am, Your majesty's very obliged and very obedient servant, without any reserve, Anne Boleyn.

2. Letter of King Henry VIII to Anne Boleyn, 1527

On turning over in my mind the contents of your last letters, I have put myself into great agony, not knowing how to interpret them, whether to my disadvantage, as you show in some places, or to my advantage, as I understand them in some others, beseeching you earnestly to let me know expressly your whole mind as to the love between us two. It is absolutely necessary for me to obtain this answer, having been for above a whole year stricken with the dart of love, and not yet sure whether I shall fail of finding a place in your heart and affection, which last point has prevented me for some time past from calling you my mistress; because, if you only love me with an ordinary love, that name is not suitable for you, because it denotes a singular love, which is far from common. But if you please to do the office of a true loyal mistress and friend, and to give up yourself body and heart to me, who will be, and have been, your most loyal servant, (if your rigor does not forbid me) I promise you that not only the name shall be given you, but also that I will take you for my only mistress, casting off all others besides you out of my thoughts and affections, and serve you only. I beseech you to give an entire answer to this my rude letter, that I may know on what and how far I may depend. And if it does not please you to answer me in writing, appoint some place where I may have it by word of mouth, and I will go thither with all my heart. No more, for fear of tiring you.

Written by the hand of him who would willingly remain yours, H. Rex

3. Raphael Holinshed's Account of the Papal Trial, 1529

From The Third Volume of the Chronicles (1587 Edition)

There rose a secret bruit in London that the king's confessor Doctor Longland, and diverse other great clerks had told the king that the marriage between him and the Lady Catherine, late wife to his brother, Prince Arthur, was not lawful: whereupon the king should sue a divorce, and marry the Duchess of Alanson, sister to the French King at the town of Calais that same summer. . . . The king was offended with those tales, and sent for Sir Thomas Seimor, mayor of London, secretly charging him to see that the people ceased from such talk.

■ ■ ■

The truth is, that whether this doubt was first moved by the Cardinal [Thomas Wolsey], or by the said Longland, being the king's confessor, the king was not only brought in doubt, whether it was a lawful marriage or no; but also determined to have the case examined, cleared, and adjudged by learning, law, and sufficient authority. The Cardinal verily was put in most blame for this scruple now cast into the king's conscience, for the hate he bore to the Emperor, because he would not grant to him the archbishopric of Toledo, for the which he was a suitor. And therefore he did not only procure the King to join in friendship with the French King, but also sought a divorce betwixt the king and the queen, that the king might have had in marriage the Duchess of Alanson, sister unto the French King.

■ ■ ■

But howsoever it came about that the King was thus troubled in conscience concerning his marriage, this followed, that like a wise and sage prince, to have the doubt clearly removed, he called together the best learned of the realm, which were of several opinions. Wherefore he thought to know the truth by indifferent judges, lest peradventure the Spaniards, and others also in favor of the Queen, would say that his own subjects were not indifferent judges in this behalf. And therefore he wrote his cause to Rome, and also sent to all the universities in Italy and Franc, and to the great clerks of all Christendom, to know their opinions, and desired the court of Rome to send into his realm a legate [i.e., Cardinal Campeius], which should be indifferent, and of a great and profound judgment, to hear the case debated. At whose request the whole consistory of the college of Rome sent thither Lawrence Campeius, a priest Cardinal, a man of great wit and experience, which was sent hither before in the tenth year of this king, as you have heard, and with him was joined in commission the Cardinal of York and legate of England.

■ ■ ■

The place where the cardinals should sit to hear the cause of matrimony betwixt the king and the queen, was ordained to be at Black Friars in London, where in the Great Hall was preparation made of seats, tables, and other furniture, according to such a solemn session and royal appearance. The court was platted in tables and benches in manner of a consistory, one seat raised higher for the judges to sit in. Then as it were in the midst of the said judges aloft above them three degrees high, was a cloth of estate hanged, with a chair royal under the same, wherein sat the king; and besides him, some distance from him, sat the Queen. . . .

Then before the king and the judges within the court sat the archbishop of Canterbury, William Warham, and all the other bishops. Then stood at both ends within the counselors learned in the spiritual laws, as well the king's as the queen's. The doctors of law for the king (whose name ye have heard before) had their convenient rooms. Thus was the court furnished. The judges commanded silence whilst their commission was read, both to the court and to the people assembled. That done the scribes commanded the crier to call the king by the name of "King Henry of England, come into the court!" With that the king answered and said, "Here!" Then called he the queen by the name of "Catherine, queen of England, come into the court!" She made no answer, but rose out of her chair.

And because she could not come to the king directly, for the distance between them, she went about by the court, and came to the king, kneeling down at his feet, to whom she said in effect as follows:

"Sir," quoth she, "I desire you to do me justice and right, and take some pity upon me, for I am a poor woman, and a stranger, born out of you dominion, having here no indifferent counsel and less assurance of friendship. Alas, sir, in what have I offended you, or what occasion of displeasure have I showed you, that you intend thus to put me from you after this sort! I take God to my judge, I have been to you a true and humble wife, ever conformable to your will and pleasure; that never contraried or gainsaid anything thereof, and being always contented with all things wherein you had any delight, whether little or much, without grudge or displeasure, I loved for your sake all them whom you loved, whether they were my friends or enemies.

"I have been your wife these twenty years and more, and you have had by me diverse children. If there be any just cause that you can allege against me, either of dishonesty or matter lawful to put me from you, I am content to depart to my shame and rebuke; and if there be none, then I pray you to let me have justice at your hand. The king your father was in his time of excellent wit, and the king of Spain, my father, Ferdinando, was reckoned one of the wisest princes that reigned in Spain many years before. It is not to be doubted, but that they had gathered as wise counselors unto them of every realm, as to their wisdoms they thought meet, who deemed the marriage between you and me good and lawful. Wherefore, I humbly desire you to spare me, until I may know what counsel my friends in Spain will advertise me to take, and if you will not, then your pleasure be fulfilled." With that she arose up, making a low curtsy to the king, and departed from thence.

The king, being advertised that she was ready to go out of the house, commanded the crier to call her again, and the crier called her by these words: "Catherine, queen of England, come into the court!"

With that Master Griffith [i.e., the Queen's General Receiver] said, "Madame, you be called again."

"On on," quoth she, "it makes no matter; I will not tarry—go on your ways!" And thus she departed, without any further answer at that time, or any other, and never would appear after in any court.

The king, perceiving she was departed, said words these in effect: "For as much," quoth he, "as the queen is gone, I will in her absence declare to you all, that she hat been to me as true, as obedient, and as conformable a wife, as I would wish or desire. She hath all the virtuous qualities that ought to be in a woman of her dignity, or in any other of a baser estate. She is also surely a noble woman born, and her conditions will well declare the same."

After that Wolsey the Cardinal said: "Sir, I most humbly require your highness to declare before all this audience, whether I have been the chief and first mover of this matter unto your majesty or no, for I am greatly suspected herein."

"My lord Cardinal," quoth the king, "I can well excuse you in this matter. You have been rather against me in the tempting hereof, than a setter forward or mover of the same. The special cause that moved me unto this matter, was a certain scrupulosity that pricked my conscience, upon certain words spoken at a time when it was, by the bishop of Bajon the French ambassador, who had been hither sent, upon the debating of a marriage to be concluded between our daughter the lady Mary, and the duke of Orleans, second son to the king of France.

"Upon the resolution and determination whereof," the king continued, "the ambassador desired respite to advertise the king his master thereof, whether our daughter Mary should be legitimate in respect of this my marriage with this woman, being sometimes my brother's wife.

"These words at once conceived within the secret bosom of my conscience, engendered such a scrupulous doubt, that my conscience was incontinently encumbered, vexed, and disquieted; whereby I thought myself to be greatly in danger of God's indignation.

"This appeared to be the case, as it seemed to me, because God had sent us no issue male—and all such issues male as my said wife had by me, died incontinent after they came into the world, so that I doubted the great displeasure of God in that behalf.

"Thus my conscience being tossed in the waves of a scrupulous mind, and partly in despair to have any other issue than I had already by this lady now my wife, it behooved me further to consider the state of this realm, and the danger it stood in for lack of a prince to succeed me. I thought it good in release of the weighty burden of my weak conscience, and also the quiet estate of this worthy realm, to attempt the law therein, whether I may lawfully take another wife more lawfully, by God may send me more issue, in case this my first copulation was not good, without any carnal concupiscence, and not for any displeasure or misliking of the queen's person and age, with whom I would be as well contented to continue, if our marriage may stand with the laws of God, as with any woman alive.

"In this point consisteth all this doubt that we go about now to try, by the learning, wisdom, and judgment of you our prelates and pastors of all this our realm and dominions, now here assembled for that purpose, to whose conscience and learning I have committed the charge and judgment, and according to which I will, God willing, be right well content to submit myself, and for my part obey the same." . . . After that the king rose up, and the court was adjourned until another day.

Here it is to be noted, that the queen in presence of the whole court most grievously accused the Cardinal [Thomas Wolsey] of untruth, deceit, wickedness, and malice, which had sown dissention betwixt her and the king her husband; and therefore openly protested, that she did utterly abhor, refuse, and forsake such a judge, as was not only a most malicious enemy to her, but also a manifest adversary to all right and justice; and therewith did she appeal unto the pope, committing her whole cause to be judged of him.

■ ■ ■

And thus this court passed from sessions to sessions, and day to day, till at certain of their sessions the king sent the two cardinals to the queen, then in Bridewell, to persuade her by their wisdoms, and to advise her to surrender the whole matter into the king's hands by her own consent and will, which should be much better to her honor, than to stand the trial of law, and thereby to be condemned, which should seem much to her dishonor.

The cardinals being in the queen's chamber of presence, the gentleman usher advertised the queen that the cardinals were come to speak with her. With that she rose up, and with a skein of milk white thread about her neck, came into her chamber of presence, where the cardinals were attending. At whose coming, quoth she, "What is your pleasure with me?"

■ ■ ■

"Forsooth, good madame," quoth the cardinal, "if it please you, we come both to know your mind how you are disposed to do in this matter between the king and you, and also to declare secretly our opinions and counsels to you, which we do only for very zeal and the obedience we bear your grace.

"My lord," quoth she, "I thank you for your good will, but to make you answer in your request I cannot so suddenly, for I was set among my maids at work, thinking full little of any such matter, wherein their needeth a longer deliberation, and a better head than mine to make answer. For I need counsel in this case which touches me so near, and as for any counsel or friendship that I can find in England, they are not for my profit. What think you, my lords, will any Englishman counsel me, or be friend to me against the king's pleasure, that is his subject? Nay forsooth. And as for my counsel in whom I will put my trust, they be not here, but they are in Spain in my own country.

"And my lords," she continued, "I am a poor woman, lacking wit, to answer any such noble persons of wisdom as you be, in so weighty a matter, and therefore I pray you be good to me a poor woman, destitute of friends here in a foreign region, and your counsel also I will be glad to here." And therewith she took the cardinal by the hand and led him into her privy chamber with the other cardinal, where they tarried for a season talking with the queen.

When this communication ended, they departed to the king, making to him relation of her talk. Thus this case went forward from court to court, till it came to judgment, so that every man expected the judgment would be given the next day. At which day the king came thither, and set him down in a chair within a door, in the end of the gallery (which opened directly against the judgment seat) to hear the judgment given, at which time all their proceedings were read in Latin.

That done, the king's counsel at the bar called for judgment.

"With that," quoth Cardinal Campeius, "I will not give judgment till have made relation to the pope of all our proceedings, whose counsel and commandment in this case I will observe. This case is very doubtful, also the party defendant [the Queen] will make no answer here, but does rather appeal from us, supposing that we be not indifferent. Wherefore I will adjourn this court for this time, according to the order of the court of Rome. And with that the court was dissolved, and no more done. The protracting of the conclusion of the matter, King Henry took very displeasantly. Then Cardinal Campeius took his leave of the king and nobility, and returned to Rome.

4. Letter of Queen Catherine to Emperor Charles V

6 November 1531

The source of this letter is *Letters and Papers, Foreign and Domestic, Henry VIII, Volume 5: 1531–1539*, ed. James Gairdner (1880).

My tribulations are so great, my life so disturbed by the plans daily invented to further the King's wicked intention, the surprises which the King gives me, with certain persons of his Council, are so mortal, and my treatment is what God knows, that it is enough to shorten ten lives, much more mine. As far as concerns this business, I have offended neither God nor the King, to whom I have always shown obedience as a true wife, and sometimes more so in this affair than my conscience approved of. Yet they treat me in such a manner that I do not know what to do, except to complain to God and your Majesty, with whom my remedy lies, and to beg you to cause the Pope to make such a speedy end of the matter as my truth merits. I pray God to pardon the Pope for his delay. In this world I will confess myself to be the King's true wife, and in the next they will know how unreasonably I am afflicted.

Your Majesty's ambassador here sent me certain articles from Rome for my council to see. I take no advice but that of your Majesty and your Ambassador, who gives me much encouragement, telling me of the victory my truth deserves, and your Majesty's grief at the delay, and your urgency with the Pope to do justice. He shows himself a learned man when there is necessity, and some of my council say that your Majesty could not have sent a better person. As my council are afraid to speak, the duty of answering rests with him, and I can find no other remedy, and this seems to me more certain and secure. Until the sentence comes with what will put out this fire, your Majesty must say, among persons who can carry the news hither, how much you feel my troubles, and how surprised you are at my treatment by the King, with anything else you may think right, for the Pope's delay makes many persons lukewarm in the matter. They (her adversaries) deter those who would speak the truth, and give so much to those who favor themselves that they come like hawks to the lure. If your Majesty speak thus, it will animate those who wish me well, and show them that there is some one who grieves at my troubles. The Ambassador's letters will give fuller information. He shows the greatest diligence in this and other matters.

5. Archbishop Thomas Cranmer's Letter to Archdeacon Hawkyns

27 June 1533

This letter details, in Thomas Cranmer's own words, the "concluding of the matter of the divorce between my Lady Catherine and the King's Grace." The source of this letter is the first volume of *The Remains of Thomas Cranmer, Archbishop of Canterbury*, ed. Henry Jenkyns. Oxford: Oxford University Press, 1833.

In my most hearty wise I commend me unto you, and even so would be right glad to hear of your welfare, and the like. These [words] be to advertise you, that inasmuch as you now take some pains in writing unto me, I would be loth you should think your labour utterly lost and forgotten for lack of writing again; therefore, and because I reckon you be some deal desirous of such news as hath been here with us of late in the King's Grace's matters, I intend to inform you a part thereof, according to the tenor and purport used in that behalf.

And first, as touching the final determination and concluding of the matter of divorce between my Lady Catherine and the King's Grace, which said matter, after the Convocation in that behalf had determined and agreed according to the former consent of the Universities, it was thought convenient by the King and his learned counsel, that I should repair unto Dunstable, which is within four miles unto Amptell, where the said Lady Catherine keepeth her house, and there to call her before me to hear the final sentence in the said matter. Notwithstanding, she would not at all obey thereunto, for when she was by Doctor Lee cited to appear by a day, she utterly refused the same, saying, that inasmuch as her cause was before the Pope, she would have none other judge; and therefore would not take me for her judge.

Nevertheless the eighth day of May, according to the said appointment, I came unto Dunstable, my Lord of Lincoln being assistant unto me, and my Lord of Wynchester, Doctor Bell, Dr. Claybroke, Dr. Trygonnell, Dr. Hewis, Dr. Olyver, Dr. Brytten, Mr. Bedell, with divers other learned in the law, being counselors in the law for the King's part: and so there at our coming kept a Court for the appearance of the said Lady Catherine, where were examined certain witness which testified that she was lawfully cited and called to appear, whom for fault of appearance was declared *contumax;* proceeding in the said cause against her *in penam contumaciae,* as the process of the law thereunto belongeth; which continued fifteen days after our coming thither. And the morrow after Ascension-day I gave final sentence therein, how that it was indispensable for the Pope to license any such marriages.

This done, and after our rejourneying home again, the King's Highness prepared all things convenient for the Coronation of the Queen, which also was after such a manner as followeth. . . .

6. The Last Letter of Queen Catherine

Written before her Death at Kimbolton Castle on 7 January 1536

The source of this letter is *Documents Illustrative of English Church History*, ed. Henry Gee and William John Hardy (London: Macmillan, 1914). Some have speculated that the letter was written after her death by sympathizers, and thus may be fictitious. See Giles Tremlett, *Catherine of Aragon*, pp. 360–65 for an account of her last days and the letter.

My most dear lord, king and husband, The hour of my death now drawing on, the tender love I owe you forces me, my case being such, to commend myself to you, and to put you in remembrance with a few words of the health and safeguard of your soul which you ought to prefer before all worldly matters, and before the care and pampering of your body, for the which you have cast me into many calamities and yourself into many troubles. For my part, I pardon you everything, and I wish to devoutly pray God that He will pardon you also. For the rest, I commend unto you our daughter Mary, beseeching you to be a good father unto her, as I have heretofore desired. I entreat you also, on behalf of my maids, to give them marriage portions, which is not much, they being but three. For all my other servants I solicit the wages due them, and a year more, lest they be unprovided for. Lastly, I make this vow, that mine eyes desire you above all things.

Catherine the Queen

Appendix II

Relevant Laws, Acts, and Oaths

1. The Text of the Opening of the *Magna Carta Libertatem* (The Great Charter of Liberty)

In this trial, More appealed to the *Magna Carta*, specifically the ancient agreement that "the English Church shall be free." The text of the beginning and the end of the *Magna Carta* follows. Regarding this document, Sir Winston Churchill remarked in 1956: "Here is a law which is above the King and which even he must not break." This reaffirmation of a supreme law and its expression in a general charter is the great work of *Magna Carta*; and this alone justifies the respect in which men have held it. Regarding the deaths of Thomas More and John Fisher in 1535, Churchill also remarked in *A History of the English Speaking Peoples*: "The resistance of More and Fisher to the royal supremacy in Church government was a noble and heroic stand." The translation below is taken from G. R. C. Davis, *Magna Carta*, Revised Edition, British Library, 1989.

I, JOHN, by the grace of God King of England, Lord of Ireland, Duke of Normandy and Aquitaine, and Count of Anjou, to his archbishops, bishops, abbots, earls, barons, justices, foresters, sheriffs, stewards, servants, and to all his officials and loyal subjects, Greeting.

KNOW THAT BEFORE GOD, for the health of our soul and those of our ancestors and heirs, to the honor of God, the exaltation of the holy Church, and the better ordering of our kingdom, at the advice of our reverend fathers Stephen, archbishop of Canterbury, primate of all England, and cardinal of the holy Roman Church, Henry archbishop of Dublin, William bishop of London, Peter bishop of Winchester, Jocelin bishop of Bath and Glastonbury, Hugh bishop of Lincoln, Walter Bishop of Worcester, William bishop of Coventry, Benedict bishop of Rochester, Master Pandulf subdeacon and member of the papal household, Brother Aymeric master of the knighthood of the Temple in England, William Marshal earl of Pembroke, William earl of Salisbury, William earl of Warren, William earl of Arundel, Alan de Galloway constable of Scotland, Warin Fitz Gerald, Peter Fitz Herbert, Hubert de Burgh seneschal of Poitou, Hugh de Neville, Matthew Fitz Herbert, Thomas Basset, Alan Basset, Philip Daubeny, Robert de Roppeley, John Marshal, John Fitz Hugh, and other loyal subjects:

(1) FIRST, THAT WE HAVE GRANTED TO GOD, and by this present charter have confirmed for us and our heirs in perpetuity, that the English Church shall be free, and shall have its rights undiminished, and its liberties unimpaired. That we wish this so to be observed, appears from the fact that of our own free will, before the outbreak of the present dispute between us and our barons, we granted and confirmed by charter the freedom of the Church's elections—a right reckoned to be of the greatest necessity and importance to it—and caused this to be confirmed by Pope Innocent III. This freedom we shall observe ourselves, and desire to be observed in good faith by our heirs in perpetuity.

TO ALL FREE MEN OF OUR KINGDOM we have also granted, for us and our heirs for ever, all the liberties written out below, to have and to keep for them and their heirs, of us and our heirs. . . . [here a long, detailed list of liberties follows].

IT IS ACCORDINGLY OUR WISH AND COMMAND that the English Church shall be free, and that men in our kingdom shall have and keep all these liberties, rights, and concessions, well and peaceably in their fullness and entirety for them and their heirs, of us and our heirs, in all things and all places for ever.

Both we and the barons have sworn that all this shall be observed in good faith and without deceit. Witness the above-mentioned people and many others.

Given by our hand in the meadow that is called Runnymede, between Windsor and Staines, on the fifteenth day of June in the seventeenth year of our reign [1215].

2. The Text of the Ordinance and Statute of Praemunire (1353)

First passed in 1353, the praemunire law forbids the assertion or support of any papal or other foreign powers in England.

Our lord the king, with the assent and by the prayer of the lords and commons of his kingdom of England, in his great council held at Westminster on Monday next after the feast of St. Matthew the Apostle, in the twenty-seventh year of his reign—that is to say in England; in France the fourteenth—for the improvement of his said kingdom and for the maintenance of its laws and usages, has ordained and established the measures hereinunder written:

First, whereas our lord the king has been shown by the clamorous and grievous complaints of his lords and commons aforesaid how numerous persons have been and are being taken out of the kingdom to respond in cases of which the cognizance pertains to the court of our lord the king; and also how the judgments rendered in the same court are being impeached in the court of another, to the prejudice and disherison of our lord the king and of his crown and of all the people of his said kingdom, and to the undoing and annulment of the common law of the same kingdom at all times customary: therefore, after good deliberation held with the lords and others of the said council, it is granted and agreed by our said lord the king and by the lords and commons aforesaid that all persons of the king's allegiance, of whatever condition they may be, who take any one out of the kingdom in a plea of which the cognizance pertains to the king's court or in matters regarding which judgments have been rendered in the king's court, or who bring suit in the court of another to undo or impede the judgments rendered in the king's court, shall be given a day . . . [on which] to appear before the king and his council, or in his chancery, or before the king's justices in their courts, either the one bench or the other, or before other justices of the king who may be deputed for the purpose, there to answer to the king in proper person regarding the contempt involved in such action. And if they do not come in proper person on the said day to stand trial, let them, their procurators, attorneys, executors, notaries, and supporters, from this day forth be put outside the king's protection, and let their lands, goods, and chattels be forfeit to the king, and let their bodies, wherever they may be found, be taken and imprisoned and redeemed at the king's pleasure.

3. The Text of King Henry VIII's Coronation Oath, 1509

At his trial, Thomas More reminded King Henry of the Coronation Oath he swore in 1509, when he rose to the throne with all the splendor and promise of the sun in midsummer days. The text of that oath follows. It is taken from volume one of *Sources of English Constitutional History*, ed. C. Stephenson and F. G. Marcham (Harper Brothers, 1937).

Archbishop: "Sire, will you grant and keep and by your oath confirm to the people of England the laws and customs given to them by the previous just and god-fearing kings, your ancestors, and especially the laws, customs, and liberties granted to the clergy and people by the glorious king, the sainted Edward, your predecessor?"

King: "I grant and promise them."

Archbishop: "Sire, will you in all your judgments, so far as in you lies, preserve to God and Holy Church, and to the people and clergy, entire peace and concord before God?"

King: "I will preserve them."

Archbishop: "Sire will you so far as in you lies, cause justice to be rendered rightly, impartially, and wisely, in compassion and in truth?"

King: "I will do so."

Archbishop: "Sire, do you grant to be held and observed the just laws and customs that the community of your realm shall determine, and will you, so far as in you lies, defend and strengthen them to the honor of God?"

King: "I grant and promise them."

4. The Text of the Oath of the Act of Succession, 1534

In 1534, Sir Thomas More, Bishop John Fisher, and others were arrested, for refusing to take this Oath, which added crucial and controversial words about the King's "supremacy" to the original Act of Succession. The source for this text is *Documents Illustrative of English Church History*, ed. Henry Gee and William John Hardy (London: Macmillan, 1914).

. . . And at the day of the last prorogation of this present Parliament, as well the nobles spiritual and temporal as other the Commons of this present Parliament, most lovingly accepted and took such oath as then was devised in writing for maintenance and defense of the said Act, and meant and intended at that time that every other of the king's subjects should be bound to accept and take the same, upon the pains contained in the said Act, the tenor of which oath hereafter ensueth:

"Ye shall swear to bear faith, truth, and obedience alonely to the king's majesty, and to his heirs of his body of his most dear and entirely beloved lawful wife Queen Anne, begotten and to be begotten, and further to the heirs of our said sovereign lord according to the limitation in the statute made for surety of his succession in the crown of this realm, mentioned and contained, and not to any other within this realm, for foreign authority or potentate: and in case any oath be made, or has been made, by you, to any person or persons, that then ye [are] to repute the same as vain and annihilate; and that, to your cunning, wit, and uttermost of your power, without guile, fraud, or other undue means, you shall observe, keep, maintain, and defend the said Act of Accession, and all the whole effects and contents thereof, and all other Acts and statutes made in confirmation, or for the execution of the same, or of anything therein contained; and this ye shall do against all manner of persons, of what estate, dignity, degree, or condition soever they be, and in no wise do or attempt, nor to your power suffer to be done or attempted, directly or indirectly, any thing or things privily or apartly to the let, hindrance, damage, or derogation thereof, or of any part of the same, by any manner of means, or for any manner of pretence; so help you God, all saints, and the holy Evangelists."

And forasmuch as it is convenient for the sure maintenance and defense of the same Act that the said oath should not only be authorized by authority of Parliament, but also be interpreted and expounded by the whole assent of this present Parliament, that was meant and intended by the king's majesty, the Lords and Commons of the Parliament, at the said day of the said last prorogation, that every subject should be bounden to take the same oath, according to the tenor and effect thereof, upon the pains and penalties contained in the said Act. . . .

5. The Text of the Act of Supremacy, November 1534

The source of this text is *The Statutes of the Realm*, Volume 3 (Great Britain, 1817).

Albeit the King's Majesty justly and rightfully is and ought to be the supreme head of the Church of England, and so is recognized by the Clergy of this Realm in their convocations; yet nevertheless, for corroboration and confirmation thereof, and for increase of virtue in Christ's Religion within this realm of England, and to repress and extirpate all errors, heresies, and other enormities and abuses heretofore used in the same, Be it enacted, by authority of this present Parliament, that the King, our sovereign lord, his heirs and successors, Kings of this Realm, shall be taken, accepted, and reputed the only supreme head in earth of the Church of England, called Anglicana Ecclesia; and shall have and enjoy, annexed and united to the imperial crown of this realm, as well the title and style thereof, as all honors, dignities, preeminences, jurisdictions, privileges, authorities, immunities, profits, and commodities to the said dignity of the supreme head of the same Church belonging and appertaining; and that our said Sovereign Lord, his heirs and successors, Kings of this Realm, shall have full power and authority from time to time to visit, repress, redress, record, order, correct, restrain, and amend all such errors, heresies, abuses, offenses, contempts and enormities, whatsoever they be, which by any manner of spiritual authority or jurisdiction ought or may lawfully be reformed, repressed, ordered, redressed, corrected, restrained, or amended, most to the pleasure of Almighty God, the increase of virtue in Christ's Religion, and for the conservation of the peace, unity, and tranquility of this realm; any usage, custom, foreign laws, foreign authority, prescription, or any other thing or things to the contrary hereof notwithstanding.

6. The Text of the Oath of Supremacy, 1559

The Oath of Supremacy, like the Oath of the Act of Succession, was required to prove one's loyalty to Henry by acknowledging his title, "supreme head of the Church of England." The Act of Supremacy was repealed by Queen Mary I in 1554, when England returned for a time to the old faith of Catholicism. After Mary's death and Elizabeth's coronation, however, the Act of Supremacy was passed again and became the law of the land. The wording of the original Oath is unknown, though the Act of Supremacy and the Oath of Succession provide some clear sense of its content. The text that follows is from the Oath of Supremacy required in 1559. This oath would later be required of all members of Parliament and all those studying for a degree at English universities; hence, Catholics were effectively barred from civic life, unless they conformed. John Donne, the great poet and relative of Thomas More, is an example of one man who, first raised Catholic, later conformed in order to take a degree, get a place, and make his way in this new world.

I, ___, do utterly testify and declare in my conscience that the Queen's Highness is the only supreme governor of this realm, and of all other her Highness's dominions and countries, as well in all spiritual or ecclesiastical things or causes, as temporal, and that no foreign prince, person, prelate, state or potentate hath or ought to have any jurisdiction, power, superiority, pre-eminence or authority ecclesiastical or spiritual within this realm; and therefore I do utterly renounce and forsake all foreign jurisdictions, powers, superiorities and authorities, and do promise that from henceforth I shall bear faith and true allegiance to the Queen's Highness, her heirs and lawful successors, and to my power shall assist and defend all jurisdictions, pre-eminences, privileges and authorities granted or belonging to the Queen's Highness, her heirs or successors, or united or annexed to the imperial crown of this realm. So help me God, and by the contents of this Book.

7. The Text of the "Treasons Act" of Parliament, 1535

After his imprisonment for refusing to take the Oath in 1534, More was found guilty of violating this "Treasons Act," passed by Parliament in 1534, on the grounds that he broke the *praemunire* law.

Be it therefore enacted by the assent and consent of our sovereign lord the king, and the Lords spiritual and temporal, and Commons in this present Parliament assembled, and by the authority of the same, that if any person or persons, after the first day of February next coming, do maliciously wish, will or desire, by words or writing, or by craft imagine, invent, practice, or attempt any bodily harm to be done or committed to the king's most royal person, the queen's, or their heirs apparent, or to deprive them or any of them of their dignity, title, or name of their royal estates, or slanderously and maliciously publish and pronounce, by express writing or words, that the king our sovereign lord should be heretic, schismatic, tyrant, infidel or usurper of the crown, or rebelliously do detain, keep, or withhold from our said sovereign lord, his heirs or successors, any of his or their castles, fortresses, fortalices, or holds within this realm, or in any other the king's dominions or marches, or rebelliously detain, keep, or withhold from the king's said highness, his heirs or successors, any of his or their ships, ordnances, artillery, or other munitions or fortifications of war, and do not humbly render and give up to our said sovereign lord, his heirs or successors, or to such persons as shall be deputed by them, such castles, fortresses, fortalices, holds, ships, ordnances, artillery, and other munitions and fortifications of war, rebelliously kept or detained, within six days next after they shall be commanded by our said sovereign lord, his heirs or successors, by open proclamation under the great seal:

That then every such person and persons so offending in any the premises, after the said first day of February, their aiders, counselors, consenters, and abettors, being thereof lawfully convicted according to the laws and customs of this realm, shall be adjudged traitors, and that every such offence in any the premises, that shall be committed or done after the said first day of February, shall be reputed, accepted, and adjudged high treason, and the offenders therein and their aiders, consenters, counselors, and abettors, being lawfully convicted of any such offence as is aforesaid, shall have and suffer such pains of death and other penalties, as is limited and accustomed in cases of high treason.

Appendix III

Responses to More's Death

1. Sir Thomas More's Trial and Execution

The Paris Newsletter Account
First Published 4 August 1535

The text of this contemporary account of More's trial and execution is taken from volume eight of *Letters and Papers, Foreign and Domestic, of the Reign of Henry VIII. Volume 8.* Ed. J.S. Brewer and James Gairdner (London: Longmans and Co., 1882), number 996.

On the 1st July 1535, Master Thomas More, sometime Chancellor of England, was brought before the judges and the accusations against him read in his presence. The Chancellor and the Duke of Norfolk turned to him and said, "You, Master More, have gravely erred against the King; nevertheless we hope by his clemency that if you repent and correct your obstinate opinion in which you have so rashly persevered, you will receive pardon." He replied, "My Lords, I thank you very heartily for your good will. I pray God preserve me in my just opinion even to death. As to the accusation against me, I fear words, memory, and judgment would alike fail me to reply to such a length of articles, especially considering my present imprisonment and great infirmity."

A chair was then ordered to be placed for him, and he proceeded as follows: "As to the first article, charging me with having always maliciously opposed the King's second marriage, I will only answer that what I have said has been according to my conscience. I never wished to conceal the truth, and if I had, I should have been a traitor. For this error, if error it should be called, I have been condemned to perpetual imprisonment, which I have already suffered for fifteen months, and my goods confiscated. For this reason I will only reply to the principal charge against me, that I have incurred the penalty of the Statute made in the last Parliament since I was in prison, by refusing to the King his title of Supreme Head of the Church, in proof of which you allege my reply to the Secretary and Council, that as I was dead to the world, I did not care to think of such things, but only of the passion of Christ. I reply that your Statute cannot condemn me to death for such silence, for neither your Statute nor any laws in the world punish people except for words or deed—surely not for keeping silence."

To this the King's proctor replied that such silence was a certain proof of malice intended against the Statute, especially as every faithful subject, on being questioned about the Statute, was obliged to answer categorically that the Statute was good and wholesome.

"Surely," replied More, "if what the common law says is true, that he who is silent seems to consent, my silence should rather be taken as approval than contempt of your Statute. You say that all good subjects are obliged to reply; but I say that the faithful subject is more bound to his conscience and his soul than to anything else in the world, provided his conscience, like mine, does not raise scandal or sedition, and I assure you that I have never discovered what is in my conscience to any person living.

"As to the second article, that I have conspired against the Statute by writing eight letters to the bishop of Rochester, advising him to disobey it, I could wish these letters had been read in public, but as you say the Bishop has burnt them, I will tell you the substance of them. Some were about private matters connected with our old friendship. Another was a reply to one of his asking how I had answered in the Tower to the first examination about the Statute. I said that I had informed my conscience, and so he also ought to do the same. I swear that this was the tenor of the letters, for which I cannot be condemned by your Statute.

"Touching the third article, that when I was examined by the Council, I answered that your Statute was like a two-edged sword, for he who approved it would ruin his soul, and he who contradicted it, his body; and that the bishop of Rochester answered similarly, showing that we were confederates, I reply that I only answered thus conditionally, that if the Statute cut both ways like a two-edged sword, how could a man behave so as not to incur either danger? I do not know how the Bishop replied, but if he answered like me, it must have been from the agreement between us in opinion, but not because we had ever arranged it between us. Be assured I never did or said anything maliciously against the Statute, but it may be that this has been maliciously reported to the King."

Then they ordered an usher to summon 12 men according to the custom of the country, and these articles were given to them that they might judge whether More had maliciously contravened the Statute. After a quarter of an hour's absence they declared him guilty of death, and sentence was pronounced by the Chancellor "*selon la lettre de la nouvelle loy*."

More then spoke as follows: "Since I am condemned, and God knows how, I wish to speak freely of your Statute, for the discharge of my conscience. For the seven years that I have studied the matter, I have not read in any approved doctor of the Church that a temporal lord could or ought to be head of the spirituality." The Chancellor interrupting him, said, "What, More, you wish to be considered wiser and of better conscience than all the bishops and nobles of the realm?" To this More replied, "My lord, for one bishop of your opinion I have a hundred saints of mine; and for one parliament of yours, and God knows of what kind, I have all the General Councils for 1,000 years, and for one kingdom I have France and all the kingdoms of Christendom." Norfolk told him that now his malice was clear. More replied, "What I say is necessary for discharge of my conscience and satisfaction of my soul, and to this I call God to witness, the sole Searcher of human hearts. I say further, that your Statute is ill made, because you have sworn never to do anything against the Church, which through all Christendom is one and undivided, and you have no authority, without the common consent of all Christians, to make a law or Act of Parliament or Council against the union of Christendom. I know well that the reason why you have condemned me is because I have never been willing to consent to the King's second marriage; but I hope in the divine goodness and mercy, that as St. Paul and St. Stephen whom he persecuted are now friends in Paradise, so we, though differing in this world, shall be united in perfect charity in the other. I pray God to protect the King and give him good counsel."

On his way to the Tower one of his daughters, named Margaret, pushed through the archers and guards, and held him in her embrace some time without being able to speak. Afterwards More, asking leave of the archers, bade her have patience, for it was God's will, and she had long known the secret of his heart. After going 10 or 12 steps she returned and embraced him again, to which he said nothing, except to bid her pray to God for his soul; and this without tears or change of color. On the Tuesday following he was beheaded in the open space in front of the Tower. A little before his death he asked those present to pray to God for him and he would do the same for them [in the other world.] He then besought them earnestly to pray to God to give the King good counsel, protesting that he died his "faithful servant, and God's first."

2. From Reginald Pole, Defense of the Unity of the Church [1536]

Pole wrote this personal appeal to Henry VIII in the year after More's death. This excerpt is taken from Pole's *Defense of the Unity of the Church*, trans. Joseph Dwyer (Westminster, MD: Newman Press, 1965). Like the later Nicholas Harpsfield, who compared More to Cicero, Pole compares More to a classical figure, Socrates, who met death through hemlock after he was condemned by an Athenian jury.

Oh! England! What do you say here? . . . Rather do you not know that you were deprived of your own parent in this finest and most loving citizen of yours? Furthermore, if anyone ever deserved from you the name of "Father of his Country," it was this man. . . .

But you, Oh! City of London! All of these things happened within your view. You saw him when he was led out from jail to plead against this charge of treason. You recall that a short time thereafter he was convicted of treason before your tribunal. You beheld him as a boy, a youth, a man and finally in his later years as he advanced up the steps of the highest honors with the very great praise and approval of all, due to his most unusual virtues. Finally, you saw him ascend to the most renowned position; and because he was your citizen and your native son you witnessed this with a certain feeling of joy . . . (229–30)

Though I myself write these things concerning his death, separated by such a great distance, I have not only many private reasons for loving him but I have rather loved and cherished him especially because of his virtue and uprighteousness, on account of which I knew him to be most useful to his native land. . . . Though indeed, [London], by nature he was your son through his citizenship, by his benefits, however, he was your father. He displayed more signs of paternal affection toward you than a most indulgent father showed toward his one and dearest son. But in no greater way did he show that he was your parent than by his death. He lost his life for the very special reason that he would not betray your security.

Wherefore we read in the histories of the Greeks that Socrates was assailed in an unjust trial by the Athenians, even as it is now well known that More was condemned to death by you. A short while later, in a theatre where people had assembled for a spectacle, these words were read aloud from a certain tragedy: "You have killed, you have killed the best man of all the Greeks!" Immediately at these words the bitter memory of the murder of Socrates went through the minds of all. . . . by how much more just anger and compassion should you, City of London, be stirred? You did not hear these words uttered by chance just once in a theatre in your country by some actor, but you were compelled to hear this charge: "You have killed, you have killed the best of all Englishmen!" brought against you by the most serious men at a time when they were speaking most seriously in every place now Christian in name. . . . (230–31)

. . . Perhaps [a critic of More and Fisher] would say that they did not see any truth at all by divine light or by the light of reason. He would say that by some kind of obstinacy from the very beginning their minds began to defend a false opinion. He would say that it seems they decided to die rather than abandon this opinion.

Truly, my Prince, I beseech you! Examine the record for a moment. Consider the words of those [i.e., Fisher and More] who spoke in this manner. But first, you yourself who knew these men, examine them! See to it that you consider what they were like during the rest of their lives. However, I ask only this of you; I ask whether you remember anyone who ever accused these men of imprudence prior to the time when this question began to be discussed publicly.

Now I am speaking of More alone. Was anyone in all your realm considered more prudent than More during his lifetime? Manifestly, no one, in the opinion of all who knew him, can be mentioned as comparable to him in talent and prudence. He excelled in prudence; therefore, when it happened in his case that he could have avoided all inconvenience and troubles, and also could have surpassed all others in honors and in favor with you—if he would only withdraw from his opinion—he deprived himself of these honors and your favor. Can we believe he acted imprudently? (311)

3. From Nicholas Harpsfield, *The Life and Death of Sir Thomas More*

The source of this excerpt is the Early English Text Society edition of *The Life and Death of Sr. Thomas More, Knight: Sometymes Lord High Chancellor of England*, ed. Elsie V. Hitchcock and R. W. Chambers (London: Oxford University Press, 1932). Harpsfield (1519–1575) was a Catholic priest and author of several books, including *A Treatise on the Pretended Divorce of King Henry VIII and Catherine of Aragon* and *Cranmer's Recantacyons*.

And the said head [of Sir Thomas More] was set upon London Bridge, in the said City where he was born and brought up, upon an high pole, among the heads of traitors: A rueful and a pitiful spectacle for all good Citizens and other good Christians, and much more lamentable to see their Christian English Cicero's head in such sort, then it was to the Romans to see the head of Marcus Tullius Cicero set up in the same City and place where he had, by his great eloquent orations, preserved many an innocent from imminent danger and peril, and had preserved the whole City, by his great industry, from the mischievous conspiracy of Catiline and his seditious accomplices (217).

Appendix IV

Psalm on Detachment

Composed by Thomas More in the Tower of London

Give me thy grace, good Lord:
To set the world at nought;
To set my mind fast upon thee,
And not to hang upon the blast of men's mouths;
To be content to be solitary,
Not to long for worldly company;
Little and little utterly to cast off the world,
And rid my mind of all the business thereof;
Not to long to hear of any worldly things,
But that the hearing of worldly phantasies may be to
 me displeasant;
Gladly to be thinking of God,
Piteously to call for his help;
To lean unto the comfort of God,
Busily to labor to love him;
To know mine own vility and wretchedness,
To humble and meeken myself under the mighty hand
 of God;
To bewail my sins passed,
For the purging of them patiently to suffer adversity;
Gladly to bear my purgatory here,
To be joyful of tribulations;
To walk the narrow way that leadeth to life,
To bear the cross with Christ;

To have the last thing in remembrance,
To have ever afore mine eye my death that is ever at hand;
To make death no stranger to me,
To foresee and consider the everlasting fire of hell;
To pray for pardon before the judge come,
To have continually in mind the passion that Christ suffered
    for me;
For his benefits uncessantly to give him thanks,
To buy the time again that I before have lost;
To abstain from vain confabulations,
To eschew light foolish mirth and gladness;
Recreations not necessary—to cut off;
Of worldly substance, friends, liberty, life and all, to set the loss
    at right nought for the winning of Christ;
To think my most enemies my best friends,
For the brethren of Joseph could never have done him so
    much good
  with their love and favor as they did him with their malice
    and hatred.
These minds are more to be desired of every man
    than all the treasure of all the princes and kings,
 Christian and heathen, were it gathered and
    laid together all upon one heap.

BIBLIOGRAPHY

Ackroyd, Peter. *The Life of Thomas More*. New York: Doubleday, 1998.

Berglar, Peter. *Thomas More*. New York: Scepter Publishers, 2011.

Bolt, Robert. *A Man for All Seasons*. New York: Vintage, 1990.

Cambridge Companion to Thomas More. Ed. George Logan. Cambridge: Cambridge University Press, 2011.

Cicero. *Tusculan Disputations*. Trans. J.E. King. Loeb Classical Library (Cicero, vol. 18). Cambridge, MA: Harvard University Press, 1927.

Cicero. *De Officiis*. Trans. Walter Miller. Loeb Classical Library (Cambrige, MA: Harvard University Press, 1913.

Cicero. *De Oratore*. Trans. E.W. Sutton and H. Rackman. 2 vols. Loeb Classical Library. Cambridge, MA: Harvard University Press, 1942.

Contemporaries of Erasmus: A Biographical Register of the Renaissance and Reformation. Ed. Peter G. Bietenholz and Thomas B. Deutscher. 3 vols. Toronto: University of Toronto Press, 1985-1987.

Cranevelt, Francis. *Literae Virorum Eruditorum ad Franciscum Craneveldium, 1522–1528*. Ed. Henry de Vocht (Louvain: Uystpruyst, 1928).

Curtright, Travis. *The One Thomas More*. Washington, D.C.: Catholic University of America Press, 2012.

Erasmus, Desiderius. *The Correspondence of Erasmus: Letters 1252–1355*. Trans. John Olin. Toronto: University of Toronto Press, 1989.

Erasmus, Desiderius. *Collected Works of Erasmus. Correspondence: Letters 1356–1534* (1523–1524). *Vol. 10*. Trans. R.A.B. Mynors and Alexander Dalzell. Toronto: University of Toronto Press, 1992.

Erasmus, Desiderius. *The Epistles of Erasmus*. Ed. Francis M. Nichols. 3 vols. (New York: Russell and Russell, 1962).

Erasmus, Desiderius. *Praise of Folly.* Trans. Clarence Miller. New Haven: Yale University Press, 2003.

Erasmus, Desiderius and Luther, Martin. *Discourse on Free Will.* New York: Continuum, 1985.

Guy, John. *A Daughter's Love: Thomas More and His Dearest Meg.* New York: Houghton Mifflin Harcourt, 2009.

Guy, John. *Thomas More.* New York: Oxford University Press, 2000.

Homer, *Iliad.* Trans. Robert Fagles. New York: Penguin, 1998.

Horace. *The Odes and Epodes.* Trans. C. E. Bennett. Loeb Classical Library. Harvard, MA: Harvard University Press, 1927.

Horace. *Satires, Epistles and Ars Poetica.* Trans. H. Rushton Fairclough. Loeb Classical Library. Harvard, MA: Harvard University Press, 1926.

Juvenal. *Juvenal and Persius.* Trans. G.G. Ramsay. Loeb Classical Library. Harvard, MA: Harvard University Press, 1979.

Kelly, Henry et al. *Thomas More's Trial by Jury: A Procedural and Legal Review with a Collection of Documents.* Boydell and Brewer, 2011.

Lewis, C.S. *English Literature in the Sixteenth Century, Excluding Drama.* Oxford: Oxford University Press, 1954.

Miles, Geoffrey. *Classical Mythology in English Literature.* London: Routledge, 1999.

Miller, Clarence. "Letters to Francis Cranevelt." *Moreana.* Vol 31.117 (March 1994), 3–66.

More, Thomas. *A Thomas More Source Book.* Ed. Stephen W. Smith. Washington, DC: Catholic University of America Press, 2004.

More, Thomas. *The Correspondence of Sir Thomas More.* Ed. Elizabeth F. Rogers. Princeton, NJ: Princeton University Press, 1947.

More, Thomas. *Dialogue Concerning Heresies.* Modernized by Mary Gottschalk. New York: Scepter Publishers, 2006.

More, Thomas. *Dialogue of Comfort against Tribulation.* Modernized by Mary Gottschalk. Princeton, N.J.: Scepter Publishers, 1998.

More, Thomas. *The English Works of Sir Thomas More.* 2 volumes. Ed. W. E. Campbell. London: Eyre and Spottiswoode, 1931.

More, Thomas. *Last Letters of Thomas More*. Ed. Alvaro Silva. Eerdmans: Cambridge, 2000.

More. Thomas. *Life of Pico*. Modernized by Russell Shaw. New York: Scepter Publishers, 2011.

More, Thomas. *Sadness of Christ*. Trans. Clarence Miller. New York: Scepter Publishers, 1997.

More, Thomas. *St. Thomas More: Selected Letters*. Trans. Elizabeth F. Rogers. Princeton, NJ: Princeton University Press, 1947.

More, Thomas. *Utopia*. Trans. George Logan. New York: Cambridge University Press, 2002.

More, Thomas. *The Yale Edition of the Complete Works of St. Thomas More*. New Haven, CT: Yale University Press, 1963–97. 15 vols.

CW 1 *English Poems, Life of Pico, The Last Things*. Ed. Anthony S. Edwards, Katherine G. Rodgers, Clarence H. Miller. 1997.

CW 2 *The History of King Richard III*. Ed. Richard S. Sylvester. 1963.

CW 3.1 *Translations of Lucian*. Ed. Craig R. Thompson. 1974.

CW 3.2 *The Latin Poems*. Ed. Clarence H. Miller, Leicester Bradner, Charles A. Lynch, and Revilo P. Oliver. 1984.

CW 4 *Utopia*. Ed. Edward Surtz and J. H. Hexter. 1965.

CW 5 *Responsio ad Lutherum*. Ed. J. M. Headley. 1969.

CW 6 *A Dialogue Concerning Heresies*. Ed. Thomas Lawler, Germain Marc'hadour, and Richard Marius. 1981.

CW 7 *Letter to Bugenhagen, Supplication of Souls, Letter against Frith*. Ed. Frank Manley, Germain Marc'hadour, Richard Marius, and Clarence H. Miller. 1990.

CW 8 *Confutation of Tyndale's Answer*. Ed. Louis Schuster, Richard Marius, James Lusardi, and Richard Schoeck. 1973.

CW 9 *The Apology*. Ed. J. B. Trapp. 1979.

CW 10 *The Debellation of Salem and Bizance*. Ed. John Guy, Ralph Keen, Clarence H.Miller, and Ruth McGugan. 1987.

CW 11 *The Answer to a Poisoned Book*. Ed. Stephen M. Foley and Clarence H. Miller. 1985.

CW 12 *A Dialogue of Comfort against Tribulation.* Ed. L. L. Martz and Frank Manley. 1976.

CW 13 *A Treatise on the Passion.* Ed. Garry E. Haupt. 1976.

CW 14 *De Tristitia Christi.* Ed. Clarence M. Miller. 1976.

CW 15 *In Defense of Humanism.* Ed. Daniel Kinney. 1986.

Oxford Classical Dictionary. Ed. Simon Hornblower and Antony Spawforth. Oxford: Oxford University Press, 2003.

Oxford Dictionary of National Biography. Ed. H. Matthew and Brian Harrison. 60 vols. Oxford: Oxford University Press, 2004.

Oxford Dictionary of the Christian Church. Ed. F.L. Cross. Oxford: Oxford University Press, 2005.

Oxford English Dictionary. Second Edition. 20 vols. Oxford: Oxford University Press, 1989.

Plato. *Dialogues.* Trans. Benjamin Jowett. 5 vols. Oxford: Oxford University Press, 1892.

Pole, Reginald. *Defense of the Unity of the Church.* Westminster, MD: Newman Press, 1965.

Quintilian. *Institutio Oratoria.* Trans. and ed. H. E. Butler. 4 volumes. Loeb Classical Library. Harvard, MA: Harvard University Press, 1921.

Shakespeare, William. *The Riverside Shakespeare.* Second Edition. Ed. Blakemore Evans. Houghton Mifflin Company, 1996.

Sidney, Sir Philip. *The Major Works.* Ed. Katherine Duncan-Jones. Oxford: Oxford University Press, 2002.

Swartz, Daniel. *Aquinas on Friendship.* New York: Oxford University Press, 2007.

Wegemer, Gerard b. *Thomas More on Statesmanship.* Washington, D.C.: Catholic University of America Press, 1996.

Wegemer, Gerard b. *Thomas More: Portrait of Courage.* New York: Scepter Publishers, 1997.

Wegemer, Gerard b. *Young Thomas More.* New York: Cambridge University Press, 2011.

Weir, Alison. *Six Wives of Henry VIII.* New York: Grove Press, 1991.

Scriptural Index

INDEX